DISCARDED

Picking Wedlock

Picking Wedlock

Women and the Courtship Novel in Spain

SHIFRA ARMON

ROWMAN & LITTLEFIELD PUBLISHERS, INC.
Lanham • Boulder • New York • Oxford

ROWMAN & LITTLEFIELD PUBLISHERS, INC.

Published in the United States of America
by Rowman & Littlefield Publishers, Inc.
4720 Boston Way, Lanham, Maryland 20706
www.rowmanlittlefield.com

12 Hid's Copse Road, Cumnor Hill, Oxford OX2 9JJ, England

Copyright © 2002 by Rowman & Littlefield Publishers, Inc.

Chapter 1 from Campbell, Gwyn E., and Judith Whitenack, eds. *Zayas and Her Sisters, 2: Essays on Novelas by 17th Century Spanish Women*. Studies on Spanish Classical Literature 1. Binghamton: Global, ICGS, forthcoming. Used by permission.

Cover image: Portrait of Philip IV of Spain and Isabel of Bourbon, from Gil González D'Avila's *Teatro de las grandezas de la Villa de Madrid* (1624). By permission of the Houghton Library, Harvard University.

All rights reserved. No part of this publication may be reproduced, stored in a retrieval system, or transmitted in any form or by any means, electronic, mechanical, photocopying, recording, or otherwise, without the prior permission of the publisher.

British Library Cataloguing in Publication Information Available

Library of Congress Cataloging-in-Publication Data

Armon, Shifra, 1956–
  Picking wedlock : women and the courtship novel in Spain / Shifra Armon.
    p. cm.
  Includes bibliographical references and index.
  ISBN 0-7425-0772-6 (alk. paper) — ISBN 0-7425-0773-4 (pbk : alk. paper)
  1. Spanish fiction—Women authors—History and criticism. 2. Spanish fiction—Classical period, 1500–1700—History and criticism. 3. Courtship in literature. 4. Women and literature—Spain—History—17th century. I. Title

PQ6140.W6 A86 2002
863'.309287—dc21

2001019734

Printed in the United States of America

⊖™ The paper used in this publication meets the minimum requirements of American National Standard for Information Sciences—Permanence of Paper for Printed Library Materials, ANSI/NISO Z39.48-1992.

Contents

Acknowledgments	vii
Introduction	ix
Chapter 1. Women and the *Novela de Cortejo* [Courtship Novel]	1
Chapter 2. "I Do": Nuptiality and Gender in Early Modern Spain	19
Chapter 3. Agency and Constraint in Courtship Plots	67
Chapter 4. The Art (and Craft) of Courtesy	109
Chapter 5. Courtship as Political Allegory	143
Afterword	191
Appendix Twenty-One Women's Courtship Narratives: Synopses of Nineteen Novellas and Two Cornices— Published by Women in Spanish Between 1647 and 1663	193
Bibliography	207
Index	225
About the Author	231

Acknowledgments

I am grateful to many colleagues, friends and family members for their support. Harry Sieber infused in me a respect for the discursive interplay of history and literature. Edward Baker continues to inspire me with his inexhaustible intellect and writerly elegance. Margaret Greer and Gwyn Campbell have also encouraged me and guided my steps. Many colleagues near and far have generously given of themselves to read and critique portions of my manuscript as it evolved. At the University of Florida I would like to acknowledge Efraín Barradas, Diana Boxer, William Calin, Diane Marting, Anne Wyatt-Brown and the graduate students of the fall 1998 Golden Age Prose Fiction seminar. I would also like to thank Susan Rosser, former director of the Center for Women's Studies and Gender Research for the opportunity to present my work-in-progress at the fall 1998 Colloquium Series. At other institutions, Mary Berg, Denise DiPuccio and Margo Persin offered valuable insights on my manuscript. For the many tranquil summers that I have spent writing in Boston, I thank Lois Grossman and Mark DeVoto for their unfailing hospitality.

Two academic institutions, Cornell University and the University of Florida, have supported and nourished my research financially. The Department of Romance Studies at Cornell University generously fomented my research in its early stages. At the University of Florida, the Graduate School, the College of Liberal Arts and Sciences and the Department of Romance Languages and Literatures have provided summer research grants as well as additional funding for translating and travel.

I would especially like to express my admiration for and gratitude to my graduate assistant, Karen Jones, whose vervy translations grace this volume. Karen is responsible for teaching me the shortcut for formatting triple em dashes on a Macintosh, for hammering the manuscript into its camera-ready form and for keeping me smiling throughout the semester that we worked together. I would also like to thank Holly Freifeld for her patient editorial assistance. At Rowman and Littlefield, I thank Serena Leigh and Michael Marino for their availability at each stage of the preparation and production process.

Introduction

> Echar al aire algunas cosas
> (Tossing about a few ideas)
> ——Baltasar Gracián, *Oráculo manual y arte de prudencia*, Aforismo 164 ["The Oracle," Aphorism 164], 1647[1]

It is exciting to discover that a literary genre commonly dismissed as inferior actually excels at something. However, before pursuing this thought further, Gracián's Aphorism 164 instructs that the enthusiast who wishes to launch an important matter first test the waters by "tossing about" the topics to be broached: "Tantéase las voluntades desta suerte, y sabe el atento dónde tiende los pies, prevención máxima del pedir, del querer y del governar" [The attentive speaker must gauge the interlocutor's response in this fashion, and thereby will know where to plant his or her feet, a necessary precursor for requesting, willing and governing]. Accordingly, I open this introduction by tossing into play those ideas that have animated and shaped my discovery. If Gracián is right, this "tossing about" procedure should help plant my scholarly feet more securely in the following pages. However, if, after 350 years, the Jesuit theologian's advice has lost its relevance and I stumble, the allusion to Gracián will still have paid off because it foreshadows a significant innovation of this volume. *Picking Wedlock* posits a close and fruitful relationship between practical wisdom (e.g., Gracián's aphorisms) and women's writings (e.g., my Introduction), a matter which is also tossed about below.

The literary genre commonly dismissed as inferior (assuming that its existence is acknowledged at all) is that of the Spanish courtship novel (*novela de cortejo*) cultivated by women writers on the Iberian peninsula in the seventeenth century. The courtship novel, oblivious to the credit to be earned had it managed to anticipate Realism, and indifferent to Cervantes's shining model, has provoked the disdain and attendant neglect of most literary historians. Blatantly reliant upon superannuated courtship conventions, the genre also poses special challenges for feminist scholarship. Although investigators have recuperated and interpreted individual texts—María de Zayas's 1647 *Desengaños amorosos* [Disenchantments of love], Leonor de Meneses's 1655 *Desdeñado más firme* [Scorned yet steadfast] and Mariana de Carvajal's 1663 *Navidades de Madrid* [Christmastide in Madrid]—these works are still viewed primarily in isolation. Yet, it seems puzzling that three female novelists all picked courtship novels within the very thirty-year period during which the genre as a whole was receding into extinction. The startlingly unanimous selection of a waning genre suggests that courtship plots excelled at a discursive function that women needed them to perform at the time. Did a common agenda, purpose or necessity prompt women writers to select a genre that enlists courtship scenarios to pattern its action? If so, how did courtship plots fulfill those needs?

Drawing from recent findings in women's history, *Picking Wedlock* begins to identify a range of social and political functions that courtship novels were uniquely positioned to fulfill. A vigorous new generation of historians has begun assembling data on gender boundaries in courtship and marriage during the seventeenth century. These researchers affirm that marriage represented elite women's principal means of social elevation in contrast to men, for whom a wider range of military, diplomatic and ecclesiastical choices were available (Wiesner). Thus, the stakes for early modern women were higher than they were for men in matters of courtship and marriage. Denise Riley offers a succinct manner of expressing this phenomenon in the concept of "gender density," a measure of the relative significance of different life-course experiences in the construction of gender. Courtship and marriage were more "gender dense" for early modern women than for men; that is, in the process of establishing social identity, they mattered more.

Picking Wedlock departs from the presupposition that "women have experienced life differently from men and that this difference is worth studying," as Constance Jordan writes in her introduction to *Renaissance Feminism: Literary Texts and Political Models* (1). Traditional scholarship has overlooked these experiential differences, positing in their place "una organización completa de la vida y de todos sus valores como enunciados inamovibles" [a systematic and exhaustive organization of life and all its values as fixed formulations] (Zavala 10). Even concepts as apparently gender-neutral as those of authorship and publication were subjected to gendering following the advent of printing, according to Wendy Wall, in her 1993 *The Imprint of Gender* (x). As the nascent print industry struggled for ascendancy in early modern England, as throughout Europe, the rhetoric over its legitimization frequently invoked gendered imagery. For example, pundits deemed the pen superior to the printing press by aligning quills with masculinity and the printing press with promiscuity. That in Elizabethan slang "being pressed" meant losing one's virginity lent further fuel to the polemic. The dictum, "Est Virgo Hec Penna: Meretrix Est Stampificata," which translates, "The pen is a virgin, the printing press a whore" (169) provides a glimpse of the powerful gendering forces with which early modern women writers contended.

However, rhetoric knows no loyalty, and women, Wall concedes, also found ways to manipulate gendered language to justify putting themselves in print. This is the strategy that author Elizabeth Joceline devised in 1624, looking not to the negatively tinged social expectation that women be whores or virgins, but to their universally admired martyrdom in the service of reproduction. Joceline's advice book, entitled *The Mother's Legacie to her Unborn Childe*, takes the form of a testament to the child who would otherwise be deprived of the mother's personal guidance were she to die in giving birth (Wall 284-285).

Joceline's case, though morbid, since in fact she did die in childbirth and her book was published posthumously, opens the door to considering that gendered language—language that speaks from a woman's position as a woman—might not only thwart, but also promote the publishing ambitions of women writers. As Judith Butler observes, "It is precisely the *expropriability* of the dominant 'authorized' discourse that constitutes one potential site of its subversive resignification" (157, Butler's emphasis). Public sympathy did not lie with virgins and whores, but with "safer" icons such as mothers, as in Joceline's case. By expropriating an orthodox scenario, women writers create the appearance of endorsing the dominant discourse while breaking the silence which that discourse ostensibly imposes upon them.

Geraldine McKendrick and Angus MacKay adduce a similar argument to explain the exceptional popularity of a group of writing women of late-fifteenth- and early-sixteenth-century Spain, the female visionaries known as *las alumbradas* [the luminaries]. These women (among them Sor María de Santo Domingo, Magdalena de la Cruz, Isabel de Texeda and Juana de la Cruz) preached and wrote a millenary message of world redemption. Their prophesies crowned Spanish monarchs and cardinals as saviors of a redeemed Christian world, a vision that dovetailed with and served the ambitions of Spanish imperialism and the crusading spirit of the counter-Reformation. This helps to explain why many of the women's excesses, their ecstasies, writings, or, in the case of Magdalena, "immaculate" pregnancies, met with a relatively benevolent or belated reaction from authorities. For McKendrick and MacKay, "the fact is that in the drive to define and protect orthodoxy the policies of both the monarchy and the Inquisition are of interest, not only because of the war waged on 'heresy'" but also due to what was accepted or tolerated within the confines of orthodoxy (96). Thus, a marginal group of women gained protection by adopting a discourse superficially supportive of the dominant group's political interests.

I maintain that a marriage-obsessed coalition of civil and ecclesiastical forces in the following century would tolerate the publication of women's courtship narratives for similar reasons. Courtship plots turned on the transition from maiden to wife through the sacrament of marriage. By creating the impression that they promoted the matrimonial control of women, these fictions reassured and gratified authorities normally suspicious of women's literary activity. As the cases of Elizabeth Joceline and the *alumbradas*, cited above, testify, Church and Crown overlooked the obvious gap between prescript (women shouldn't write) and practice (certain writing women) for the sake of what they perceived to be an affirmation of their own power. This "hypocrisy" served female novelists well, for although at first glance courtship novels appear conservative of patriarchal gender boundaries, the closer readings propounded in chapters 3, 4 and 5 of this volume reveal a different story.

Not all scholars allow that a disjunction between doctrine and practice could empower women. For example, while Mary Elizabeth Perry agrees that "María de Zayas, like many of her contemporaries, recognized that this prescriptive literature did not describe the women they knew" ("Crisis" 30), for her, such inconsistencies only threatened women's welfare and incited their ire ("Crisis" 35). In her words, "The growing gap between prescription and actualities increased tensions that promoted a widespread malaise of cynical hypocrisy and gendered violence" ("Crisis" 24). However, Zayas's happy ending (*fin felice*) curtails this cynical malaise, not by closing the gap between "prescription and actualities" but by exploiting it. That Zayas's central female character, Lisis, does not eschew hypocrisy, but rather harnesses it for her own purposes illustrates how contradictions between experience and precept might not only endanger women in some instances, but empower them in others.[2] While it might be argued with Perry that "Zayas wrote with some anger" ("Crisis" 35) about this hypocrisy, another courtship novelist, Carvajal, wrote with equanimity. The discontinuity between normative precept and lived experience that Perry laments actually constituted an essential precondition that enabled women's courtship discourse to come into being. In effect, if authorities had practiced what they preached they would have prevented women from publishing courtship plots altogether; had the frontiers of gender actually been policed as strictly as sermons and manuals decreed, female novelists could not have transgressed or even imagined transgressing those frontiers in writing.

Women's courtship fictions excel at reminding female readers that their subjectivity extended beyond the paradigm of the *perfecta casada*, or obedient wife. "It would be an error," writes George Mariscal, "to think that the dominant ideology (or the often misunderstood 'power') always already blocked or co-opted the potential for action. Power may indeed be everywhere, but it is not homogeneous, and relations of power are not articulated in a single way once and for all" (211-212). Female novelists after Cervantes unlock a doctrinally unassailable discursive site, that of courtship narratives, to rearticulate power relations between women and men.

Chapters 1 and 2 of *Picking Wedlock* set the stage for performing three critical readings that elucidate the interplay of genre and gender in women's courtship narrative. With regard to genre, operations of courtship constitute a fundamental plotting mechanism of this body of women's writing. Because the currently prevailing term, "courtly novel" (*novela cortesana*), fails to reflect the genre's commitment to courtship and also runs linguistically aground on the ambiguous Spanish word *cortesana* [courtly, courtesan], chapter 1, "Women and the Courtship Novel [*Novela de Cortejo*]," advocates replacing the usage "courtly novel," with the more descriptive label "courtship novel" (*novela de cortejo*).

Chapter 2 "'I Do': Nuptiality and Gender in Early Modern Spain," adduces a composite picture of gender in seventeenth-century Spain by balancing images and precepts concerning gender against evidence that points to the lived experience of sexed beings. Often, a society's gender ideals differ significantly from its practices. *Picking Wedlock* reconstructs early modern gender formations as a nexus of cultural, normative, socioeconomic and subjective factors. This fourfold approach helps to correct the reductive tendency to equate prescriptive admonitions about gender with the everyday life experience of males and females. On this basis, chapter 2 establishes the primacy of marriage for satisfying the courtly ambitions of Spanish noblewomen, yet also reveals that the female life-course flowed in and out of wedlock with greater fluidity than has previously been thought. Therefore even the most abnegate of wives could not be expected to remain in that state for very long, enjoying many other life-course experiences unencumbered by wifely constraints.

Chapters 3, 4 and 5 analyze women writers' mobilization of the mimetic, didactic and rhetorical energies, respectively, of courtship novels to contest a hegemonic story of women's oppression. Chapter 3, "Agency and Constraint in Courtship Plots," explicates the mimetic aspect of women's courtship novels. By lavishing descriptive detail on their female characters' life-course experiences before, during and after matrimony, women novelists refute the conflation of female identity with the ideal of the *perfecta casada* [perfect wife] promoted in normative writings of the time. Chapter 4 "The Art (and Craft) of Courtesy," makes evident the courtship novel's instructive impulse by enlisting the concept of "discretion," a habit of practical intellect cultivated by the elite to promote their interests at Court. Not unlike Gracián's *The Oracle*, cited above, courtship plots taught their readers the practical wisdom necessary to realize their connubial (or non-connubial) goals.

Chapter 5, "Courtship as Political Allegory," frames courtship within the context of imperial dynastic politics. Zayas, Meneses and Carvajal dedicated their courtship novels to powerful political figures. Each dedicatee favored a different matrimonial solution to Spain's succession crisis, a crisis that coincided with, and probably abetted, the final flowering of the courtship novel genre after 1647. Chapter 5 decodes the allegorical language of courtship to unlock the political import of each novel.

An appendix summarizes the nineteen novellas and two cornices (frame tales) on which *Picking Wedlock* relies. It is hoped that this resource will facilitate assimilation of a body of narrative not yet familiar to many readers, and that the number of courtship plots available to study will increase as scholarly interest in women's courtship novels continues to grow.

Notes

1. Carlos Hernández-Sacristán compares this "tossing about" technique to "presequencing," a category of conversation analysis (*"The Art of Worldly Wisdom* as an Ethics of Conversation," in *Rhetoric and Politics: Baltasar Gracián and the New World Order*, eds. Nicholas Spadaccini and Jenaro Talens, Hispanic Issues, Vol. 14 [Minneapolis: University of Minnesota, 1997] 291-292). All translations in this volume, except as noted otherwise, are by Karen Jones.

2. Lisis's hypocritical purposes included: throwing an engagement party to wriggle out of an engagement, pretending that the recitation of the *desengaños* [tales of disillusionment] "convinced" her to enter Orders when she had actually orchestrated it solely to convince her cousin Lisarda to reject her fiancé, choosing enclosure just to spite a former suitor, etc. See chapter 3.

1: Women and the *Novela de Cortejo* [Courtship Novel]

> Taking women seriously involves reconstructing their actions within the context of the relations that men and women instituted between themselves. It involves viewing relations between the sexes as a social construct whose history can and should be an object of study (Davis, Farge, 2).

Introduction

Of all the literary genres circulating in seventeenth-century Spain, the so-called *novela cortesana* [courtly novel] most attracted women writers.[1] Three female novelists—María de Zayas (*Novelas amorosas*, [Love stories] 1637; *Desengaños amorosos,* [The disenchantments of love] 1647), Leonor de Meneses (*El desdeñado más firme,* [Scorned yet steadfast] 1655) and Mariana de Carvajal *(Navidades de Madrid,* [Christmastide in Madrid] 1663)—cultivated this supposedly waning genre[2] during the reign of Philip IV (1621-1665). The purpose of the present volume is to elucidate the convergence of women novelists in a genre characterized, according to Agustín González de Amezúa, by its urban setting, aristocratic characters and erotically motivated plot (11, 12).

The best-known courtly novels (barring four arguably picaresque narratives)[3] are Cervantes's *Novelas ejemplares* [Exemplary novellas], first published in 1613. Nonetheless, in subsequent decades, women writers adopted the genre and made it their own through their unique treatment of the courtship plot. Unfortunately, the term "courtly novel" as it is currently formulated clouds the privileged role that the genre grants to courtship and to marriage, thereby occluding the very features of the form that specifically accommodated women. For this reason, I propose replacing "courtly novel" with "courtship novel," a demonstrably more useful and accurate term, one that situates women's affinity for the form within the interlocking operations of gender and genre in early Spanish fiction. I have dedicated this chapter to demonstrating the advantages of replacing the prevailing generic label, "courtly novel" (*novela cortesana*), with that of "courtship novel" (*novela de cortejo*) and to enumerating the lexical and historiographical shortcomings of the term "courtly novel." To contextualize the terminological revision that I propose, it will be useful to begin by introducing González de Amezúa's influential opuscule, the *Formación y elementos de la novela cortesana*

[Structure and elements of the courtly novel], where he first defines the taxonomic category of the courtly novel. After outlining the scope and reception of González de Amezúa's new classification, I will argue etymologically and sociologically for replacing his term with that of "courtship novel." Three distortions implicit in González de Amezúa's approach obscure women's contribution to the early history of the novel in Spain. To underscore the urgency of substituting "courtship novel" for "courtly novel," these distortions are explicated below.

From Courtly Novel to Courtship Novel

The sub-genre "courtly novel" was first identified, named and explicated by Agustín González de Amezúa in his 1929 address to the *Real Academia Española de la Lengua* [The Royal Spanish Academy of Letters] entitled, *Formación y elementos de la novela cortesana* [Structure and elements of the courtly novel], González de Amezúa's *Discurso* [Discourse] not only initiated an astonishingly productive new direction in Golden Age studies, it has also survived a half century of scrutiny and debate, largely intact. González de Amezúa established three criteria to define the courtly novel: urban setting, aristocratic characters and erotically motivated plot (11, 12). These traits are intended to distinguish the genre from other varieties of fiction such as the pastoral romance (rural landscape/aristocratic characters), the picaresque novel (urban landscape/socially marginal characters) and the romance of chivalry (aristocratic characters/exotic landscape).

Like the term "novel" itself, which gained currency only centuries after the vernacular prose fictions were first written and read,[4] "courtly novel" is also a belated category. Nonetheless, it has proven to be an enduring label, resisting the rival *novela corta romántica* [short romantic novel] (Pfandl 1929), *novela corta* [brief novel] (Place 1926; Pabst 1953; Rodríguez 1979), *novela amorosa* [love-themed novel] (Rodríguez 1987) and *novela barroca* [baroque novel] (Ripoll 1991). In 1983, Pacheco-Ransanz defended the ongoing utility of "courtly novel" as the taxonomic phrase of choice owing to its applicability to a large body of otherwise unassimilable prose works:

> González de Amezúa definió la novela cortesana en función de la condición social de sus protagonistas, la localización urbana de los relatos y el ambiente erótico de la acción. Estas características le permitieron agrupar sin gran esfuerzo un buen número de textos del siglo XVII difí

ciles de catalogar en otras categorías, justificando así el acierto inicial y el valor práctico de su invención crítica. (115)

(González de Amezúa defined the courtly novel in terms of the social status of its protagonists, the urban setting for the tales and the erotic atmosphere in which the action takes place. These characteristics permitted him to group together, without too great an effort, a good number of seventeenth-century texts that were difficult to place in other categories, thus justifying his initial innovation and the practical utility and merit of his critical invention.)

However, Amezúa's "acierto inicial" [initial innovation] presents linguistic, functional and historical drawbacks. From a linguistic standpoint, the term "courtly" proves semantically vague. The difficulty here lies in the fact that the Spanish adjective *cortesana* [courtly] carries contradictory connotations in its masculine and feminine forms, so different, in fact, that in Boscán's translation of Castiglione's *The Book of the Courtier,* when the time comes to compile a portrait of the ideal female courtier, Boscán prefers the term *dama* [lady] to that of *cortesana* [lady-in-waiting or lady of the court].[5] The *Diccionario de Autoridades* [Dictionary of authoritative sources] of 1728 defines *cortesano* [courtly] as "Lo perteneciente ò próprio de la Corte" [that which belongs to or is characteristic of the court], or "comedido, atento, urbáno, cortés" [obliging, attentive, urbane, courteous], while *cortesana* [the feminine-gender variation of the same term] is taken to mean, "la mujer libre, que vive licenciosamente" [a free woman who lives licentiously]. When the adjective *cortesano* flips into the feminine form to modify the word *novela,* it evokes the second definition of the noun *cortesana,* that of loose women. Certainly, allowing that adjectives are gendered by the substantives that they modify, the term *novela cortesana* might be understood merely as a *novela* about matters of Court, but it might equally be argued that it describes a *novela* concerning licentious women.

The great literary haven of freewheeling women in early fiction was the picaresque novel, as for example in López de Úbeda's *La pícara Justina,* [Naughty Justina] Castillo Solórzano's *Las harpías en Madrid* [The harpies in Madrid] and Francisco Delicado's *La loçana andaluza.* [The lively Andalusian lass]. In the "courtly" novel, by contrast, when *damas cortesanas* [lascivious women] appear they tend to play marginal roles, and are designated as inferior beings, predisposed as such to unruliness.[6] Two unruly women who illustrate this point are Don Gaspar's *lusitana dama* [Portugese lady] of Zayas's *desengaño,* "Estragos que causa el vicio" ["The vicissitudes of vice"] (472), and don Álvaro's concubine, Juliana, in Carvajal's "Quien bien obra siempre acierta" ["Kindness always pays"]. For seventeenth-century Spanish readers, to identify a woman as Portuguese was itself maligning. Even if Don Gaspar's Portugese lover had not shown herself to be a character of dubious morals, she would have elicited a negative response from readers by recalling Spain's humiliating loss of Portugal in 1640. Likewise, Carvajal's narrative already brands Don Álvaro's *esclava de casa* [domestic servant], Juliana, as an outsider to elite social circles, and therefore probably a negative element by the *clavo,* or slave-brand on her cheek, (Carvajal, *Navidades* 113) her extramarital relations with Don Álvaro, and the evil stepson that their relations produced. Since *damas cortesanas* [lascivious women] comprise but a small proportion of the female characters in the "courtly novel" and then generally only in minor roles, it makes little sense to risk overstating their prominence by including *cortesana* in the name of the genre. Instead, I propose replacing the ambiguous feminine adjective *cortesana*, possibly connoting wantonness, with the equally polyvalent, but far more relevant word, *cortejo* [courtship].

Cortejar, to court, from which the noun *cortejo* or courtship derives, converges two meanings fundamental to the courtship novel plot. Carlos de Coloma's 1609 *Guerra de Flandes* [War in Flanders], documents one prevailing definition of courtship as "Asistir, acompañar a uno contribuyendo a lo que sea de su agrado" [to attend to or accompany another, contributing in whatever way possible to that which might please him].[7] Plot in courtship novels consists largely of maneuvering into a more favorable position at Court. Courtship understood as a calculated social strategy becomes apparent through the novels' obsessive monitoring of inheritances won and lost, knighthoods, titles and sinecures awarded, dowries and brideprices negotiated or promised, detailed accounting of jewels, liveries, gowns and furnishings; in short, through a persistent trope of reckoning status. Far more than a mercenary streak, these socioeconomic cues point to an abiding concern with courting favor on the social pyramid of Court.

The second definition of *cortejar* in the seventeenth century, "galantear, requebrar, obsequiar a una mujer" [to treat a woman gallantly, to pay her amorous compliments, to shower her with gifts] relates to initiating an amorous relationship.[8] Like the English equivalent, courtship, the French *courtiser* and the Italian *corteggiare, cortejo* acquired the romantic connotations associated with it today with the rise of the great Courts of the Renaissance. The medieval Spanish term for wooing, *doñear,* betrayed the lady-centered ideal of courtly love.[9] Beginning in the fifteenth century, however, the process of bringing together two lovers became associated with the art of persuasion, or courting favor, a much more reciprocal, and at the same time, more mediated exchange than the static medieval concept of *doñear*. For Catherine Bates, courtship at the Elizabethan Court had become a:

rhetorical procedure that was strained, tortuous, and formalized. Strategies of persuasion, knowing, testing were designated to bridge an emotional, epistemological, and psychological gap that had opened up between the two partners in love . . . perceived as two remote and distanced individuals between whom communication was presented as difficult and highly pressurized. (10)

A flourishing trade in conduct manuals in the sixteenth and seventeenth centuries further attests that all varieties of public self-fashioning at court, whether political or amorous, were fraught with the pressure of performing before an exacting audience.[10]

Courtship as acts of deference to someone from whom one might expect political favor mingles with courtship as an overture to union in early modern Spain because women often held the key to men's ambitions at court. "Women, especially royal women, were at the center of the early modern European political world," according to Magdalena Sánchez.[11] Prior to Bourbon imposition of Salic law, Spanish women could occupy the throne and inherit titles of nobility, entailments and wealth. Among the highest nobility, it was permitted for a man to pass on his wife's title to his descendents, so a count who married a duchess could thereby become a duke-consort, and his son, a duke.[12] Upon her death, a noblewoman bequeathed her titles and riches to her husband, who, by marrying strategically in sequence, could move "up" the social ladder. In this manner, courtship leading to marriage represented another in the courtier's repertoire of strategies of social ascent. [13]

However, gender exerted differential force on the meaning of courtship for men and for women. Noblemen seeking to better themselves in the social hierarchy of Court could enhance their status by many means, as for example through military, diplomatic and financial service to the king, by rising through ecclesiastical ranks, or even through participation in public cultural spectacles (jousts, *certámenes*, [poetry contests] etc.). Meanwhile, early modern European women's work rhythms were largely shaped by "individual biological and social events such as marriage, motherhood, and widowhood," according to social historian Merry Wiesner. She continues, "A man's stages of life were often differentiated by his place in an occupational or professional hierarchy, while a woman's depended on her marital status" (83). This disparity of access to channels of social convection for men and women led to a corresponding difference in the relative importance of courtship and marriage for the two sexes: matrimony mattered more to women. This may explain why women novelists gravitated almost exclusively to the courtship plot while men cultivated a broader range of narrative genres reflecting their proportionally broader spectrum of socioeconomic activity.

Male authors had favored the courtship novel in its inception and early development. As Theresa Ann Sears writes of marriage in Cervantes' *Novelas ejemplares,* "marrying his desiring heroes to their virginal beloveds allows Cervantes to both [sic] evoke desire for its literary pleasures, and at the same time, to drain it of its erotic force by channeling it into a socially acceptable form" (152). Once that balance between post-Tridentine utility and erotic delight had been achieved, courtship novel convention was reified in a set of generic formulae that soon became depleted. However, a new challenge overtook the old, as women infused the hollow medium of the courtship plot with matters of their own. The *novelas de cortejo,* in which marriage provides the teleological and thematic impetus for plot, offered women an accommodating discursive field for reconstructing the self both within and beyond existing gender paradigms. By adhering to a genre firmly rooted in an orthodox conception of courtship and marriage, Zayas, Carvajal and Meneses could satisfy counter-Reformation scruples while re-envisioning two life-course events disproportionately vital to women: courtship and marriage.

The older term "courtly novel" not only misrepresents female characters in the courtship novel as unruly or licentious, as demonstrated earlier, but also obfuscates the prominence of courtship as a primary structuring element of plot, thereby eliminating the possibility of recognizing the courtship novel's appeal to female novelists. Shifting usage from "courtly novel" to "courtship novel" highlights the primacy of courtship in the courtship novel plot while correcting the misapprehension that intemperate female characters (*damas cortesanas*) dominate the genre.

However, the term "courtly novel" is not the only aspect of González de Amezúa's *Formación* [Structure] that pleads for revision. González de Amezúa's celebratory *Discurso* [Discourse] to the Real Academia de la Lengua [Royal Academy of the Spanish Language] in 1929 purveys a vision of the courtship novel genre better suited to titillating the *Real Academia*'s male membership than to explicating a literary form honed and crafted by novelists of both sexes. As I demonstrate below, González de Amezúa's *Discurso* exaggerates the lurid aspects of courtship novel plots and downplays women's agency in the courtship process. These distortions can serve a cautionary function, for they anticipate and expose errors that readers of today are likely to reproduce. By elaborating three sites of historical slippage evident in González de Amezúa's *Formación y elementos de la novela cortesana* [Structure and elements of the courtly novel], my intention is not to detract from the author's indisputable contribution to Spanish literary historiography, but rather to insert an overdue and necessary corrective to the ongoing redaction of that account.

Historicizing Courtship: Three Distortions

González de Amezúa's *Discurso* applies three anachronistic presuppositions to the seventeenth-century texts that it claims to elucidate. First, the *Discurso* imposes modern psychological concepts onto works pertaining to a period before intersubjectivity was "naturalized" as a model of human affect. Second, it overprivileges a sensationalist and self-centered model of desire, and, third, it attributes a male viewpoint to all characters in courtship, whether male or female. Revisiting the *Discurso* with an eye to recognizing differences between courtship in absolutist Spain and courtship now can help to minimize the risk of reproducing these distortions,[14] and can promote a more historically sensitized and gender inclusive approach to the courtship novel.

Distortion 1: Psychologizing the Past

González de Amezúa assumes that the departure point for plot in the courtship novel (*novela de cortejo*) is that of "love": "El fondo de la intriga es también, invariablemente, con muy raras excepciones, el amor" [the basis of the intrigue is also, invariably, with very few exceptions, love] (48). Paradoxically, this formulation is both too general and too specific to be effective in defining courtship novels. It is too general insofar as one agrees with narrative theorist Peter Brooks that, "[d]esire is always at the start of a narrative" (38), making it an insufficiently specific criterion for distinguishing one literary form from another. Even González de Amezúa concedes that, "variadísimas y ricas especulaciones . . . sobre el amor pululan entonces en *toda suerte de libros*" [extraordinarily varied and rich speculations on love teem in *all sorts of books*] (51, emphasis added). On the other hand, González de Amezúa's notion of love presupposes a specific approach to human affect that had not yet gained currency in the 1600s: that of modern psychology.

For Amezúa, love is a compulsive drive, "la fuerza del amor" [the force of love] (49), a degraded version of the troubadour's pure adoration:

> el amor no buscará cadalsos ni graderías, sino callejas oscuras y misteriosas; no anidará en donceles con estampa de trovadores, sino en unos mozos inquietos, libertinos y tornadizos, quienes, como decía con enérgica frase un orador de entonces, serán "idólatras de ídolos de sangre y carne"; no habrá en aquella honesta separación y diferencia de las Cortes de Amor, sino la tenue y huidiza de unos leves *mantos de humo;* en suma, amor se hará real, humano, pecador las más veces. (50)

(love will not seek out all manner of public places in order to display itself openly, preferring instead dark, mysterious alleyways; it will not make its dwelling in young noblemen with the fine appearance of troubadours but rather in fickle, libertine, restless youths who will become, as an orator of the day said so energetically, "worshippers of false idols of flesh and blood"; that honorable separation between these two types of love, set out so clearly by the Courts of Love, will cease to be, becoming instead as tenuous and elusive as flimsy veils of smoke; in short, love will become real, human, sinful in most cases.)

González de Amezúa's love story is one of interiorized instincts and drives rather than external stimuli. It is a twentieth-century story that occludes the plotting mechanisms of seventeenth-century texts. By portraying the *mozos inquietos* [fickle youth] of the courtship novel as though compelled by uncontrollable forces of love to violate the social contract in their back-alley forays, G. de Amezúa reduces their "idolatry" to lust, eliminating any distance between stimulus and response, and thereby construing male aggression to be what he elsewhere characterizes as a "despótica ley" [despotic law] (45).

Ascribing autonomy and compulsivity to the *galanes* [gallant beaux] of the courtship novel confuses the impassioned subject postulated centuries later by Romanticism, with the Renaissance's Humoralist Man. Erotic desire was not understood in early modern Europe as libido, a driving force that charges the individual from within. Rather, men and women were viewed as humorally constituted sites continuously challenged to maintain equilibrium. When a strong emotion did "burn" one of the humors, as a consequence of external stimulation by food, environment, beauty, etc., this conflagration was thought to leave behind a residue called "adust melancholy" or *atrabilis* that itself gave rise to a host of new symptoms. Thus, whereas libido is postulated as part and parcel of a healthy modern being, Renaissance medicine distinguished between love, which is characterized by harmony and balance, and passions excited by external contaminants which produced imbalance and pathology (Soufas 6, 7).[15]

Distortion 2: Ambition and Desire

A second problem for the *Discurso* is that eroticism itself as an explicit *topos,* theme or pretext for action is an anachronistic criterion to impose on non-comedic vernacular writings of the early modern period.[16] In post-Tridentine literature, libidinal satisfaction, except where matrimonial intentions are evident, is proscribed as an explicit literary motive.[17] Physical yearning is textualized as neo-platonic or heavenly desire, sensuality, linked to temptation and sin. However, not only is the free play of *erotic* desire held at bay; *any* assertion of individual will at the expense of orthodox values is chastened. The premiere emblem of personal striving in early modern fiction is the *pícaro* [rogue], whose goal is survival and self-advancement. However, characters that condone the picaresque get-ahead ethos in Golden Age letters are portrayed as monstrous caricatures.

Three examples suffice to illustrate that the pursuit of individual happiness was not yet assimilated as a positive value in early modern Europe. First is the well-known case of the demented squire Don Quixote, who frees galley slave and self-proclaimed *pícaro,* Ginés de Pasamonte. Rather than exalting Don Quixote's defense of Pasamonte's unfettered freedom, Cervantes's text portrays Don Quixote's actions as lunatic. Second, at the conclusion of *Lazarillo de Tormes* [The life and adventures of Lazarillo de Tormes] (1554) the wandering rogue, Lázaro, finally finds an ally in the person of an archpriest. However, this supposed "protector" proves to be just as ignoble as Lázaro's previous masters, extorting the sexual services of Lázaro's wife in exchange for granting Lázaro a small measure of security. Finally, footloose Berganza, whose autobiographical picaresque narrative comprises the substance of Cervantes's novella "El coloquio de los perros" [The dog's colloquy] can at best be considered a talking mutt born of a monstrous witch. At worst, the text gives us to understand that Berganza may be no more than a figment of the imagination of a more repentant *pícaro* [rogue], that of Ensign Campuzano, who "over-hears" the dog's tale in the course of a syphilitic fit.[18] Still viewed during this period as a social pariah, criminal or monster, the *pícaro* who placed personal advancement above collective values had yet to attain the stature of a cultural hero.[19]

The nobility was granted no greater leeway in pursuing personal satisfaction at the expense of others than was the street-rogue. When Tirso's *Burlador* [Libertine] Don Juan fails to repent a lifetime of self-satisfaction, for example, he is taken down (literally) at the end of the play to hell. The primacy of a discrete subject's search for self-realization would not be fully textualized until the Romantics recast the *caballero andante* [knight-errant], not as Christian soldier or deluded antiquarian, but as an exemplary model of individualistic quest. Meanwhile, in Golden Age letters, so elaborately do absolutist and counter-Reformation discourses attenuate and refract the *fuerza de amor* [force of love] that it became something qualitatively different than that which modern readers have come to expect.

Once erotic desire and personal ambition are relinquished as the predominant impetus for plot, what remains to motivate courtship? The desire that marriage satisfies in women's courtship novels proves reiteratively not to be "erotic" but rather, pragmatic.[20] Lisis, the frame-tale protagonist of María de Zayas's *Desengaños amorosos* [Disenchantments of love], for example, dreams of balancing men's wishes against women's needs: "¡Oh, quién tuviera el entendimiento como el deseo, para saber defender a las hembras y agradar a los varones!" [Oh, but were it possible to possess as much understanding as desire, in order to know how to defend the females of the species and please the males!] (470). Other desires include those of preserving or enhancing aristocratic standing, pleasing parents, avoiding sin or amassing wealth. Zayas's "La inocencia castigada" [Her innocence punished] and Cervantes's "La fuerza de la sangre" [The strength of blood-ties] provide just two among many instances of courtship plots that strip courtship and marriage bare of any pretense of romantic desire.

Inés, of "La inocencia castigada," "aceptó [su] casamiento, quizá no tanto por él [su hermano], cuánto por salir de la rigurosa condición de su cuñada que era de lo cruel que imagainarse puede." [accepted her marriage, perhaps not so much because of him (her brother), but rather in order to escape her sister-in-law, who, because of her demanding nature, was wont to be as cruel as humanly possible] (265). For Inés, marriage satisfies the desire to escape from an oppressive sister-in-law. Her spouse's character, even his identity, remain incidental to her assent. The more fully to evacuate any hint of erotic desire from Inés's courtship, Zayas defers naming Inés's husband until late in the tale (282).[21]

Courtship responds to equally pragmatic concerns in Cervantes's novella, "La fuerza de la sangre," where a carefully orchestrated courtship scene salvages Leocadia's honor, lost when Rodolfo raped her. The motive that drives Leocadia to the altar to wed her assailant is not love, but only the very practical necessity of reintegrating into a society that would otherwise ostracize her. *Amor pecador* [sinful love] functions not as the axis of plot, but as a tripping mechanism, comparable to that of the *Licenciado's* [Licentiate's] madness, the Gypsy maid's family romance or the Extremaduran's possessiveness[22] in Cervantes's other tales. As Harry Sieber observes, an originary novelty disrupts the status quo in the *Exemplary Novels,* giving rise to the complications of its plot. That novelty may take many forms, only one of which is lust: "O por elección, or por rapto, o por locura o por otros motivos, los personajes—como los lectores en el acto de leer las novelas—se encuentran en situaciones diferentes y anormales, en fin, 'novelescas'" [perhaps by choice, perhaps by force or because of insanity or other reasons, the characters—like those in the act of reading the novels—find themselves in situations that are different, bizarre, abnormal, all in all, "novel-like"] ("Preliminar," *Novelas ejemplares* I, 15). The term "courtship novel" unhinges courtship from miscreance, recasting it in the neutral guise of a pragmatically motivated activity by which women and men secure and improve their social standing.

Distortion 3: A Male Domain

Action in "La fuerza de la sangre" unspools in relation to Leocadia's dishonor and her strategic response to this challenge. Although her rapist, Rodolfo, matches González de Amezúa's profile of the *mozo libertino* [libertine youth], plot revolves around the female protagonist, Leocadia, in Toledo, not the male antagonist, Rodolfo, in Italy. This observation gives rise to the third of the three object lessons that the *Discurso* can offer: its unstated assumption that courtly novels are about men. Notice the figurative language in the following passage, in which González de Amezúa idealizes the union of two lovers in a prototypical courtly novel: "y en las sombras densas de la noche. . . irrumpirá el amor en desbordado torrente de requiebros y dulzores, que impregnan también nuestras novelas de su sutil perfume" [and in the night's dark shadows, love will overflow its banks, bursting forth in a torrent of amorous admiration and sweetness that pervades our novels with its delicate scent] (45-46). Love from this viewpoint erupts in torrents in a dense shadowy place to impregnate with its subtle perfumes. Is this vision of courtship universal to both sexes, or would a female-focalizer[23] exalt other aspects of the experience?

There is little evidence that courtship novels privilege male focalizers or actors. In twenty-one courtship plots written by the three women novelists, María de Zayas, Leonor de Meneses and Mariana de Carvajal, between 1647 and 1663, female characters focalize action or share focalization in every one.[24] Therefore it is likely that courtship novels represent conflicts, experiences, rhythms and pleasures of both male and female characters. Female-focalized courtship scenes are not difficult to find. Mariana de Carvajal's "El amante venturoso" ["The lucky lover"] supplies one example. Teodora, an unmarried maiden living in her parents' house, has recently been seized by fascination for her neighbor, Carlos:

> El día siguiente, mandó llevar los bastidores de sus curiosas bordaduras a una sala que caía frontero de la casa de Carlos, dando a entender lo hacía por el calor, para ver despacio a su nuevo dueño. Fiaba en las guardas de los balcones, por estar adornados de espesas y tejidas celosías y lustrosas vidrieras. (78)

> (The following day, she commanded that the frames that held her unique embroidery be sent to a parlor that looked upon Carlos' house across the way—on the pretense that she did so because of the heat—in order to look upon her heart's new master at her leisure. She trusted that the balconies would shield her, for they were adorned with densely woven latticework and lustrous panes of glass.)

Hidden securely behind intricate architectural screens and veils of protocol, Teodora revels in the voyeuristic sensuality of being courted without being seen.[25]

The contrast between Carvajal's fiction and G. de Amezúa's treatise is striking. In "El amante venturoso" [The lucky lover], *curiosas bordaduras* [unique embroidery] replace *desbordados torrentes* [bursting torrents]; the pace is *despacio* [slow]; pleasure is exclusively the woman's, and no consequences are implied. This is a courtship that remains within bounds, delighting in prolongation rather than culmination, in freedom from risk rather than the perils of union itself. In this respect, it is reminiscent of the happy courtship that María de Zayas concedes to the otherwise unfortunate heroine of "Mal presagio casar lejos" [Only disaster awaits a bride far from home]:

> demás de gozar las más noches de músicas, los días de paseos, toros, cañas y encamisadas, máscaras y otras fiestas que el príncipe hacía en servicio de doña Blanca, estaban [las damas] muy medradas de galas y otras dádivas, y a vueltas de esto gozaban también de sus galanteos. Y si ellas deseaban que el año no se acabara, doña Blanca lo deseaba más. (347)
>
> (besides having taken much pleasure in the many nights of musicians, the days full of afternoon strolls, the bullfights, the stunning displays of horsemanship and the silly torch-lit improvisational skits, the masked balls and other festivities and diversions the prince had arranged in order to woo Lady Blanca, the ladies in waiting were benefitting from all the new gowns and other gifts and they also revelled in the prince's gallantries. And if they wished that the year would never end, so did Lady Blanca, even more fervently.)

Without over-privileging the focalizing impact of female characters in the courtship novel, there is doubtless much to be gained by beginning to recognize and to analyze the interplay of multiple perspectives in early women's fiction.

To conclude the foregoing critique, despite certain lexical and conceptual limitations, González de Amezúa's 1929 *Discurso* continues to teach much about courtship novels. Particularly, as its author observed, the genre's characters are aristocrats operating in an urban as opposed to bucolic setting.[26] However, licentious female characters, when present, play only circumscribed roles. Plot need not be erotically motivated, but rather departs from a range of pragmatic issues related to courtship and marriage that often focalize women's concerns. There is no evidence that a male perspective predominates.

Picking Wedlock

While "courtly novel" has been a useful and enduring critical category, this term mutes women's contribution to the genre and restricts the kinds of questions that can be asked about courtship narratives. Revisiting the phrase *novela cortesana* seven decades after its coinage affords the opportunity, in Natalie Zemon Davis's words, to "take women seriously," that is, to apply current developments in women's social and literary history to early fiction in general, and to the courtship novel in particular. By replacing the luridly tinged vagaries of *cortesanía* [courtliness, or relating to courtesans] with the external action of courtship, the term "courtship" helps to defamiliarize a corpus of writing that predates the advent of modern psychology. This distancing can help the reader to "take seriously" women's predilection for courtship plots during a period of emergent female subjectivity in post-Cervantine letters.

The new rubric "courtship novels" recalls that courtship, understood in both its political and romantic senses, holds the key to explaining the genre's appeal to aristocratic women writers. Chapter 2, "'I Do.': Nuptiality and Gender in Early Modern Spain" historicizes the construction of gender in seventeenth-century Spain in order to elucidate early modern noblewomen's participation in both political and pre-nuptial courting. Following Joan Wallach Scott's model for (re)writing the social history of gender, chapter 2 evidences four distinct areas of gender experience (cultural, normative, juridical and subjective). Gender expectations in the early modern period varied widely from one area of experience to the next (laws empowering women versus treatises restricting them, for example) and from one life-course stage to the next (unmarried maiden to wife, wife to widow, for instance). These fissures and contradictions in the social construction of gender allowed women to recognize that courtship and marriage, rather than monolithic exercises in submission and oppression, were transformative, at times harrowing, life passages, nuanced at every step of the way by obstacles and opportunity, choice and control.

The courtship novel provided female novelists a consecrated framework in which to anatomize the degree of agency and constraint available to themselves as women during courtship and marriage. Courtship plots encrypt, depict and rescript power struggles enacted between men and women in three domains of interaction: the domain of society and its institutions (family, church, law, etc); the domain of social discourse (the rhetoric of self-representation that will be called "courtesy"), and the domain of dynastic politics at the Hapsburg court. Chapters 3, 4 and 5 address each of these domains respectively.

Notes

1. It is more prudent to write "most" rather than "exclusively" not only because research on early modern women's writing is so active at the moment that exceptions to categorical statements could turn up at any time, but also in the event that Calalina de Erauso, the picaresque autobiographical heroine of the *Vida i sucesos de la monja alférez* [Life and exploits of the nun-ensign] turns out to have been a real historical personage after all. However, even as recently as 1997, Encarnación Juárez, who situates *La monja alférez* [The nun-ensign] within the genre of female fictionalized autobiography, is forced to concede that, "Al no existir el autógrafo de la autobiografía no se puede afirmar categoricamente que Catalina de Erauso fuera la autora de ella" [Since the autobiography is not signed, it is not possible to categorically affirm that Catalina de Erauso was its author] ("La autobiografía como búsqueda y afirmación de identidad" [The autobiography as search for and affirmation of identity"], in *La Chispa '95: Selected Proceedings of the 16th Louisiana Conference on Hispanic Languages and Literatures*, ed. Claire Paolini [New Orleans: Tulane University, 1995] 185n2).

"In the sixteenth century, three women wrote Spanish romances of chivalry: Leonor Coutinho (*Don Belindo*), the anonymous author of *Palmerín de Oliva* [The flamenco artist from Oliva] and *Primaleón* [Cousin-tigress] and Beatriz Bernal (*Don Cristalián de España* [Don Cristalián of Spain]). See Amy Kaminsky, ed., *Water Lilies: An Anthology of Spanish Women Writers from the Fifteenth through the Nineteenth Century* (Minneapolis: University of Minnesota Press, 1996), 84. In the seventeenth century, Ana Francisca Barca de Bolea penned a religio-pastoral work, the *Vigilia y octavario de San Juan Bautista* [The vigil of abstinence and poetic musings of St. John the Baptist], ed. María Angeles Campo Guiral (Huesca, Spain: Instituto de Estudios Altoaragoneses, 1994), which contained a novel entitled "Fin bueno en el mal principio" [A good ending from a bad beginning].

2. Walter Pabst views Zayas as the last novelista cortesana of note (*La novela corta en la teória y en la creación literaria* [The short novel in literary theory and creation], trans. Rafaél de la Vega [Madrid: Gredos, 1972], 493). Augustín González de Amezúa dates the demise of the genre to the 1630s (*Formación y elementos de la novela cortesana: Discurso leído ante la Real Academia Española* [Structure and elements of the courtly novel: A discourse read before the Royal Spanish Academy] [Madrid: Real Academia Española, 1929], 99). Caroline Bourland catalogues only fourteen new novellas from 1647 to 1693 as compared to dozens in the first third of the century ("Aspectos de la vida del hogar en el siglo XVII según las novelas de Doña Mariana de Carbajal" [Aspects of home life in the seventeenth century according to the novels of Doña Mariana de Carbajal], in *Homenaje ofrecido a Menéndez Pidal* [Homage to Menéndez Pidal], Vol. II [Madrid, 1925]).

3. "Rinconete y Cortadillo" [Rinconete and Cortadillo], "El casamiento engañoso" [The deceptive wedding], "La ilustre fregona" [The illustrious kitchen maid] and "El coloquio de los perros" [The dogs' colloquy].

4. Northrop Frye offers a prescient analysis of this process in *Anatomy of Criticism: Four Essays* (Princeton: Princeton University Press, 1957).

5. Capítulo primero: Cómo la Duquesa dió el cargo al Manífico Julián de formar una perfeta Dama [Chapter one: How the Duchess put Manífico Julián in charge of forming a perfect Lady]. Baldassare Castiglione, *El cortesano* [The courtier], trans. Juan Boscán, ed. Marcelino Menéndez Pelayo (Madrid: Consejo Superior de Investigaciones Científicas, 1942), 224.

6. Here, a notorious exception proves the rule. Casandra, of Juan Pérez de Montalbán's memorable, "La mayor confusión" [The greatest confusion] seduces her own son, raises the daughter born of that union in secrecy, and later fails to prevent the same son from marrying his own daughter/sister. Curiously, Church authorities viewed with benevolence the first two editions of this conspicuously lascivious tale. See Evangelina Rodríguez, *Novela corta marginada del siglo XVII Español* [The marginalized short story of Spain's seventeenth century] (Valencia: Universidad de Valencia, 1979).

7. Carlos de Coloma, *Guerra de Flandes,* 1629, book I chapter 6, quoted in *Enciclopedia del idioma: Diccionario histórico y moderno de la lengua española (Siglos XII al XX)* [Encyclopedia of the language: Historical and modern dictionary of the Spanish language] , 3 vols. (Madrid: Aguilar, 1958).

8. César Oudin, *Tesoro de las dos lenguas francesa y española* [Thesaurus of the French and Spanish languages] (Paris, 1607); Lorenzo Franciosini, *Vocabulario español e italiano* [Spanish and Italian vocabulary] 2 vols. (Rome, 1620); Francisco Sobrino, *Diccionario nuevo de las lenguas españoals y francesas* [New dictionary of the Spanish and French languages] (Brussels, 1705), quoted in *Enciclopedia del idioma* [Encyclopedia of the language], 1958.

9. See for example Jacques Joset, ed., *Juan Ruiz, Arcipreste de Hita. Libro de buen amor* [Juan Ruíz, Archpriest of Hita. The Book of Good Love] (Madrid: Taurus, 1990), cc 450b, 527b, 616d, 633a, 1336d 1342a.

10. Castiglione's *Il cortegiano* [The book of the courtier] underwent at least fifty editions and translations in the sixteenth century (*Enciclopedia universal ilustrada* [Illustrated universal encyclopedia] [Barcelona: Espasa, 1912]). In Spain, Boscán's 1534 translation was reprinted at least fourteen times (Harry Sieber, "Literary Continuity, Social Order, and the Invention of the Picaresque," in *Cultural Authority in Golden Age Spain*, ed. Marina Brownlee and Hans Ulrich Gumbrecht [Baltimore: Johns Hopkins University Press, 1995], 144).

11. Two female rulers Magdalena Sánchez foregrounds are Charles V's daughter, Empress María (1528-1603), co-regent of Castile with her husband Maximilian II from 1548-1551, and Philip III's sister, Isabel Clara Eurgenia (1566-1633), joint ruler of the Netherlands with Archduke Albert, and later sole ruler from 1621-1633 (*The Empress, the Queen and the Nun: Women and Power at the Court of Philip III*, Johns Hopkins University Studies in History and Political Science, Series 2.116 [Baltimore: Johns Hopkins University Press, 1998], 183-184).

Other female rulers included Princess Margarita of Savoy, who governed Portugal for six years until the 1640 Restoration, Ana and Mariana of Austria, who acted as regents of France and Spain during Louis XIV and Charles II's minorities, and Luisa of Portugal, an Andalusian heiress who married the Duke of Bragança, and rose to royalty with him, becoming Queen of Portugal following his death in 1656. See John H. Elliott, *The Count-Duke of Olivares* (New Haven, Conn.: Yale University Press, 1986).

12. This is the case of Rodrigo de Silva, who became Duke Consort of Híjar in 1621 upon marrying doña Isabel Margarita Fernández, IV Duchess of Híjar, Lécera y Aliaga, VI Countess of Belchite and Countess of Valfogona and Guimerá. Of this match, the Archbishop of Zaragoza attested that the bride was one of the greatest heiresses of Spain in the seventeenth century "por el número y honor de sus estados, por la representación de su sangre y por la claridad de sus virtudes" [because of the number and value of her estates, the importance of her bloodline, and her many shining virtues]. Quoted in Ramón Ezquerra Abadía, *La conspiración del Duque de Híjar (1648)* [The Conspiracy of the Duke of Híjar] (Madrid, 1934), 76-79.

13. James Boyden documents one such advantageous marriage, that of Ruy Gómez de Silva, whose marriage to Doña Ana de Mendoza de la Cerda gave the untitled favorite of Philip II aristocratic cachet, a vast inheritance, the right for his eldest son to inherit the title of Count of Mélito and valuable landholdings with their accompanying incomes (*The Courtier and the King: Ruy Gomez de Silva, Philip II, and the Court of Spain* [Berkeley and Los Angeles, Ca.: University of California Press, 1995], 24-38).

14. An allusion to Keith Whinnom's now-classic essay, *Spanish Literary Historiography: Three Forms of Distortion.* (Exeter, England: University of Exeter, 1967).

15. "The varying symptoms that passion produces such as insomnia, hallucinations, desire for darkness and solitude, discontentment, and villainous tendencies are also characteristics associated with insanity" (Teresa Scott Soufas, *Melancholy and the Secular Mind in Spanish Golden Age Literature* [Columbia, Mo.: University of Missouri Press, 1990), 7).

16. In 1561, Fray Luis de León scandalized censors by translating *oscula* as *beso* [kiss], and *ubera* as *pecho* [breast] in the "Song of Songs"; somehow in Latin the poem's sensuality hadn't quite hit home. As León's subsequent imprisonment and trial attest, his Inquisitors found it extremely difficult to reconcile eroticism, even when deployed figuratively, with Christian dogma. In his written defense, León wrote: "Ansi que a este el texto le offende, y yo ya que le puse en romançe no pude escusar de offendelle, porque no tenia otros vocablos que romançar oscula, ubera, amica mea, fermosa mea, y lo semejante, sino diziendo besos, y pechos, y my amada, y mi hermosa, y otras cosas asi, porque no sé otro romançe del que me enseñaron mis amas que es el que ordinariamente hablamos" [And so this text offends you, and I, for having translated it to our colloquial tongue, could have done nothing but offend you because I had no other words for "oscula" [kisses], "ubera" [breasts], "amica mea" [my beloved], "fermosa mea" [my beauty], and so forth than "kisses" and

"breasts" and "my love" and "my beauty" and so on, because what I know of our vulgar language is limited to what my housekeepers taught me, and this is the way we ordinarily speak it] (*Cantar de Canteres de Solomón, 1651* [Song of Songs], ed. José Manuel Blecua, Biblioteca Románica Hispánica, Vol. 22 [Madrid: Gredos, 1994], 18-19).

17. Prior to 1640, lasciviousness was prohibited by the Spanish Indexes only insofar as it promulgated heresy or errors of faith. However, with the advent of Sotomayor's 1640 Index, "Prohíbense así mismo los libros que tratan, cuentan y enseñan cosas de propósito lascivas, de amores o otras qualesquiera, como dañosas a las buenas costumbres de la Iglesia Christiana aunque no se mezclen en ellas heregías y errores en la Fe, mandando que los que los tuvieren, sean castigados por los inquisidores severamente" [And thus are prohibited those books which deal with, speak of, or teach about things that are intrinsically lascivious, whether they deal with love affairs or other inciteful themes, as they are harmful to the morals of the Church and the faithful even if heresies and religious errors are not mixed into their pages; thus it is ordered that those who possess such books be severely punished by the officers of the Inquisition]. *Novissimus Librorum Prohibitorum et Expurgatorum Index* [Index of books most recently prohibited and expurgated] Madrid, 1640, Regla VII, quoted in Jesús Martínez de Bujanda, "Literatura e Inquisición en España en el Siglo XVI" [Literature and the Inquisition in Spain in the sixteenth century], in Ángel Alcalá, ed., *Inquisición española y mentalidad inquisitorial* [The Spanish Inquisition and the inquisitorial mentality] (Barcelona: Ariel, 1984), 583.

18. The Ensign Campuzano records a conversation between two dogs that he swears that he heard take place outside his window while he was undergoing sweat treatments at the Hospital of the Resurrection. That "conversation," the dogs' colloquy, consisted of Berganza relating his life's story to his companion, Cipión.

19. For Peter Brooks, the *pícaro* represents the very crudest aspect of desire, the desire to survive: "A rock-bottom paradigm of the dynamic of desire can be found in one of the very earliest novels in the Western tradition, *Lazarillo de Tormes* (1554), where all of the hero's tricks and dodges are directed initially at staying alive" (*Reading for the Plot: Design and Intention in Narrative* [New York: Vintage-Random House, 1984], 38).

20. A historical counterpart to this pragmatic view of courtship is found in the prevailing institution of dynastic diplomacy, by which monarchies allied themselves with one another through marriage. The following excerpt from a letter written in 1554 describes the future King Philip II's marriage to Mary Tudor of England: "The Queen is very happy with the King and the King with her. . . . [T]he best of it is that the King fully realizes that the marriage was concluded for no fleshly considerations, but in order to remedy the disorders of the Kingdom and preserve the Low Countries" (Boyden, *Courtier and King*, 46).

21. Once wed, Inés finds herself opportuned by a stealthy and persistent suitor, who finally succeeds at dishonoring her through magic. Although the law exonerates Inés on the grounds that sorcery disabled her free-will, her husband

and brother insist on her guilt. The secret punishment that they devise is to immure Inés alive for six years.

22. See Shifra Armon, "The Paper Key: Money as Text in Cervantes's 'El Celoso Extremeño' and Camerino's 'El Pícaro Amante,'" *Cervantes: Bulletin of the Cervantes Society of America* 18 (1998), 96-114.

23. Focalization, as formulated by Gerard Genette and adapted by Shlomith Rimmon-Kenan, allows "who sees" within a narrative to be distinguished from the point of view of "who speaks." The example given by Rimmon-Kenan is that of James Joyce's *Portrait of an Artist*, in which the narrative agent is an adult, but child-like language and perspective indicate the focalization of a child (*Narrative Fiction: Contemporary Poetics* [London: Methuen, 1983], 71-85).

24. Ten *desengaños*, eight novelas of the *Navidades,* two framing plots and Meneses's *Desdeñado.*

25. Carmen Martín Gaite symbolizes woman's liminal social position with the image of the woman in the window.

26. Country scenes prompted by exile, flight or excursions away from the metropolis represent a superficial change of costume or setting rather than a fundamental shift in modality. Thus, in Mariana de Carvajal's "Amar sin saber a quién" [Her mystery lover], an island hunting estate sets the scene for courtly spectacles, jousts, etc.

2: "I Do": Nuptiality and Gender in Early Modern Spain

> Mi vida ... [h]a variado de fases muchas veces—tantas, que me parece haber vivido en muchas generaciones diferentes.
> (I've gone through many stages in my life—so many that it seems as though I've lived in many different eras.)[1]
> —Carmen de Burgos "Autobiografía"

> when daughters inherit, control of their marriage becomes very important.
> —James Casey, *The History of the Family*, 85.

Writing gender into the historical account of courtship and marriage restores layer to layer of possible interpretations of marriage tropes in the courtship novel even as it disallows anachronistic readings based on subsequent events. The point of reconstructing this nexus of associations is not to limit the interpretative drift that women's courtship plots have undergone across three and a half centuries, nor even to fix a unified reading within the period in which they were published. Readership had become too diverse and too dispersed in the latter seventeenth century to predict a unitary pattern of reception,[2] and there is no reason to deny future readers the creative engagement with the text that enlivened it for them. What historicizing can accomplish is to indicate a range of possible readings at the time of circulation, and to exclude a range of readings that would have been unlikely to come into play until later developments had taken place.

Gender changes over time. The boundaries of household and family, public and private, the historically significant and the historically trivial were drawn very differently in the seventeenth century than they are today. Even within the early modern period, according to Natalie Zemon Davis, "sex roles were sometimes tightly prescribed and sometimes fluid, sometimes markedly asymmetrical and sometimes more even" ("Women's History" 88). Joan Wallach Scott's formulation of gender is useful for the task of delineating gender boundaries at the Hapsburg Court while respecting their instability because it embraces multiple aspects of human experience and perception that can change over time. Gender for Scott, "is a constitutive element of social relationships based on perceived differences between the sexes, and gender is a primary way of signifying relationships of power" (1067). As a constitutive element of social relationships based on perceived differences between the sexes, gender involves four areas of human experience: cultural symbols, normative concepts that limit the interpretation of those symbols, sociopolitical relationships and identity formation. By investigating courtship and marriage experiences and expectations for men and women in these four areas, a range of possible interpretations and meanings of courtship plots at the time of their initial circulation can emerge. This horizon of interpretability is further nuanced by recalling, with Scott, that "gender is one of the recurrent references by which political power has been conceived, legitimated, and criticized" (1073).

The organization of this chapter, consistent with Scott's schema, is fourfold. The first two areas of human experience to be investigated are cultural symbols and the doctrines that color their interpretation. Women's fiction draws its imagery from the fund of symbols available at the time, and tempers those symbols to comply with (or subvert) societal expectations. Therefore the first section below presents an overview of iconographic models of femininity in early modern Spain while the second visits the realm of normative discourses on gender with special attention to marriage treatises. In the third section, marriage is seen to function as a primary node in the distribution of social, legal and economic prerogatives. In the seventeenth century, as now, theory clashed with practice; women's lived experience of gender did not necessarily conform to official paradigms, but this disjunction only comes into focus when the hegemonic discourse is contrasted with historical conditions. Clearly it would be naive to imagine that women's experience of marriage matched the fantasy painted in Luis de León's marriage treatise, *La perfecta casada* [The perfect wife]. If it did, there would have been no need to write such a treatise. Therefore symbolic and preceptive gender models must be weighed against the actual choices available to women before, during, after and outside of marriage. Finally, section four attempts to reconstruct the subjective experience of femininity given the circumstances described in the preceding three sections. Aristocratic women and men's life-stages are contrasted with one another to illustrate how marriage came to weigh more heavily in women's identity formation than in men's. Women writers gravitated toward courtship plots, it is argued, precisely because courtship heralded the most significant transformation in early modern women's lives: the obligatory transformation from maiden to wife.

Cultural Symbols of Femininity

The bibliography covering cultural and normative aspects of wedlock in early modern Spain is extensive and growing. It would be impossible to convey all of the findings in this burgeoning field in one section, chapter or even a separate book. Entire volumes have been published on representations and contestations of gender within a single region, as for example, Seville in Mary Elizabeth Perry's *Ni espada rota ni mujer que trota* [literally, Neither broken sword nor wandering woman[3]]. Here, only those cultural codes most relevant to women's courtship novels are identified.

Novelists Mariana de Carvajal, María de Zayas and Leonor de Meneses belonged to an aristocratic milieu. The symbolic codes available to them and to their readers contained conflicting messages regarding gender divisions in courtship and marriage. Saints were a primary signifier of female virtue for unmarried maidens as well as a potent recruiting tool of the counter-Reformation, "un instrumento beligerante y propagandístico que se vale del Santo que la encabeza para conseguir sus fines" [a belligerant and propagandistic instrument that used the saint chosen as a figurehead of the movement in order to achieve its ends] in Concha Torres Sánchez's words (113). Widely read *Flos Sanctorum,* or Lives of Saints, in the seventeenth century included that of Alonso de Villegas (1589-1592) and that of Pedro de Rivadenayra (1599-1601) (Torres Sánchez 115).

Fervor toward saints was fomented by harnessing an element of local pride. A systematic effort was made to renew (and create) saints specific to a particular region. As Sara Nalle observes:

> But the times demanded more than the rescue of saints endangered on foreign soil; militant, native exemplars of sanctity had to be put before the people to lead them in faith and succor them in times of hardship. In addition to new saints such as Diego de Alcalá, Ignatius Loyola, or Teresa de Ávila, during the Counter-Reformation numerous older Spanish miracle workers were called up from reserve and put on active duty in the defense of their cities. Ávila invented the cult of San Segundo while nearby Segovia rediscovered San Frutos. León turned to San Froylán. Madrid found San Isidro Labrador, Toledo celebrated Santa Leocadia, and Cuenca resurrected San Julián, the city's second bishop. (26)

In sacred art and sculpture, as well as in popular hagiographic literature, virgins and martyrs epitomized the feminine qualities of chastity, self-sacrifice, humility and faith. For Mary Elizabeth Perry, the ascendancy of the Virgin Mary and locally revered martyrs "proporcionaron un modelo de perfección femenina a partir del cual se juzgaba a las mujeres" [provided a model of feminine perfection, a standard by which women were judged] (52). At the same time, virgin martyrs such as Saints Justa and Rufina of Seville (Perry 41-44) were also clearly insubordinates who defied secular authority for the sake of their beliefs. It was impossible to tell the story of their heroic resistance to their Roman persecutors without opening women's eyes to the possibility of female agency. A less dramatic but no less virtuous image of female martyrdom promulgated during this period was that of the long-suffering wife, whose travail would only be rewarded in the world to come. Bartolomé Murillo's canvases of the Virgin Mary in her *mater dolorosa* [doleful mother] aspect glorify a meek and mortified Mother of God (Perry 46-49). The final reward for a lifetime of submission is graphically symbolized on Murillo's Immaculate Conception canvases by a bevy of rose-tinged cherubs surrounding the Virgin.

Not all female exemplars were martyrs. Mary's mother, Saint Ann, was frequently depicted teaching Mary to read from a book. This image of a saintly mother-daughter pair engaged in book-learning reappeared in graphic arts throughout the seventeenth century (Luna 86), and had the effect of promoting female learnedness. For example, the noblewoman d. Mencía de Mendoza testified that "it is a well-known fact that literate women read aloud to illiterate women books such as the Scriptures and Lives of Saints" (McKendrick 101). Another learned female figure was the Old Testament prophetess Holda who counseled and comforted the Children of Israel during a vacuum of male leadership (Kings 22:14). In the prologue to the 1510 Spanish translation of St. Angela, of Foligno's *Book,* the translator compares this Italian mystic to Holda, for while men remained "ciegos con sus carnales exposiciones y entendimientos" [blinded by their carnal writings and knowledge], St. Angela saw clearly and instructed them (Surtz 11, 12 n70).

Closer to home than the saints was the model of the Bride of Christ. Conventual enclosure was widespread among seventeenth-century noblewomen, constituting what Elisja Schulte van Kessel has called "social security," especially for wealthier urban women (151). The essential qualities of a nun, according to Fray Hortensio Paravicino, writing in 1641, were those of "self-inflicted pain, suffering in silence, humility and total submission to her confessor and to God" (Sánchez 81). As abject as these qualities may appear, they also accrued power to the woman known to possess them. A reputation for devotion was crucial for the nun who wished to exert her influence in the political realm. "Religious devotion gained [nuns] the favor and sympathy of the Spanish populace, the respect of ambassadors and nuncios, and the continued affection and regard of their relatives," according to Magdalena Sánchez who concludes that "ultimately, their spiritual practices (which were both private and public) lent greater weight to their petitions and their arguments" (6).

As these examples illustrate, sacred images of feminine duty could paradoxically lend themselves to liberating interpretations for women. It would be erroneous to discount the transgressive potential of images of female submission such as martyrs, saints and obedient nuns, especially since women encountered them in the context of a competing secular iconography, which provided alternative stories about singlehood, courtship, motherhood and marriage. Fernando de Rojas's *Tragicomedia de Calixto y Melibea* [Tragicomedy of Calixto and Melibea], uncensored until 1640, represents just such a competing secular iconography. Rojas's prinicipal female character, Melibea, rebels against parental authority in pursuit of carnal pleasure. Although she loses her love, Melibea remains defiant to the end. Rojas's "tragicomedy" also popularized the bawd or *lena* figure found in Plautus and Terence's Roman comedies, a powerful female procuress who not only undermined the sexual mores of society, but did so for personal gain that granted her financial security outside of marriage (Nicholson 297-298). Another poetic figure that contested an ideology of wifely submission was that of the *bella malmaridada,* or unhappily married beautiful wife, an image that Anne Cruz has shown permeated both popular and learned poetry.

The stock of available subversive gender models multiplied manyfold with the revival of classical learning in the Renaissance. Visual arts inspired by ancient Greek and Roman myths depicted Olympians and mortals, male and female alike who failed to toe the gender-boundaries by which Catholic readers would later judge them. Diana, the resolutely chaste huntress, Athena, the warrior goddess and virtuous, albeit suicidal, Lucrecia, were joined by scores of goddesses and mortal women swept up in a vortex of beauty and pursuit. Some mythical models, like Venus and Psyche, acceded voluntarily to Adonis and Amor; others struggled, but resistance by no means guaranteed chastity. The rape of Europa by Jupiter and the abduction of Persephone by Pluto were two favored motifs of Italian and Flemish painting that glorified the triumph of male aggression over female volition. More ambiguous was the representation of Daphne, dissolving into a botanical specimen at Apollo's first touch. Although her loss of personhood was represented as Jupiter's tragedy, this popular image also conveyed the lose-lose dynamics of resistance for woman, for whom the price of virtue was shown to be entrapment in a subhuman form.[4]

Yet, it was doubtless the theaters or *corrales* that most systematically exposed the public, both male and female, to potentially heterodox modes of thought and conduct. At first glance, women in the *comedia* [Golden Age tragicomedies] appear to be weak and passive. As Denise DiPuccio observes:

> With regard to love, most *comedia* heroines, including those of the mythological plays, are passive objects of desire. In courtships involving love triangles or pairs, few women take the lead. Even when the men are in weakened positions, or dead, the women remain passive.... Two options are open to *comedia* heroines who refuse marriage or do not love properly: the convent or death. The myth plays add another solution to the list. Metamorphosis subdues rebellious women as effectively as seclusion. (45)

Love was a common theme and, as DiPuccio notes, erotic impulses were usually channeled at the end into matrimony, seclusion or transformation into a static object as in Daphne's sudden reconstitution as a laurel bush.

Dogmatic admonitions interwoven into the dramatic dialogue reinforced an official image of silenced femininity. In act 2 of Calderón's *No hay burlas con el amor* [Love is no laughing matter] d. Pedro, evokes the Woman of Valor paean of Proverbs 31.10-31 (popularized in León's *La perfecta casada*), to put woman in her place: "Bordar, labrar y coser / sepa sólo; deje al hombre / el estudio" [To embroider, to work and to sew are the only things she need know; leave studying to men] (vv. 1458-1460, p. 94). Nonetheless, dramatic appeal lay neither in the control of desire, nor in those characters who obeyed precept, but precisely in enactments of the ungovernability of passion. Before order was restored in the final scene, love had had its way with a colorful parade of viragos, androgens, cuckolds, clowns, monarchs, rebels, swains, maidens, sorcerers and bawds.[5]

In the *comedia*, overt moral infraction was generally castigated and contained on-stage, but more subtle transgression of the social order often met with reward. Gender role reversals are a case in point. When d. Juana of Tirso's *Don Gil de las calzas verdes* [Don Gil of the green breeches] dons her green tights, she not only covers herself in the guise of a handsome adolescent male, she also recovers a precious aspect of herself: her honor. Gender-crossing is represented as a superficial and temporary change, justified by its effectiveness in securing a more profound and permanent stratum of being, that of d. Juana's reputation (identity) as a virtuous woman.

The representation of a male character by an actress or vice-versa was rewarded both on-stage—d. Gil got her man—and off—actresses in breeches and actors in drag received warm receptions from the public.[6] As a result, Eric Nicholson observes, "both presentation and representation mock the gender-determined boundaries of dress and public behavior, as laid down by ecclesiastical and civil authorities in accordance with the scriptural law against cross-dressing [Deut 22:5]" (303). Positively inscribed spectacles of role reversal denaturalized gender by revealing its arbitrary and constructed character. For a brief, almost subliminal moment, the public, particularly the female public occupying the women's section, or *cazuela,* was made aware that gender norms otherwise believed to be inviolable were even less than skin deep, mere masks susceptible to voluntary metamorphosis. By visually dramatizing the logical extension of the Baroque cult of appearances, public theater imparted the subversive possibility that gender boundaries were not fixed, but open to realignment. Festive masking, disguise and cross-dressing likewise enliven the pages of women's courtship novels, although when men cross-dress to win women's trust and ultimately deceive them, as in Zayas's "Amar sólo por vencer" ["Loving only to conquer"], the results can be anything but liberating for the woman (see chapter 3).

Furthermore, the theater paid actresses highly for engaging in glamorous public work, granting them independence, visibility and prestige. If acting were not quite a reputable activity for young women of the day,[7] it was nonetheless highly admired and valued. Actresses' popularity and wealth demonstrated that women could participate successfully in creating public culture, an encouraging message for aspiring female poets, painters, musicians—and novelists.

A significant feature of the Court society to which Zayas, Meneses and Carvajal belonged was the blurring of boundaries between theater and non-theater, between spectacle and life. The courtier enacted a display of sociability or "self-fashioning" (Greenblatt) whenever he or she appeared publically, a display aimed at impressing upon others the certainty of the actor's social worth. The title of Domna Stanton's study of courtiers and dandies, *The Aristocrat as Art,* speaks eloquently to the preoccupation with "striving always to be 'recognized as better than the rest,' a sight 'to feed the spectator's eyes'" (19).[8] The semiotics of courteous self-presentation receives extensive treatment in chapter four; here the phenomenon warrants remark for exerting an equalizing effect in the competition between men and women for favor at Court. A chronological shift in the criteria of social ascent may be perceived that starts with a medieval conception of social worth based on brute strength and military prowess, and graduates toward a Renaissance conception of sociability, based on an ideal of courteous gentility. Although the courtier idealized by Castiglione had proven his military mettle in distant lands, at Court he was called upon to downplay his martial achievements and to appeal to others precisely through such feminine qualities as musical ability, beauty and refined speech. Whether at Versailles or at the Buen Retiro Palace of Philip IV, described by Brown and Elliot as a "magnificent theater in which the principal actor [Philip IV] was permanently on stage" (31), "the self, transformed into a system of signs that includes body, gesture, adornment, manners, and speech, gear[ed] its strategy to the captivation of others and to the imposition of its superiority" (Stanton 7). This shift in the parameters of social achievement placed women on a more even footing with men for they too excelled at verbal and spectacular arts.[9]

While the arts of sociability permitted women to compete successfully with men for status and recognition, within the courtly ideal of gentility, fine distinctions based on sex abounded. As Castiglione opined, "a woman should in no way resemble a man in her ways, manners, words, gestures and bearing. Thus just as it is very fitting that a man should display a certain robust and sturdy manliness, so it is well for a woman to have a certain soft and delicate tenderness, with an air of feminine sweetness in her every movement."[10] Likewise, while both men and women dressed in expensive fabric at Court, women's attire emphasized their exposed white arms and shoulders and small waists, made smaller-looking by vast *guardainfantes* or hoop-skirts, while male attire featured exposed legs and "increasingly prominent and beribboned" codpieces (Matthews Greico 56). Women's courtship novels, which displayed the writer's social virtues in print rather than in manner, responded to these conflicting gender pressures—to surpass men in courtly contests on one hand, and to please them on the other—with a range of mimetic, instructive and persuasive strategies that are explicated in chapters 3, 4 and 5.

To summarize, multiple cultural archetypes of femininity precluded the possibility of an untroubled and univocal story about what women were expected to be. Although, gender identities, according to Mary Nash, "are, to a large extent, consolidated and disseminated through images of women" (26), chaste and docile iconography competed with insubordinate and lustful imagery. The figure of Mary could incite the desire to surrender to the Church or the desire to expand one's book-learning. Lives of Saints paradoxically taught resistance as well as submission. The *comedia* prescribed matrimony as the antidote to social chaos while revealing how much more fun could be had in a world turned upside-down. Ideals of courtly self-presentation both rewarded mastery of the art of sociability and dictated a fashion of feminine helplessness. To this chorus of conflicting messages about appropriate gender roles must be added an array of cultural mechanisms that Joan Scott calls "normative" controls (1067), which promulgated "right" interpretations of circulating cultural symbols, and displaced "wrong" ones. The following section is devoted to delimiting these normative mechanisms, whether repressive, as in Inquisitorial prosecution and the "entangling alliance of politics and art" (Cruz, Perry *Culture* xiii), characteristic of Baroque absolutism, or propagandistic, as in prescriptive literature on women's place in society.

Normative Limits of Interpretation

Normative literature helps to establish the "shoulds" that regulated women's lives, the official line that women were expected to toe. These ideological models, often taking the form of treatises and manuals, are by definition didactic and heavy-handed, commonly revealing grossly patriarchal and misogynist assumptions that can leave the modern scholar aghast. Nonetheless, indignation is not a helpful response to a body of texts which, it will be recalled, tell only one-fourth of the story of gendering pressures experienced by early modern women. Outrage only drowns out the possibility of perceiving that normative dicta were inconsistent, internally incoherent and unevenly applied over the course of women's lives. To avoid attributing to these wishful models a greater impact on women's daily lives than they probably exerted, it is useful to view them as only one "literature among discourses" (Spadaccini). Golden Age treatises that aimed to regulate relations between the sexes circulated among many other versions of this age-old story, including women's courtship plots.

Historians and culture critics have begun documenting the cultural controls that inhibited the free play of symbolic discourse on gender in early modern Spain. Cruz and Perry name as institutions of counter-Reformation control: the edicts of the Council of Trent (1545-1563), witch trials, oratory and devotional practices and spectacles. Traub, Kaplan and Callaghan, for whom gender is always contested rather than imposed, produce a similar list of sites of struggle:

> That which signifies the subject's emergence takes place within the highly contested terms of cultural struggle. . . . The terms of gender were reconfigured over the course of two centuries, sometimes subtly in the diurnal round of domestic relations, and sometimes dramatically, as in the instance of witch persecutions. That the terms of gender were a matter of intense social debate is evinced by the range of domains in which gender struggle was played out—village ritual, stage plays, conduct books, broadsides, pamphlet wars, and law courts. (2-4)

Gender was broadly understood as a way of containing women's innate unruliness. Women were considered by natural law to be intellectually, morally and physically inferior to men, as "proven" by the second creation story (Jahvist narrative) of Genesis 2, in which woman is formed after Adam, derivative and subordinate, from his rib.[11] Saint Paul reasoned that Eve, not Adam, committed the Original Sin because she rather than Adam was "seduced" by the serpent into disobeying the word of God (1 Tim 2:14). In the sixteenth century, Huarte de San Juan adduced a "scientific" explanation for the serpent's (devil's) choice: the snake realized that women were more ignorant than men, so that Eve would be more easily deceived.[12] Woman's alleged inferiority caused her "fall," justified man's subsequent domination over her and demanded her indoctrination and containment, without which, it was thought, her uncivilized nature would unravel the social fabric. Again, in Huarte de San Juan's words, "su sexo no admite prudencia ni disciplina"[13] [her sex admits of neither prudence nor discipline].

Unlike Huarte de San Juan, who despaired of impressing prudence or discipline on women, many contemporary theologians did consider women educable, relying on Books of Hours, Lives of Saints, and conduct manuals to provide instruction and correction. Still, the proliferation of manuals and mirrors dictating all aspects of maidenly, wifely and even widowly duty reveals great disparities. No consensus was reached concerning woman's education, proper domestic pursuits or, indeed, the best method for instructing her. Instead of promulgating a uniform message, theologians presented a scramble of more and less severe gender prescriptions. This divided front undercut the authority of the most severe pronouncements and exposed the relativity of the debate. These variations are more readily observed by comparing and contrasting key guidebooks for women published between the fifteenth and seventeenth centuries.

Jardín de las nobles doncellas [Garden of the noble maidens] was one of the more magnanimous treatises available in the fifteenth century for female moral instruction.[14] Directed to Isabel I in 1468 as she prepared to ascend to the throne of Castile, Fray Martín Alonso de Córdoba's volume rehearses the biblical creation myth, describes women's "good" and "less good" qualities, and addresses the question of her education. Among woman's "good" qualities, he lists: modesty, honor piety and selflessness, and among the "less good," intemperateness, prattling, stubbornness and fickleness (Esteban Mateo 88). Princesses and queens should be granted access to higher learning as a concession to their rank, according to Fray Martín, an opinion tepidly echoed by the queen's first confessor, Fray Hernando de Talavera, professor of Theology at the University of Salamanca. Chapter 8 of Talavera's *De cómo se ha de ordenar el tiempo para que sea bien expendido* [On how time must be disposed so that it may be well-spent] permits learning only insofar as it assists in saving the soul (Esteban Mateo 89).

The sixteenth century saw the publication of two massively circulated guidebooks for women: Juan Luis Vives's 1523 *Instruction of the Christian Woman*, dedicated to Catherine of Aragon, then Queen of England, and Fray Luis de Leon's 1583 *La perfecta casada* [The perfect wife], dedicated to a Spanish noblewoman, d. María Varela Osorio. Because Vives believed that fear alone could make a woman receptive to moral teaching, the first section of his treatise is menacing in tone: "la hembra . . . no se siente cohibida más que por el miedo. Si este miedo no existe, toda coerción natural queda relajada, y si tiene propensión al mal, en él se precipita y no sale buena, si ya por su propio carácter y temperamento no fuere tal"[15] [Only fear inhibits a female. If this fear does not exist, all innate constraint becomes relaxed, and if she has any inclination to evil, she will throw herself headlong into it and will emerge from it corrupted, assuming that, due to her character and temperament, this wasn't already the case]. In general, Vives casts women as disorderly, impervious to reason and highly susceptible to corruption. In the *Instruction*, Vives advocates women's reclusion in the home, and limits the range of their activity to domestic concerns.[16] However, in keeping with the doctrine of fear expounded above, he also wished her to read books that frightened her into acting properly. Far from forbidding women to study, Vives felt that learning inoculated women against sinning through ignorance: "No es fácil que hallen mujer mala si no es la necia. . . . La doncella que por su natural virtud, o por efecto de su buena índole, o, simplemente por sus letras, hubiere aprendido a poner ojo en estas y otras consideraciones semejantes"[17] [With difficulty will you find a bad woman who is not ignorant. A maiden, due to her innate virtue, or as a result of her good nature, or simply because of her studies, would have learned to be wary of these and other similar considerations].

If Vives's principle motivational tactic was one of intimidation, Fray Luis de León in *La perfecta casada* (1583) preferred to glorify marriage ("el primero y más antiguo de todos los estados" [the first and most ancient of all civil status]) and the duties of the wife, elevating them to a sacred plane. Presented as a wedding gift to d. Ana Osorio, *La perfecta casada* glosses Proverbs 31: 10-31, explicating in its turn each poetic "figure" of the ideal wife: "mi oficio . . . será . . . señalarle con las palabras, como con el dedo, cuanto en mí fuere, sus hermosas figuras, con todas sus perfecciones, y hacerle que vea claro lo que, con grandísimo artificio, el saber y mano de Dios puso en ella encubierto" (A doña . . . Osorio) [my work, to the best of my abilities, will be to point out to you with my words, as with a finger, the lovely examples (of Proverbs) listing all of the perfections (of the perfect wife) and enable you to see clearly that which the skillful hand and ingenious mind of God has hidden there]. For León's Woman of Valor, marriage is an honorable and important vocation (*oficio*) ordained, not as punishment for an original sin, but in Paradise before the Fall. In León's conception, marriage blesses both humans and God with its transcendent and joyful effects. Its purpose is "para que se conserven los hombres, y para que salgan de ellos los que nacen para ser hijos de Dios, y para honrar la tierra y alegrar el cielo con gloria" [so that mankind may be preserved, and to beget children of God, in order to honor the Earth and to brighten the heavens with glory].

Turning from these initial hyperboles, León's text dwells largely in the everyday affairs of household management. Following Proverbs, *La perfecta casada* stresses the wife's role as able governess of a prospering domestic economy. The wife should "no sólo bastecer a su casa, sino también adelantar su hacienda; no sólo hacer que lo que está adentro de sus puertas esté bien proveído, sino hacer también que se acrecienten en número los bienes y posesiones de fuera" [both sustain the home and augment the estate as well; she should not only make sure that that which is behind the doors of her home is provided for, but it should also be her duty to increase the number of exterior goods and possessions] (VIII). Nonetheless, León betrays a less than flattering view of woman's "thin and cold" temperament, which ill suits her to confront such mental challenges as: "el estudio de las ciencias ni . . . los negocios de dificultades" [the study of sciences or . . . difficult undertakings] (III). Citing a popular saying, he commends the home that boasts oxen for tilling, and a wife for guarding the hearth: "el buey para que are, y la mujer para que guarde" [oxen for tilling and reaping, women for home and keeping] (III), thereby implicitly equating woman to a beast of burden. León exalts the role of child-rearing in chapter 18, and in 19, echoes Vives's reservations regarding artifice in appearance, because conspicuous beauty arouses doubt regarding the wife's virtue.

The tradition of women's instruction did not end with Vives and León. At the end of the sixteenth century, precisely as the first wave of escapist secular fiction—chivalric and pastoral romance—was peaking in popularity, Malón de Chiade issued a fiery protest against women who read for pleasure. His vituperative *La conversión de la Magdalena* [The conversion of Mary Magdalene], dedicated to Beatriz de Cerdán y de Heredia, asks how a woman inflamed with such tripe can devote herself to pious texts: "¿Cómo se recogerá a pensar en Dios un rato la que ha gastado mucho en Garcilaso?"[18] [How can she who has wasted so much time on Garcilaso compose herself in order to contemplate God?] Continuing along similar lines as De Chiade, Fray Alonso de Herrera expresses the view in his *Espejo de la perfecta casada* [Reflection of the perfect wife] of 1637 that education only incites women to disorder.[19]

Another frequent target of the debate over how best to control sexual relations between the sexes was the ostentation demanded of both men and woman at Court. Mariló Vigil surveys an extensive bibliography on sumptuary propriety in which moralists diverged considerably among themselves in their recommendations. His overview helps correct the harsh impression that an isolated treatise might convey regarding sumptuary norms of the period. For example, Fray Vicente Mexía, writing in 1566 approves of women's adornment on three grounds. First, he compares woman to a building whose external appearance should reflect the beauty within.[20] Second, Mexía gave leave for wives to arouse their husbands, "que en nada les ofenden ni defrauden antes les provoquen a querer y exercitar lo mismo que de su estado son obligados" [that in no way should they be reviled nor their hopes dispelled but rather they should be incited to love one another and practice that which their married state requires of them]. Finally, he claims that since women have always dressed ostentatiously and it had never been censured or caused any harm before, it must therefore be an acceptable practice today, as he reasons (somewhat hazily), "Pues no es de creer que tanta multitud de personas . . . fuesen todos tan ignorantes, que . . . viniesen a caer todos juntos en un yerro tan público como éste sería siendo malo."[21] [Therefore it is inconceivable that such a multitude of people . . . could be so ignorant as to . . . all err as egregiously as they would be found to have erred if this were indeed some kind of evil.] On the other hand, for Gaspar de Astete, writing in 1598, women do not harm themselves with their cosmetics and fancy dress; the problem is the harm that they "inflict" on the bystander. "Si tú vas por las calles vestida con suntuosos vestidos," Astete warns, "no echas de ver que llevas tras de ti los ojos de todos, y atraes los sospiros de los mancebos, y engendras en ellos el fuego de la concupiscencia. . . . Y aunque te parece que tú no pierdes ¿no ves que pierdes a los otros?"[22] [If you walk through the streets dressed in sumptuous gowns, do you not notice that all eyes are upon you, and that you draw the sighs of all the young gentlemen, and that you provoke them to fiery lustfulness. . . . And although it may seem to you that you lose nothing in all this, do you not see that you drive these men to perdition?] However, other commentators objected more strenuously to provocative dress, framing the decadent excesses of both men and women in the context of Spain's overall political and moral malaise. Fray Pedro Galindo's *Verdades morales* [Moral truths] criticizes parishioners who spend so much time getting ready for Mass that they arrive after it is almost finished. Galindo reprimands women whose dress exposes their shoulders, back and chest ("el mayor incentivo de la lujuria" [the greatest incitement to lust]), women so oblivious to their own "nudity" that when they go to confession all they repent is having spoken harshly to their cat.[23]

In conclusion, preceptive literature promoted the sacrament of marriage and justified the institutionalized inequities for women that it entailed. Gender divisions were purported to issue from a moral or even divine imperative to curb vice and protect society from women's naturally ordained debilities. Nevertheless, as this overview has shown, apart from the universal call for matrimony, Spanish theologians failed to arrive at any consensus with respect to such fundamental issues as women's education, daily pursuits or appearance. At the fissures between their conflicting appeals, and, more importantly, at the great divide between ideology and their female readers and parishoners' lived experiences arose the chance to imagine alternative courtship scenarios.

Socioeconomic Relationships

The socioeconomic interactions of everyday life offered women a third site at which to contest gender restrictions. Courtship novels demanded that their readers already be familiar with many material gendering practices—marriage and inheritance law, judiciary protocols, and dowering customs, for example—which enter the narratives in the form of obstacles to overcome, or resources for women to exploit (see chapter 3). The purpose of this section is to equip the twenty-first century reader with a set of historical schema that contemporary readers presupposed when interpreting women's courtship novels, but which the modern scholar must acquire through concerted inquiry. I begin this approach to the daily lived experience of gender in early modern Spain by recalling the canonical definition of marriage that would obtain throughout the early modern period. This definition is followed by an overview of the social, legal and economic ramifications of marriage that combined to impart a distinctly utilitarian (as opposed to romantic) character to early modern nuptiality. Three historical examples serve to illustrate marriage's utility for social convection at Court. Outside of marriage, monasticism and widowhood broadened the socioeconomic parameters of gender available to women. These additional positions will also be examined.

Legal and Socioeconomic Aspects of Nuptiality

Session Twenty-Four of the Council of Trent stipulated that after banns had been publicized, a couple was to be married before the wife's parish priest, in the presence of two or three witnesses (Gacto 38). Once wed, the bride fell under the jurisdiction of her husband's legalized authority, known as *patria potestad,* under which wives were largely defenseless against accusations of sexual misconduct. For example, in the case of a wife's alleged adultery, Spanish law granted unlimited authority to the husband: "Si muger casada ficiere adulterio, ella, i el adulterador amos sean en poder de el marido, i faga dellos lo que quisiere, i de quanto han, assi que no pueda matar al uno i dexar al otro."[24] [If a married woman commits adultery, both she and the adulterer are to be remanded to the authority of her husband, and he may do with them as he wishes, and however many of them there are, the husband may not kill one and allow the other to live.] This authority also extended to prospective husbands toward their betrotheds. No corresponding provision was made for the woman whose husband was unfaithful, nor could a wronged wife counter her husband's accusation with one of her own against him. If a husband legally killed his wife for adultery, her dowry and her partner's goods became his property. A father who discovered that his daughter was acting unchastely on his property could legally kill her and her lover (McKendrick 15, 16).

In contrast to women's disadvantaged legal position in questions of honor, inheritance rights situated women in a decisive position with respect to the distribution of wealth and power in early modern Spain. According to David Reher, "women played a relevant role in property transmission because they always conserved their patrimony and bequeathed it separately to their offspring, even though during marriage it was administered by their husbands" (52). A wife and a husband equally owned their possessions and equally shared the profits that they produced. The husband was responsible for his wife's debts, but the wife was exempt from responsibility for those of her husband. However, wives could not sign contracts without the husband's permission, and could not prosecute or defend in court, although they retained the right of appeal (McKendrick 16, 17). If a husband died, the widow could retrieve her dowry and the *arras* or marriage pledge, but during wedlock, these remained in her husband's custody (Gacto 40).

"En lo que toca a su dote," reads a letter heralding the happy denouement of Carvajal's novel, "La dicha de Doristea" ["Doristea's good fortune"], "pasa a veinte mil ducados, sin la herencia de la hermana de su madre . . . que pasan de diez mil" [In reference to her dowry, it exceeds twenty thousand ducats, excluding the inheritance from her mother's sister. . . which alone is more than ten thousand ducats] (62). Courtship novels do not hesitate to quantify the worth of marriageable daughters in terms of their anticipated dowries and inheritance. The two commodities that the families of the bride and groom exchanged in marriage were lineage and wealth. Wealth was transacted by means of dowry, a compensation package of moneys, properties and privileges presented by the father of the bride to the groom to offset the burden of the daughter's future upkeep. This added a financial incentive to matchmaking. According to Olwen Hufton, even among non-nobility, "marriage settlements for children were interpreted, in the language of the day, as 'the weightiest business' a family could undertake" (16). Strictly speaking, dowry did not consist in a transfer of assets from the bride's family to the husband, for the husband was obliged to match the dowry with an *arras*, or endowment to the bride, the amount of which by Spanish law could not exceed one-tenth of the groom's goods.

The dowry was not considered merely an expenditure; it was an investment by the father-in-law which would ideally help to secure his own family's fortune. By generously dowering their daughters, foreigners, "New Christians" and lower nobility who sought to integrate themselves more fully into the ranks of the aristocracy, tempted young men of unblemished or higher pedigree to receive their daughters' hands in matrimony. For Juan Hernández Franco, this use of dowries, in effect, to buy honor represented a significant factor in the assimilation of *conversos* [recent converts to Christianity] into Old Christian Spanish society (17). Wealthy husbands who could afford to forego a large dowry in exchange for marrying a woman of superior breeding but limited means deployed the inverse strategy. Brown and Elliott recount the case of the Genoese banker, Carlos Strata, who penetrated into the highest echelons of Spanish Court society by marrying a Spanish noblewoman. Strata "lived the life of a merchant prince" in the fashionable Carrera de San Jerónimo zone of Madrid, where he entertained the King himself and was privy to the highest affairs of state (36, 37). Patterns of social ascent through marriage receive fuller treatment later in this chapter.

The dowry system depended upon women's juridical right to own and bequeath wealth and privileges. Prior to Bourbon imposition of Salic law in the eighteenth century, Spanish women could legally occupy the throne and could inherit property, titles of nobility, entailments, wealth and incomes from landholdings. According to Bartolomé Clavero, these rights gave women a crucial role in preserving and in consolidating privilege among the aristocracy: "En este punto, no se discurra sobre los derechos de la mujer en Castilla, baste pensar en la importancia que la sucesión de las mujeres en los vínculos alcanzó en orden a su acumulación en las líneas principales de la nobleza mediante las uniones matrimoniales de titulares de mayorazgos" [At this point, we will not question the rights of women in Castille, for it is enough to ponder the importance that the succession of women in matrimonial ties accrued with regards to their accumulation in the foremost ranks of the nobility through conjugal unions with those who held titles of entailed estate due to primogeniture] (242). Property inheritance law or *mayorazgo* was not strictly patrilinear; at times women were legally favored over more distant male relatives to inherit. For example, a royal edict promulgated on April 5, 1615, decreed that

> las hembras de mejor línea y grado no se entienden estar excluidas de la sucesión de los mayorazgos, vínculos, patronazgos y aniversarios que de aquí adelante se fundaren: antes se admitan a ella y se prefieran a los varones más remotos, así a los varones de hembra como a los varones de varones, si no fuere el caso que el fundador les excluyere y mandare que no sucedan.[25]

> (females of the best lineage and rank should not be understood to be excluded from the inheritance of primogeniture, entail, endowment due to familial discretion, or annuity: rather such a woman would be included and given preference over distant male relatives, both maternal and paternal, unless the executor were expressly to exclude them or decree that they not be named as legitimate heirs.)

Even when a more remotely related male superseded the closer female, he was obliged to provide her dowry: "es nuestra voluntad que el tal varón que así sucediere, porque no es en igual grado, sea obligado a darle la renta de tantos años en los primeros años que lo poseyere, de los frutos del dicho mayorazgo, para ayuda de su casamiento o religión" [it is our will that a man who inherits in such a manner, because he is not of direct descent, be obligated to give his female relative a percentage of the income he derives in the first years from his inheritance, and so help her marry or enter a convent]. In this manner, the edict protected non-inheriting women as well.[26]

Early modern elite families were willing to incur debt to provide a handsome dowry to their daughter. Often the bride's family raised money for her dowry by purchasing municipal bonds called *censos,* a form of borrowing responsible for much of the Spanish aristocracy's debt during this period. Historian Henry Kamen calls dowries, "the most common single cause of indebtedness among the higher aristocracy" (245). He illustrates the magnitude of the problem by analyzing the duke of Infantado's debt, over 41 percent of which derived from the cost of marrying his daughters to other dukes (238-245). In 1623, Olivares tried to address the problem by reviving a law of 1573 that had established a ceiling on dowries by linking them to the income of the bride's father (Casey 83).

The formation of new households produced profound demographic and economic ramifications not only for the families of the couple, but for the society as a whole. For David Reher:

> Marriage was unquestionably the most important of all of these life-cycle events. It led to demographic reproduction and set in motion a series of mechanisms which were essential for the survival of society. Marriage-related mobility was a source of redistribution of active population and, as long as it was accompanied by some sort of property devolution, as it normally was, it heralded the foundation of separate family economies and the diversification of previously existing ones. (82)

The chief beneficiaries of marriage were the families of the prospective couple, who calculated the match with the care that today might be lavished on a major stock-market transaction. When the Duke of Híjar was ready to marry his eldest son, Jaime, he engaged an agent to research and negotiate the transaction for him, as Híjar himself is recorded as declaring in court in 1648: "Y para casar al primogénito Jaime encargó otra negociación a don Luis Fernández de Córdoba, marqués de Priego y duque de Feria" [And in order to marry his eldest son and heir, Jaime, he entrusted another negotiation to d. Luis Fernández de Córdoba, Marquis of Priego and Duke of Feria] (Ezquerra Abadía 132). Unlike modern corporate "redistributions" and "diversifications," however, aristocratic marriage in the seventeenth century also yielded secondary gains for the traded commodities, the bride and groom themselves. For husbands, marriage provided the sexual services of a wife, patrilineal successors and social status. Women acquired in their husband a supervisor, disciplinarian and guard. They also gained a sexual partner, the social legitimacy and honor attendant upon becoming wives and mothers, economic support and a hereditary conduit for their own wealth. As we shall see, however, misalliance gravely affected the balance of vested interests in matrimony; the lower the bride's status, the less power she wielded as a wife.

Two patterns of social elevation through marriage have been mentioned at this point: that of dowry as a source of wealth for cash-poor noblemen, a pattern that resulted in female ennoblement[27] and that of male ennoblement through marriage to women of higher rank (Carlos Strata). The second pattern, that of male ascent traces its origins to the feudal practice whereby local chieftains would favor their best vassals by granting them their daughters' hand in marriage. The groom married "up" the social scale, gaining honor through the match, while the bride, who married "down," nonetheless commanded respect in her new household due to her superior birth. For the medieval chieftan, making sons-in-law of the best warriors of his camp ensured the loyalty of his greatest potential rivals. An alternate pattern, however, is recorded as early as the medieval epic poem, *El Cantar del Mío Çid* [The poem of the Cid]. In this type of exogamous transaction, the father of the bride offered dowry wealth to a socially more elevated groom, so that the bride married "up" to the new husband's status. The groom was enriched by the dowry, but gained a bride of inferior birth, a social liability. As depicted in the *Cantar,* such a system endangered the bride, whose husband scorned her lowly rank:

> The rub came when he [El Çid] went on to tell the high-born Infantes: "You are my sons, for I give you my daughters." The problem with this remark, familiar enough in any dowry society, was that it inverted the hierarchy of early feudal Europe, by placing wealth above honor. The inevitable tragedy followed; the restlessness of the Infantes at their dependence on their upstart father-in-law, and their eventual repudiation of their wives as a means of deliberately dishonoring him. (Casey 82)

El Çid made his fortune by personally reconquering territories taken by the Moors. However, as Christian kingdoms consolidated power in the north and central regions of the peninsula and Islamic rule gradually retreated to the south during the thirteenth through sixteenth centuries, local lords were called upon less to defend their own estates and more to supply a distant king with the arms and troops that demonstrated their fealty. In this manner, wealth supplanted military superiority as the chief mechanism for maintaining power. The aristocracy turned to dowry to attain the resources they needed, causing the first marriage pattern, that of women marrying "up" the social ladder, to gain correspondingly in prominence.

Marriage and Social Ascent: Three Historical Cases

If the *Cantar* is correct in its critique of female ascent through dowry, then women whose husbands married them for wealth (and despite their lineage) could expect less respect in their new homes than their medieval foremothers enjoyed. Women's courtship novels, as chapter 3 makes evident, lend credence to this supposition by representing dowry-driven marriage transactions as a significant obstacle to the bride's well being. But whether matrimony enriched or elevated the husband or the wife, it is clear that wives bore tremendous potential for their husband's social ascent, wielding a degree of economic power that the normative patriarchal discourse preferred to occlude.

In chapter 1, it was stated that aristocratic women often held the key to men's aspirations at Court. More precisely, an advantageous marriage could enhance a nobleman's position in three strategic areas: influence, status and/or wealth. Since women's status at Court depended largely upon the heights to which their husbands and offspring ascended, the wife also benefitted by elevating her spouse. In this sense, upward male convection served the common good of both marriage partners. Three examples of male social ascent by means of a bride's resources are delineated below. In the first, careful analysis of an entitlement document reveals that d. Juan de Arce, a nobleman whom Charles II (the last Hapsburg king of Spain) elevated to the title of count, actually received this honor not on his own recognicence, but in recognition of his wife's family's achievements. The second case demonstrates that Philip II's favorite acquired the credibility and clout necessary to operate on the King's behalf by wedding a wife of exceptional pedigree. Finally, the stellar rise to power of the Duke of Medina de las Torres in the final years of Philip IV's reign is attributed to his successive marriages to increasingly powerful women

In 1692, King Charles II elevated d. Juan de Morales Arce Reinoso to the title of ount on the merits of his wife's genealogy. At first, the entitlement document published by Serrano y Sanz, appears to claim that the king honored d. Juan in gratitutde for the service to the Crown of his two male relations: d. Fernando de Arze, *Alcalde de Hijosdalgo* [Chief Judge for the civil court of noblemen], and Cardinal d. Diego de Arce Reinoso, inquisitor general under the reign of Philip IV. However, the text's legalistic language and the fact that it presents d. Juan's paternal antecedents before his maternal ones obscures the fact that d. Juan was related to d. Fernando and d. Diego through his mother and his wife, so it is primarily to these women that he owes his new title.

The document consists largely of genealogical lists enumerating honors, titles and estates acquired through each of d. Juan's relation. Particular attention is paid to relationships linking d. Juan to Alcalde d. Fernando and Cardinal d. Diego. The entitlement document opens by cataloguing Juan and then his father's credentials, which include military knightships and property-holdings. Next, the credentials of d. Juan's mother, d. Maria de Arze y Reinoso are enumerated. D. María was the Alcalde d. Fernando's sister and Cardinal d. Diego's niece.

> y [hixo lexítimo] de Doña María de Arze y Reinoso su muxer, hermana entera de Don Fernando de Arze, Cauallero del órden de Alcantara, Comendador de Belbis y Nauarra, Alguazil maior de la Inquisizión de Toledo y del mi Consexo, sobrina de Don Diego de Arze y Reinoso, Obispo, Inquisidor Jeneral, del mi Consexo de Estado. (Serrano y Sanz I 53)

> (and [legitimate son] of Lady María de Arze y Reinoso his wife, sister of the esteemed gentleman Fernando de Arze, Knight of the Order of Alcantara, Commander of Belbis and Navarre, Honorary Inquisitor of Toledo and of my Tribunal, niece of the esteemed gentleman Diego de

Arze y Reinoso, Bishop, Chief Ecclesiastic Justice of my Council of State.)

It appears at this point in the text that d. Juan's mother's consanguineous relationships to Fernando and Diego (Fernando's sister, Diego's niece) qualify Juan to receive the posthumous honor due to them. Later, the document reveals that d. Juan owes even more to his mother: he inherited the *mayorazgo* of Candalixa through his maternal grandfather, and the *mayorazgo* and property of the village of Casarente via his maternal grandmother, as the text states: "Don Diego de Arze y Reinoso . . . nieto de Don Juan Antonio de Morales, vuestro Abuelo, Poseedor que fue de la Casa y Maiorazgo de Candalixa, y de Doña Isabel Mesia de Bera Portocarrero, su muxer, dueña de la Casa y Maiorazgo de Casarente" [D. Diego de Arze y Reinoso, grandson of d. Juan Antonio de Morlaes, your grandfather, who possessed the house and entailment of Candalixa, and of d. Isabel Mesia de Bera Portocarrero, his wife, owner of the house and entailment of Casarente] (Serrano y Sanz I 55).

However, d. Juan's debt to his mother is compounded by the fact that he also took his wife from her side of the family. D. Baltásara Petronila de Arce, Suárez y Mosquera was d. Juan's first cousin on his mother's side—his mother's niece and her brother, Alcalde d. Fernando's daughter and "vnibersal heredera de Don Fernando de Arze" [universal heir of d. Fernando de Arze] (Serrano y Santz I 54, 55). While d. Juan could only claim to be d. Fernando's nephew by marriage, his wife was d. Fernando's daughter and heiress. The line of descent from d. Diego is likewise more directly traced through d. Baltásara. Underscoring d. Baltásara's closeness to the alcalde and the cardinal is the fact that she, and not her husband, had been named heiress to *both* of their fortunes: "hallándose la dicha Doña Balthasara, vuestra muxer, heredera de los seruizios del dicho Don Fernando de Arze su padre, . . . y asi mismo heredera de los de Don Diego de Arze y Reinoso, su tio" [said d. Baltásara, your wife, found herself heir to the worldly goods of said d. Fernando de Arze y Reinoso, her father, and heir of those of her uncle d. Diego de Arze y Reinoso as well] (Serrano y Sanz I 54).[28] D. Baltásara's ties to her father and uncle constitute a far more compelling argument for conferring the title than do her husband's more attenuated links to those figures.

Structurally, the decree simultaneously understates and foregrounds d. Baltásara's importance in qualifying Juan to receive his title. By listing Juan and his father's (largely irrelevant) credentials first, and the mother and niece's considerably more significant connections to Diego and Fernando later, the text ratifies an expected patrilineal bias. More damagingly, this order has the effect of burying María and Baltásara's qualifications beneath the weighty catalogues that precede them. At the same time, precisely because d. Baltásara's credentials are listed after those of her husband, they are more closely identified with the king's summarizing words, "in recognition of, and partial reparation and repayment for everything just mentioned," ["de todo ello"]: "Y en memoria y alguna enmienda y remunerazion *de todo ello,* y por mas honrar y sublimar vuestra persona y Casa . . . he venido en hazeros merzed de titulo de Conde en Castilla, para vos y vuestros herederos y subzesores" [and in order to honor and sublimate your person and house, I have come to bestow upon you the title of Count of Castilla, for you and your heirs in perpetuity] (Serrano y Sanz I 53, 54, my emphasis). Although d. Juan is the official recipient of both the document and the title of count, on September 7, 1692 d. Baltásara became no less a countess for that. Earlier that year, when she published her three volume philosophical treatise, the *Tractatus Logicae* [Treatise on Logic] she was already publicly enjoying her new title, as its frontispiece illustrates: "Tractatvs Logicae . . . Dictatvs a Domina Balthasara Petronila Arce et Suarez, *Comitisa* Tvrris de Arce, et Domina de Bentrances, Figueroa, Iinzo, aliisque locis" [Treatise on Logic. . . By Lady Balthasara Petronila Arce and Suarez, Countess of Turis of Arce and Mistress of Bentrances, Figueroa, Jinzo and other lands] (Serrano y Sanz I 55, my emphasis). It might be too forceful to conclude that d. Juan serves in these proceedings as a mere legal conduit through whom the king could ennoble d. Juan's wife. Nonetheless, this text offers a glimpse at the matrilineal vectors of inheritance responsible for Juan's social ascent, and reveals the subtle ways that those vectors are assimilated into a discourse of patriarchal privilege.

A pair of final examples demonstrate the enormous potential for social ascent held in the hands of marriageable women. As James Boyden recounts in his study of Philip II, the king elevated his favorite, Ruy Gómez, by sponsoring his marriage in 1553 to a noblewoman of great fortune and impeccable pedigree. The bride, d. Ana de Mendoza de la Cerda, stood to inherit the House of Mélito, an illustrious branch of the Mendoza dynasty, as well as extensive landholdings in Calabria, Italy. Along with the aristocratic cachet that this match entailed, Ruy Gómez gained vast wealth—the income from landholdings in Castile alone was estimated at 22,000 ducats per year—to enable him to project an image appropriate to his position as royal favorite (24-38). "Ruy Gómez de Silva's marriage marked the culmination of his rise from obscurity," according to Boyden, and "was to be crucial to the future course of his career and especially to the establishment of his own house of Pastrana" (23).

The preceding examples involved single marriages, that of d. Juan Morales de Arce to d. Baltásara Petronila de Arce, Suárez y Mosquera, and that of Ruy Gómez to d. Ana de Mendoza de la Cerda. However, truly astonishing careers could be forged by marrying sequentially "up" the ladder of social rank. The biography of d. Ramiro Núñez Felipe de Guzmán represents one such ascent. D. Ramiro rose to power in the final years of Philip IV's reign in large measure by means of successive marriage alliances with three key women. First, he married the only daughter of the Count-Duke of Olivares, María. The count-duke favored his son-in-law with a substantial *mayorazgo*, leaving him duke of both San Lúcar and Medina de las Torres. The *mayorazgo* was written in such a way that d. Ramiro would retain the lands and title in the event of María's death. When she did die, the aspiring widower assumed the title of Duke of Medina de las Torres, and remarried, this time to the wealthy Italian heiress, d. Ana Caraffa, Princess of Stigliano.[29] After her death, the duke married d. Catalina Vélez de Guevara, countess of Oñate, thereby acquiring his self-styled title, Duke-Duke-Count of Oñate (Villa-Urrutia 22, 23). With his new credentials, Medina de las Torres approached the apex of the Hapsburg Court hierarchy. In 1661, d. Luis de Haro, who had succeeded his uncle the Count-Duke of Olivares to the position of *privado* [confidant, minister] to the Crown, died, leaving the field open to new political forces. The triumvirate that emerged closest to Philip IV were the Count of Castrillo, the Count of Peñaranda and the Duke-Duke-Count. His ascent ended here, however, for in his will, Philip IV explicitly barred Medina de las Torres from joining the five-man committee which was to govern with Queen Regent Mariana following the king's death (Kamen 328).

Women's dowry, inheritance rights and family connections were valuable winnings in a high-stakes game that eligible primogenitors and their families vied to acquire. The preceding examples illustrate the enormous potential for social ascent held in the hands of early modern women. Women's capacity to inherit and bequeath wealth and titles permitted Ruy Gómez de Silva in the sixteenth century and Medina de las Torres in the seventeenth to become powerful political figures of their generations. The Count of Arce also married "up," acquiring his new title in tacit recognition of his wife's lineage and inheritance.

However, what these examples do not show, is that, without men, women's enviable social resources were of little avail. Despite women's power to elevate men, their social situation relied upon marriage, the mechanism that legitimized their powers of biological reproduction and juridical bequest. Fertility was only permitted free rein within the sacrament of matrimony; exercised out of wedlock, it brought dire consequences including moral opprobrium, social ignominy and bastard offspring stripped of legal and social standing. Without legally recognized descendants to whom to pass on their credentials, women's landholdings, titles and entails were frozen assets with no marketplace value. Marriage activated women's powers for the betterment of both husband and wife, the difference being that, for wives, this was practically the only path to betterment available. The contingency of woman's social situation relative to men's and the limits of her economic autonomy can be seen at two junctures, that of the widow and that of religious women. However, within the constraints that these stations entailed, there were still niches of empowerment such as patronage and prophesy.

Monasticism and Widowhood: Alternatives to Wedlock

Since Catholicism permitted monastic enclosure for women as well as for men, it would first appear that life in Orders represented a democratizing force in early modern society. In fact, convent life did offer various advantages over the secular world, which Electa Arenal and Stacey Schlau eloquently summarize as follows:

> Convents became repositories for daughters of the nobility and wealthy urban classes, prisons for the "dishonored" or "disobedient," and sanctuaries for the studious, who had little access to higher education. Convents became home to many women who were unmarriageable because they were illegitimate. They offered the opportunity to forsake the biological family for a spiritual (and possibly divine) one. The demands of families, the dangers of childbirth, the frequent confusion and violence of sexual experience, as well as strife, illness, and death, dulled the comfort of family life for many women. Despite regimentation and restrictions, women in the convent forged a female subculture that offered a viable alternative to life in their family homes. (3)

Nonetheless, to call convents an "alternative" is to overlook that these foundations still tended to reproduce the economic, caste and patriarchal inequalities of the secular world. All but the most reformed mendicant Orders, for example, consciously perpetuated class and caste divisions. The Carmelite Constitution numerically limited the number of poor nuns that could be admitted at any one time: "atenta la renta y limosna de que se vive . . . mandamos que los que son de pobreza, no excedan las religiosas que son para el choro de treze o quatorze en ninguna manera. Y en los que tuviera renta no excedan de veinte" [in consideration of the income and alms which sustain us, we order that the number of poor women accepted to undertake devotional duties never exceed thirteen or fourteen for any reason. And that the number of those with income does not exceed twenty] (Torres Sánchez 54). As might be expected, a caste system rigidly separated the poorer women from their wealthy sisters. "Legas" [sisters of charity excluded from devotional activity], "freilas" [nuns who served as adjuncts to the military Orders] or "monjas de medio Hábito" [domestic nuns] were the serving nuns and "monjas del coro" [nuns of the choirstalls] or "monjas de velo negro" [nuns of the black veil] were the aristocratic women whose duties were devotional (Torres Sánchez 68). There was also a hierarchy of choice convents used and patronized by the nobility. In Madrid, the Descalzas Reales, founded by Charles V's daughter, Juana, was the convent preferred by royal women (Sánchez 62). Santo Domingo el Real, and the Franciscan Convent of the Immaculate Conception were also elitist, while Vallecas and the Hieronymite Conception were not (Muñoz Fernández 41).

It was also impossible to escape patriarchal oppression within the convent. Each convent, it is true, was presided over by a prioress elected by the sisters. However, Muñoz Fernández emphasizes, not even this leadership figure could perform the intercessionary duties of the priest: "Excluidas del ministerio sacerdotal . . . las mujeres han venido ocupando dentro de la Iglesia espacios institucionales secundarios. Nunca se le ha reconocido plenamente al estatuto de monja el campo de funciones que se abre ante los hombres consagrados, clérigos o monjes" [Excluded from the priesthood, women have come to occupy secondary institutional niches within the Church. Never has the work of nuns been fully acknowledged in the field of duties that is open to men of the cloth, clerics or monks] (9). To the contrary, the prioress and her daughters were subject to male confessors and priests in all spiritual and financial matters.

Unlike men, women could not hope to pursue lucrative careers within the Church. Universities, monastic orders, the Papal hierarchy and the Inquisition offered many opportunities for the male ecclesiastic to enrich both himself and his entire family. For social historian Juan Hernández Franco, educating a son in the Church represented "otro ejemplo de estrategia familiar para reproducir y perpetuar el prestigio" [another example of a family's strategy for extending and perpetuating prestige] (17). A priest could bequeath his properties and wealth directly to a sister's son, or he could establish religious endowments or foundations in his nephew's name. By means of uncle-nephew transmission, wealth and prestige earned in service to the Church could reinfuse the family with new resources in each successive generation.[30] Women contributed biologically to this pattern of indirect inheritance. For example, the priest's sister in the example above gave birth to the nephew that would receive his bequest[31] but women within the Church could not themselves generate capital or hereditary honors; to the contrary, convents demanded that nun's families pay a dowry to offset the cost of their reclusion.

One narrow band of opportunity for women within Orders to gain renown, if not wealth, was that of prophesy. That prophesy was religious woman's only means to distinguish herself helps to explain the statistical finding that there were proportionately more prophetesses than prophets in the early modern period (Surtz 7). Doctrinal support for female prophesy came from the *Summa theologica*, where Thomas Aquinas reasoned that by virtue of having a soul equal to man's, woman is equally predisposed to receive the Word of God:

Prophecy is not a sacrament but a gift of God . . . and since in matters pertaining to the soul woman does not differ from man as to the thing (for sometimes a woman is found to be better than many men as regards the soul), it follows that she can receive the gift of prophecy. (3:2698 qtd. in Surtz 6)

As noted above, the fifteenth and sixteenth centuries witnessed a flowering of female prophesy in Spain. In addition to the *alumbradas* [enlightened women] cited earlier, Ronald Surtz names as spiritual progenitors of Saint Teresa: the deaf fifteenth-century mystic Teresa de Cartagena, Princess Constanza de Castilla, who became Sor Constanza, prioress for fifty years of the Convent of Santo Domingo in Madrid, and Hieronymite sister, María de Ajofrín, the "scourge of Toledo." Just as these fifteenth- and sixteenth-century visionaries found sanctuary in orthodox religious discourse for affirming a uniquely feminine encounter with God, seventeenth-century secular female novelists "picked wedlock," a doctrinally untouchable haven, to shelter the "untold story" of their engagements with society.[32]

The situation of aristocratic widows further underlines women's contingent relationship to men, be they uncles, ecclesiastics, husbands, confessors or kings. A widowed noblewoman who had counted on her husband's position at Court for support was obliged to turn to relatives and protectors for help following his death, especially if many offspring relied upon her support. This was the plight of author Mariana de Carvajal, whose husband, Baltasar Velásquez, died in 1656. On the other hand, dowagers of means enjoyed creative freedom in choosing the terms of their estate's disposition.

When Mariana de Carvajal was widowed, she assumed full responsibility for managing the affairs of the couple's progeny, which totaled six daughters and three sons. Her own inheritance, "algunos cortijos y casas" [a few homes and country estates], according to *Prueba de sangre* [Proof of bloodline] records published by Serrano y Sanz, also included a *mayorazgo* [entailed inheritance] but apparently these holdings produced insufficient revenues to ensure all of her children's futures. Among her protectors Carvajal could count her husband's brother, Cristóbal Velázquez, *Gobernador de Orbitelo* [regional governor] of Naples, as well as the Archbishop of Toledo, d. Baltasar Moscoso, who helped Carvajal's eldest daughter to gain entry into the Convent of the Recoletas in Granada. The eldest son, Rodrigo, educated at Alcalá and Salamanca, was granted a Knighthood of Santiago, and obtained the post of *abogado de presos de la Inquisición* [lawyer for prisoners of the Inquisition] (Serrano y Sanz I 236, 237).

To support her family, Carvajal was obliged to petition Philip IV for additional aid. In her letter of petition, also published by Serrano y Sanz as her *Memorial*, [Memorial], Carvajal requested "un avito para uno de los dichos sus hijos, o casar de sus hijas como la suplicante elijiere y nombrare" [Knighthood for each one of her aforementioned sons, or the right to arrange the marriages of her daughters to grooms of the petitioner's choosing] (Serrano y Sanz 241, 242). Carvajal's *Memorial* offers several insights into women's reliance on men, on one hand, and their potential strength within the patriarchal system, on the other.

On the reliance side is the obvious fact that the letter represents a petition from a female subject impoverished by the death of her husband. Furthermore, the widow appears to be eclipsed by her husband's merit and her children's need: the request is filed in recognition of d. Baltasar's twenty-three years of labor and for the sake of her children's welfare: her own achievements and penury are not mentioned. Nonetheless, to conclude that the document testifies solely to widows' defenselessness or effacement is to overlook three factors that point in the direction of an alternate interpretation. First, Carvajal insists on retaining the right to select her daughter's groom herself, even if the match is funded by the Crown: "como la suplicante elijiere y nombrare" [of the petitioner's choosing]. Second, she requests either the granting of a dowry *or* the awarding of a knighthood: "un avito para uno de los dichos sus hijos, o casar de sus hijas;" [knighthood for each one of her aforementioned sons, *or* the right to arrange the marriages of her daughters] that is, she equates the value of assurances for a daughter's future with those for a son rather than favoring the male offspring categorically over the female.[33] Third, Carvajal has written to the king in her own name instead of having her brother-in-law or the archbishop petition on her behalf. This presupposes confidence in the efficacy of her own signature before the king and illustrates the importance of writing as a strategy of female self-assertion.

It must be recalled that it was not until after her husband's death that Carvajal was to write both her *Memorial* to Philip IV and the *Navidades,* dedicated to Viennese ambassador Eusebio Von Pötting. Like the *Memorial,* it is possible that Mariana de Carvajal's courtship novel, the *Navidades de Madrid* [Christmastide in Madrid], also represented an attempt to solicit some form of protection or compensation from its dedicatee to help alleviate the hardship that her husband's death had incurred, a possibility that is pursued in chapter 5.

The logical extension of these speculations regarding Carvajal's motives for writing the *Navidades* is that necessity was the mother of her literary inventions. Noël Valis makes a similar case for the "financially saddled mother of nine" who penned the *Navidades* so soon after she became widowed (256). Had she not been in want, Carvajal might have devoted herself to what Elisja Schulte van Kessel has dubbed "matronage," (148) the charity practiced by wealthy secular women. Charitable work was one of the few honorable activities to which women could contribute outside their home, and it therefore served as "respectable excuse for evading certain family obligations"

(Schulte van Kessel 149). Moreover, a handful of wealthy lay women in Spain "matronized" convents as a means to gain honor and secure their descendant's futures. For historian Ángela Muñoz Fernández, the importance of women's monastic centers is twofold: they served as a vocational outlet and they also played an important role in consolidating the founder's interests, "intereses que transitan ese reducido camino que une lo individual a lo familiar. . . . Es, bajo la figura del patronato, en combinación con la institución del mayorazgo, cómo estos móviles son perpetuados por los individuos de un linaje" [interests that traveled that narrow road that connects the concerns of the individual to the concerns of the familial. . . It is in the guise of trusteeship, combined with the institution of *mayorazgo*, that these motives are perpetuated on behalf of persons of a given lineage] (30).

To foreground the role that elite urban women could play in the foundation of centers of female devotion, Muñoz Fernández cites the case of Isabel I's chambermaid, d. Beatriz Galindo. Widow of the Catholic Monarchs' secretary, d. Francisco Ramírez, d. Beatriz Galindo became the "matroness" of two convents devoted to one of Queen Isabel's most passionate causes, the cult of the Immaculate Conception. In so doing, Beatriz gained exclusive burial rights for herself and her descendants in the main chapel of the convent church that she had built, as well the right to display her family's coat of arms (Muñoz Fernández 31, 32). Furthermore, in "matronizing" the Hieronymite Convent of the Conception, Beatriz stipulated that her descendants "sean reçebidas en el dicho monesterio en el número de las pobres, sean antepuestas a todas las otras"[34] [be received in said convent as the poor are, that they be given priority over all other candidates for entrance]. In this manner, the widowed d. Beatriz exploited an institution devoted to spiritual immortality to win earthly prestige and privileges for herself and her descendants.

To conclude this condensed overview of early modern women's socioeconomic horizons of possibility, Golden Age women inhabited a zone of limited agency that nonetheless afforded more choices and greater complexity than normative writings of the period would concede. As noted above, wives' legal position in marriage was precarious with respect to questions of honor, but somewhat more secure in the area of ownership and inheritance, and once a husband died, widows were relieved of many onerous marital duties and restrictions. Financially well-off dowagers could give free rein to their ambitions for themselves and their families by founding religious institutions that would commemorate their piety and shelter their descendants, while poorer widows would require assistance to support their families. Enmeshed in a web of interdependencies which granted men superior economic and legal prerogatives, women articulated their worth in terms of reproductive utility, dowry and their capacity to inherit and bequeath titles and estates. This capacity could only be realized within matrimony, however, for economic advancement through the Church was all but closed to women. Limited church-related opportunities for women included prophesy and religious "matronage."

Subjective (Psychological) Identity

"[I]dentity is always in flux among ethnic, racial, age, professional, and other markers," affirms ethnologist Ruth Behar.[35] Although preceptive literature attempted to reify Golden Age women's identity in wedlock, the socioeconomic data reviewed above effectively rebuts this distortion and supports Behar's view. As observed above, women did not spend their entire lives wedlocked; at one time or another (or simultaneously), women also occupied roles as unwed daughters, widows, neighbors, exiles, sisters, step-sisters, princesses, nuns, etc. These roles and phases, largely neglected by iconography, custom and even law, nonetheless belonged to women's developmental experience as much as (or more than) marriage itself. Courtship novels punctuate their obsessive concern for matrimonial closure with hints that women indeed led other lives. The courtship novel, by providing a literary environment for anatomizing and asserting these unacknowledged aspects of female selfhood within a doctrinally safe genre, played an important, and as yet unrecognized role in articulating early modern women's subjectivity. Our capacity to tune in to this discourse of emergent selfhood in the courtship novel, however, depends upon gaining familiarity with early modern gender roles as they shifted for men and women diachronically along the life-course. The following section synthesizes the findings presented earlier in this chapter to trace changing gender expectations for early modern men and women from childhood to old age.

Two conditions of women's lived experience of gender form a paradoxical pair. On one hand, woman's worth, to a much greater extent than man's, was measured by her ability to attract a husband and fulfill her obligations as a wife. On the other hand, this conflation of woman and wife clashed with demographic reality. Later marriage age, a scarcity of eligible husbands and higher death rates for men led to women spending extended periods of time outside of wedlock even as marriage rates rose. During unwed periods, women escaped the rigorous demands made on wives. For this reason, gender exerted less pressure on women's lived identity than might be imagined by consulting marriage treatises, legal codes or demographic data on nuptiality rates.

Two premises inform this section. The first is that gender is not fixed, but mutable. To assume that a "coherent and unitary female self" (Fisher and Halley 8) exists or ever did exist is to underestimate the developmental trajectory of the human life-course. Women and men are subject to different gender expectations during different life-course stages. For example, in early modern courtship women were called upon to be alluring, in wedlock, docile and submissive, anemic during menstruation, robust in childbirth, in motherhood to be fiercely protective of their young. To imagine all of these contradictory gender qualities simultaneously is to construct an impossible, a monstrous being. As Denise Riley queries:

> Can anyone fully inhabit a gender without a degree of horror? How could someone "be a woman" through and through, make a final home in that classification without suffering claustrophobia? To lead a life soaked in the passionate consciousness of one's gender at every single moment, to will to be a sex with a vengeance—these are impossibilities and far from the aims of feminism. (22)

For Riley, it is imperative to acknowledge the mobility of gender expectations over time, for "if woman is more accurately conceived of as a state which fluctuates for the individual, depending on what she and/or others consider to characterize it, then there are always different densities of sexed being in operation" (Riley 22). To paraphrase Luce Irigaray, it is more accurate to think of gender not as one, but as many, not stable, but mobile throughout the life-course.

The second assumption is that women and men differ in the pace at which they move from one set of age-linked gender expectations to the next. Human development is characterized by a series of transitions that differ for women and for men. According to sociologists Mercer and Nichols, "the social regulation of many transitions leads to the observation that women's developmental trajectories may differ considerably from those described for men because of different societal expectations or social circumstances" (3). Gender was "denser" or more imposing for early modern women at certain life-course stages, and denser for men at others. Gender expectations for women were less intense in childhood, more pronounced after puberty, most severe during marriage, and less intrusive in widowhood. By contrast, men experienced greater "density of sexed being" during their boyhood education away from home, while matrimony, which represented just one among many possible arenas of social convection and identification available to them, was a less crucial life-course passage. Tracing these differences helps to account for the concentration of female novelistic activity in a genre that focuses on the transition from daughter to wife (the courtship novel), while male novelistic activity condensed in novels that problematized boys' separation from home (the picaresque, followed by the "modern" novel) (see El Saffar below).

During early childhood, gender differences between girls and boys in Spain's Golden Age were apparently minimal. In conduct literature for parents in pre-industrialized Europe, the upbringing of male children was not distinguished from that of female children, according to Elizabeth Segal (166). In accordance with this observation, historian Richard Kagan finds that the earliest years of childhood "were ones of relative freedom and indulgence for children of either sex, first-born or otherwise. Tended first by a wet nurse, later pampered by the servants . . . the child's early years were, especially in comparison with the years after seven or eight, characterized by a rather lax discipline" (7). St. Teresa of Ávila provides anecdotal support that she and her siblings of both sexes shared sexually undifferentiated pastimes and tastes. She opens her confessional autobiography stating that her father encouraged all nine of his progeny to read vernacular books in their youth: "Era mi padre aficionado a leer buenos libros, y ansí los tenía de romance para que leyesen sus hijos, éstos" [My father was a keen reader of good books, and among them he had secular works of fiction that he particularly desired that his children read] (95, 96). In the same chapter she recounts how she and her closest brother, inspired by the Lives of Saints, aspired to be martyred in the service of God: "Como vía los martirios que por Dios los santos pasavan . . . deseava yo mucho morir ansí . . . y, juntávame con este mi hermano a tratar qué medio havría para esto. Concertávamos irnos a tierra de moros, pidiendo por amor de Dios, para que allá nos descabezasen" [I greatly desired to die in martyrdom, to follow the same routes as the saints had to God . . . my brother and I, together, attemted to determine how this could best be acheived. We agreed on a plan to go to the moorish territory, evangelizing in the name of God, so that, there, the Moors might decapitate us] (98). Teresa and her brother also shared the dream of becoming hermits. They invented the game of "hermitage," constructing huts out of stones, which inevitably collapsed.[36]

Perhaps because these early years were relatively free from gendering, childhood was often overlooked altogether in the regulatory literature on femininity. In 1599, Fray Juan de la Cerda tried to close this loophole and extend gender consciousness down to little girls or *niñas,* declaring that "niña y doncella no es lo mismo . . . porque niña es llamada comúnmente hasta diez años; y desde allí es llamada doncella hasta que la mujer toma marido; y este nombre de doncella le conviene hasta los veinte años de edad porque desde allí ya le cumple casarse"[37] ["little girl" and "maiden" are not equivalent . . . because a woman is called "little girl" until she is ten, and from then on she is called "maiden" until she takes a husband, and this term, "maiden," is appropriate until she is twenty, because, from then on, it is her duty to marry].

If male and female children were not socialized differently, they were differentiated according to family rank. Kagan notes that Spain's strong inheritance laws, created profound differences between the socialization of an eldest son and that of his younger brothers:

> Paternal authority was exerted most forcefully in the case of the eldest son. . . . He was carefully watched over, disciplined and controlled. . . . [T]he family's fortune, prestige and good name were too valuable to allow him to run free. The eldest son was therefore often a homebody, allowed outside the father's watchful eye only in special circumstances, usually educated in or near the home, and rarely allowed on his own to attend university. (4)

Theoretically, this extra measure of vigilance toward a firstborn child, whose future was more secure than those of his siblings, could create psychic fissures among brothers at least as profound as those between brother and sister.[38]

After first communion at the age of six, children stopped wearing special childhood gowns and began wearing clothing modeled after that of adult men and women (Kagan 7). As they entered this zone of intensified gendering, formal schooling began (often outside the home) for boys:

> At this point sons of the aristocracy, in accordance with the medieval tradition of wardship, might be sent to become pages at the royal court, while others were placed in the residence of a friend or relative to be trained in the arts of chivalry and war. Other children were boarded at a variety of monasteries and schools, and youths who were destined for the church might enter the household of a prelate. (Kagan 9)

Writing in 1643, Hernando de Salazar affirmed that puberty began for boys at the age of fourteen and for girls at the age of twelve (Kagan 8n16). Maidens, or *doncellas,* were supposed to be subject to close domestic surveillance until marriage. At home, they learned the rudiments of literacy, catechism, needlework and household management, or attended conventual boarding schools (McKendrick 18, 19). Young men continued training outside the home. Whether their ultimate goal was clerical or military, schooling was regimented, and the discipline severe (Kagan 13). In Ruth El Saffar's view, this teaching style exacted a profound psychic toll on boys. Systematically separating young boys from their mothers and routinely beating them to teach them their lessons caused them to repudiate more "feminine" aspects of their being and to lose touch with women, nature, land and home (178). For El Saffar, the purpose of Renaissance schooling was to cultivate "the ability to cast aside desire for home and mother and, by extension, concern for feelings and the body that would determine the young man's capacity to take up power in the world" (180). Removal from maternal nurture was calculated, according to this view, to create a subject fit to rule the early modern nation-state.

El Saffar's analysis is suggestive, but flawed. Certainly, the trend of guarding maidens at home while their brothers underwent an increasingly brutal schooling away from home represented a significant gendering pattern of the early modern period, but it should not be overstated. To claim that only girls were permitted to continue their maternal attachment overlooks the facts that both girls and boys were suckled by strangers, that the primogenitor of the family was often educated close to home and that boarding schools for aristocratic girls also existed. Furthermore, El Saffar exaggerates the discontinuity between medieval child-rearing practices and those of the Renaissance. As noted above, aristocratic boys in the Middle Ages were "put out" in vocational apprenticeships or as pages at a distant court (Kagan 9). Although boys' training in the Renaissance became massified and increasingly depersonalized, Walter Ong's assessment, echoed by El Saffar, that the learning of Latin constituted a "Renaissance puberty rite for boys"[39] must be weighed against equivalent medieval puberty rites such as that of ascending from the rank of page to that of squire. Despite exaggerating gender differences in pre-pubescent Renaissance schoolchildren, however, El Saffar does innovatively incorporate a fluid rather than a static model of gender into her analysis. More importantly, she links literary developments, for example, the rise of the picaresque novel, to historical shifts in gendering patterns such as the enforced separation of boys from maternal care. If the male-authored picaresque novel registered men's increasing alienation from their "feminine" nature, women's courtship novels can analogously be seen to respond to a post-Tridentine obsession with stamping women into the undifferentiated mold of wife.

Rituals of courtship marked the transition from maidenhood to mariage. "Courtship stands in a peculiarly ambivalent and indeterminate relation to marriage," writes Catherine Bates, "for it remains a preliminary process—what happens before marriage, or outside the conjugal unit—and therefore exists temporarily 'outside' the law that conjugality represents" (19). Far from a mere vestibule to the "housing together" (*casarse*) of matrimony, courtship was a lawless maze of conflicting temptations and paradigms. As such, it incited not only the opprobrium of moralists, but also the fascination of readers and writers for whom this "ambivalent and indeterminate" passage promised for-bidden delight and relief from the omnipresent stereotype of the suffering wife.

In early modern society, prenuptial courtship was characterized by tension between a medieval courtly love tradition that exalted extramarital relations, and the stern exhortations of the counter-Reformation to abstain from premarital sex. As early as the 1570s, the Inquisition "launched an all-out campaign to teach Spaniards that sexual relations outside of marriage were a mortal sin" (Nalle "To sin" n.p.). Although the Church's morality campaign did indeed coincide with a decline in illegitimate births and an increase in the number of baptized infants,[40] it is difficult to determine whether Spain was really "swept by a wave of chastity" during this period or whether changes in birth-control practices or technologies produce the desired results without changing sexual habits (Matthews Greico 67). It is clear, however, that a significant fraction of the population of early modern Spain faced a very Melibea-like dilemma when they reached young adulthood.[41] Bound by filial obedience to parents or guardians and inculcated with the expectation to wed, these young women lived for extended periods (see below) outside the precincts of matrimony, faced with the choice of sexual continence or experimentation, as well as with the risk that publicity of such an episode would one day disqualify them from ever marrying.

Since so much of the legal and preceptive writings on the control of women is based on the conflation of womanhood with wifehood, it is worthwhile to ask how great a percentage of the adult female population was married at any given time, and how great a proportion of early modern woman's life was spent in (and out of) the intense control of wedlock. According to David Reher, "The timing and incidence of marriage can be viewed as the result of availability and ability: the availability of a mate, and the economic and social ability to get married" (171). The disproportionate ratio of survival for females to males, the prolonged absences and high death-rates among males imposed by Spain's constant wars, and an inheritance system that made it difficult for any but the eldest son to wed, diminished the field of eligible husbands and reduced the probability of marriage for many young women.

Despite the rise in legitimate birth rates cited above, Spain underwent severe population decline in the sixteenth and seventeenth centuries. Epidemics at the turn of sixteenth century are estimated to have taken half a million lives.[42] The expulsion of Moriscos (baptized Moslems and their descendants) in 1609 reduced Spain's population by another 300,000 (Bennassar 92-94). Two trends exerted an especially adverse affect on the male population: emigration to the New World and war. New World emigration was officially granted at a rate of approximately four hundred people per year, but Domínguez Ortiz estimates that illegal emigration may have increased this number tenfold (87-90). Commanding the largest army in the Christian world, Spain occupied an estimated 70,000 men in military service after 1590 (Thompson 103).[43] Movement of soldiers from the peninsula to foreign battlefields drained the marriageable male population still further.[44] Against this backdrop of overall population decline accompanied by a disproportionally high survival rate for women, biological reproduction within the bounds of matrimony came to assume politically redemptive overtones. Martín González de Cellorigo explicitly linked the revitalization of Spain to population growth, and its shrinkage to national failure. This conviction led to Cellorigo's nearly heretical (and unheeded) opposition to the expulsion of the Moriscos on the grounds that this measure would only further deplete the country's strength.

Under these demographically unfavorable conditions, marriage rates exhibited great flux. Between 1590 and 1640, nuptiality in Castile plummeted by a staggering 20 percent. Beginning in the 1640s, how-ever, rates rose dramatically, continuing to surge throughout the peri-od of female courtly novel activity (1647-1663). Singlehood rates obeyed the expected inverse trend. Among women aged twenty-five and under, singlehood peaked in the 1630s and fell throughout the period from 1647 through 1663 (Reher 152, 153). This correlation between soaring marriage rates, declining singlehood and the rise of women's courtship novels lends further support to the claim that the genre arose at least partially in response to an increase in "density" or gender-pressure associated with the transition from maiden to wife.

Another angle from which to view the incidence of matrimony is that of marriage age data. In fact, women did not marry as early as they had in previous periods. As Matthews Greico observes, "since men and women married at an increasingly late age throughout the early modern period (an average of twenty-five to twenty-eight years), they were sexually mature for a good decade before being able to experience sex legitimately" (67). Thus, even though marriage rates were rising, women remained in the no (wo)man's zone of non-marriage for longer periods of time, their subjectivity hidden between the ideological cracks of a society that insisted that Christian women be wives. Fortunately, women's narratives of courtship and marriage delivered to their readers a vision of life between those cracks, emplotting contradictions between lived reality and patriarchal fantasies of subjugation, granting female characters a degree of agency that society would pretend that they lacked, and registering empowering strategies that transcended the frontiers of women's officially prescribed position (see chapters 3, 4 and 5).

A suitor proposed not to the bride-to-be, but to her father or protector. Whether or not the daughter's permission was deemed essential to the transaction is difficult to assess. Her verbal assent constituted part of the marriage ceremony, yet socialization for daughters to obey their parents' will, and lack of alternatives for disobedient and/or unwed daughters made refusal an extremely remote possibility. As Vives laments, closing chapter 18 of the *Instruction,* "¡O cuán gran locura es empezar el misterio del amor sacratísimo con la enemistad! .... Ahora hombre se casa con el dinero y el dinero se toma por mujer, que no la mujer" [Oh, what complete folly it is to begin the mystery of the most sacred love with enmity! . . . Now man marries money and takes money as his wife, instead of woman] (198). On the other hand, Vives opens the same chapter by idealizing a scene from Virgil's *Aeneid* in which Lavinia responds wordlessly to her parents' announcement of her engagement, "teniendo los ojos puestos en tierra, de vergüenza le caían lágrimas por su hermosa faz hilo a hilo" [keeping her eyes cast down, tears of shame fell streaming down her beautiful countenance], demonstrating, according to Vives, that maidens should never speak when their parents are arranging their marriage, "sino dejarlo todo en manos de ellos" [but rather leave everything in their hands] (181). As the pressure for enrichment through dowries increased in the sixteenth and seventeenth centuries, it may be supposed that Spain's cash-starved aristocracy perpetrated with increased frequency the "gran locura" [complete folly] of non-consensual marriage. Certainly, as chapter 3 makes clear, the problem of imposed marriages of convenience structures many women's courtship narratives.

"Marriage was seen not merely as woman's natural destiny," Olwen Hufton writes, "but also as a metamorphic agent, transforming her into a different social and economic being as part of a new household, the primary unit upon which all society was built" (28). Marriage represented a radical conversion from an indistinct and ill-defined maiden into a new and valid social entity, the wife. According to social historian Merry Wiesner, early modern European women's work rhythms were largely shaped by "individual biological and social events such as marriage, motherhood, and widowhood." She continues, "A man's stages of life were often differentiated by his place in an occupational or professional hierarchy, while a woman's depended on her marital status" (83). In much the same vein, Elisja Schulte van Kessel writes,"Any woman left without a husband in either this world or the next relinquished all hope of achieving a prestigious position in society" (149). Mary Elizabeth Perry echoes this appraisal, characterizing marriage as "una de las pocas vías hacia la respetabilidad" [one of the few ways to achieve respectability] for women, in contrast to men, who enjoyed access to many more channels of social convection. This discrepancy in the work rhythms and opportunities for social advancement for men and women comprised a primary source of gender pressure in the early modern period.

Although wives were subordinate to their husbands, they occupied a higher rung of the household hierarchy than anyone else except him. The same vertical disposition of power that raised rulers over their subjects, yet made male subjects despots in their own home, also empowered women with respect to those beneath them on the ladder of domestic power: children and servants. As Traub, Kaplan and Callaghan shrewdly observe:

> If the ruler were imagined as a parent, the parent was also given the rights and responsibilities of a ruler. In order for the subject to enact the monarch's will, he or she required a measure of authority in his or her own right. While husbands officially had rule over wives, both parents had rule over other members of the household, such as children and servants, male and female. Thus the analogy of state to family effected the structural subordination of its subjects while it simultaneously imparted to (at least some of) them a measure of authority. (3)

Inversely, Lou Charnon-Deutch demonstrates that this "structure of dominator/dominated" evident, for example, in María de Zayas's fiction, victimized men in the arena of empire just as it victimized women at home with respect to their husbands. Charnon-Deutch writes, "Men . . . have created a patriarchal culture that relies on the domination of an inferior other only to find that they are also susceptible to becoming the despised other in a larger community of world politics" (131). In the royal household, of course, the metaphor of domestic kingship became literalized, and the household as a microcosm of the state came to assume special significance. Among the ruling elite, matrimony was an instrument of imperial diplomacy that could consolidate the power of the empire, of which the royal family was a synechdochal miniature. The link between dynastic marriages and the courtship novel is taken up in chapter 5, where the political ramifications of courtship touched on here and in chapter 1 receive fuller consideration.

Despite the crushing insistence on matrimony, women did not spend their entire adult life subject to patriarchal rule, not only because they contracted matrimony later, but also because husbands traveled and husbands died. A woman running her husband's estate during protracted commercial or military absences, ignorant of his whereabouts or continued existence, found herself on the periphery of marriage law. Mary Elizabeth Perry recounts that there were so many women living independent of men in Seville during the Age of Conquest that the Venetian ambassador to Spain in the year 1525 characterized Seville as "Una ciudad en poder de las mujeres" [a city controlled by women] (*Espada* 23).

Widows were not subject to the same degree of social control as wives. Upon the death of her spouse, a widow reverted to a less defined, less "gender-dense" status. In fact, she assumed many responsibilities normally accorded to the male, while shedding the restrictions of a wife. The elite woman became legal head of her household and the executrix of her children's estates. According to Perry, she could buy and sell property, sign contracts and dictate her own will (24). In Seville, although women were categorically barred from joining *gremios* or trade brotherhoods, once a woman was widowed, she could inherit and run her deceased husband's shop (24-26).[45]

Widowhood was a recurrent life-course phase for many early modern women. Census data collected at the end of the sixteenth century indicates that between 15 and 20 percent of Castilian households were headed by widows (Bennassar 81, 82). This number is particularly surprising in light of the prevalence of the practice of remarriage; of 118 marriages contracted in Pedralba, Valencia between 1623 and 1675, one in three was a remarriage (Kamen 40). Enrique Gacto documents that in seventeenth-century Tarragona, 14 percent of all marriages involved widowers and 23 percent involved widows (81). Author Leonor de Meneses spent less than half of her adult life wed, despite having married twice. Between her first six-year marriage and her second three-year marriage, she spent twelve years widowed. (Whitenack 2, 3).

When a widow lacked financial resources to support her family, widowhood became a more difficult challenge. Many widows became companions or servants in more prospering households, while others were provided for by relatives on properties that would revert to the family upon their death In Mariana de Carvajal's case, cited above, the probable consequence of the author's husband's early death was to deprive most of Carvajal's five remaining daughters the means to marry.

Sara Matthews Greico estimates that as many as 25 percent of the European elite never wedded. Contributing significantly to this figure was the popularity of religious vocation for both men and women. Torres Sánchez records that 11 percent of the inhabitants of Salamanca, both male and female in 1591 lived in religious enclosure (33). Women who took the veil did not precisely relinquish marriage; rather, following the model of the early Christian virgins, they became *sponsa Christi*, or Brides of Christ (Schulte van Kessel 158). Either their parents paid a dowry in cash, incomes or land to the foundation for their upkeep, or their dowry was paid for by charity endowments established for that purpose. Like wives, novices were obliged to follow their Celestial Husband's laws. *Leyes de la Esposa* [Laws for the wife] is even the title of María de Ágreda's unfinished autobiography (Hernández Sánchez-Barba 144).

In light of the prominence of religious enclosure during this period, to argue that the reclusion motif so evident in Zayas's *Desengaños* [Disenchantments] represents a proto-feminist innovation is to confuse twenty-first-century enthusiasm for institutions promoting female solidarity with the seventeenth-century literary practice of verisimilitude.[46] Convents were a familiar facet of life, one through which many women would pass, either in lieu of, or following secular matrimony. Family ranking was an important factor in determining whether a daughter would marry an earthly or a Divine spouse. Only daughters, such as the Count-Duke of Olivares's daughter María, or Leonor de Meneses, were normally made legal heirs of their parents' estate, so it was important that they marry in order to bequeath their estates. Elder daughters in families with sons could be wed or sent into Orders as was the case with Mariana de Carvajal's eldest daughter. Younger daughters, like younger sons, generally entered Orders if their parents' resources permitted. This was the case of four of "matroness" Beatriz Galindo's granddaughters, who were sent into the Hieronymite Convent that Beatriz had endowed for them (see above). Through reclusion, illegitimate daughters, such as Lope's daughter, Madre Marcela de San Félix, could reclaim a measure of dignity withheld by the outside world (see below).

Nuns experienced gender differently than did their secular counterparts. For one thing, daughters could take greater initiative in selecting this path. Monasticism had become fashionable, and it was awkward for a family to deny their daughter this saintly vocation. Even if parents did object, a daughter who defied them could count on Church support for this decision.[47] Another gender attenuating factor was that nuns eschewed any outward displays of feminine vanity such as cosmetics or attractive clothing. To the contrary, counter-Reformist sisters were encouraged to be virile in their spiritual practices, evangelism and endurance of monastic privations. María de San José, a disciple of Teresa of Ávila, uses masculine martial imagery to pay tribute to her spiritual mother in her *Libro de recreaciones* [Book of re-creations] of 1585:

> For not only has [St. Teresa] roused weak women to take up Christ's Cross, but she has shamed the men, and dragged them out to the field of battle; and when they had turned their backs on discipline and primitive virtue, made them follow the banner of their woman Captain. . . . She began like another Deborah to inspire the army of God, promising victory to their side and never staying behind in the tent, but exposing herself to the greatest dangers and affronts. (*Recreación* I, qtd. in Arenal, Schlau 96)

Elsewhere, María refers to Teresa as a "Padre Madre monstruosa/ doctora de doctores" [Monstrous Father-Mother/greatest defender of the faith] (MS III, 361, qtd. in Arenal, Schlau, 44).

Finally, convents more than any other life-stage or vocation available to women, supported female learning. Reading was an important part of a novice's training. The Carmelite Constitution directs the novice's instructor, "que la ayuden en enseñarlas a leer" [that you help them learn to read] (Cap. 19. qtd. in Torres Sánchez 111). Although nuns did not read Fray Luis de León's *La perfecta casada,* his approved editions of Saint Teresa's *Life, Interior Castle* and *Way of Perfection* circulated throughout the Carmelite network of convents where they served as guides to contemplation and spiritual training (Sánchez Torres 169) as well as a model for aspiring conventual writers for centuries to come.

Like every other aspect of life, reading materials were strictly regulated in convents. "El leer los libros profanos de comedias y Fábulas amatorias, o novelas y poesías de amores indecentes y torpes, es cosa prohibida a las religiosas" [The reading of profane books of titillating plays and narrative, or novels and poetry featuring indecent and lascivious love, is a forbidden thing for nuns], drones an instruction book for nuns of the day.[48] Carmelite prioresses were instructed by their Constitution to give their daughters access to, "en especial Cartujanos [*Vita Christi* of Ludolph Carthusian], Flos Sanctorum, Contemptus mundi, Oratorio de Religiosos, lo de Fray Luis de

Granada y del padre Fray Pedro de Alcantara" [in particular, *Vita Christi*, Flos Sanctorum, Contemptus mundi, prayers of the pious, the works of Fray Luis de Granada and those of Fray Pedro de Alcantara] (Cap. 8. qtd. in Torres Sánchez 111). Nuns were also read aloud to, for example, during mealtimes.[49] Additionally, convents were sometimes sites of cultural production. For example, Lope de Vega's daughter, Marcela de San Félix wrote plays, colloquies and poetry for her sisters within the walls of San Idelfonso convent. In the secular world, where she was branded as illegitimate and overshadowed by her father's renown as Spain's premiere playwright, it is unlikely that Marcela would have found a comparable outlet for her talents (Arenal and Schlau 229-292).

The four stages of early modern elite woman's life outlined above are childhood, maidenhood, secular or religious marriage and widowhood. A final option that existed briefly in the sixteenth century was that of the *beata,* or unprofessed religious recluse. *Beaterios,* "un proyecto comunitario de mujeres donde la vida secular, profana y cotidiana se combina con la religión de forma natural, sin solemnidades rituales pautadas, sin claras fronteras divisorias" [a communal project created by women where secular, profane and daily life combines with religion in a natural way, without the formal structured ceremonies, and without clear dividing lines between them] (Muñoz Fernández 117) were less regimented than convents. *Beatarios* located in or near Madrid in the early sixteenth century included those of San Pedro, Catalina de Siena, Tristán, Cubas and Santa Librada in Alcalá de Henares. By 1520, all had fallen under conventual rule (Muñoz Fernández 105-120).

As women's life-stages are enumerated, it might appear that conventual and secular marriage mutually excluded one another. Certainly women who professed in Orders were wedded to Christ for life. Papal reconsideration of the perpetuity of vows would not take place until the first decade of the twentieth century, when Pious X proposed its reform.[50] However, secular marriage did not preclude reclusion at a later stage. Women could enjoy a frivolous youth, marriage, motherhood, and widowhood, and still choose to die a bride of Christ. Torres Sánchez records the curious case of a twenty-four-year-old Belgian widow named María del Mol who came to lodge at a Carmelite convent in Salamanca with her servant and two daughters in 1633. After she fell ill, d. María decided to profess, and both daughters and her servant followed suit (77, 78).

While it is evident that women's subordination in marriage was the ideological linchpin of the counter-Reform, and one of the "recurrent references by which it legitimated its power" (Joan Scott 1073), the improbability that a woman would spend a significant percentage of her life yoked to a single tyrannical husband attenuated the oppressive impact of marriage on women's lived experience. In fact, a woman was likely to spend the early part of her adult life in protracted maidenhood, marry more than once, spend periods of time during her marriage apart from her husband, move in and out of widowhood, and possibly enter Orders at a later stage. The earlier that a woman took vows, the longer time she would spend within a community supportive of women's education, removed from male predation and the vanities attendant upon winning men's favor, cultivating a spiritual fortitude that was explicitly gendered male. The life-course of a twice-married woman who elected to profess in her later years would proceed as follows: child / maiden / wife / widow / wife / widow / nun.

This fluidity of gender expectations throughout woman's life-course, as well as the relatively circumscribed impact of marriage on her daily lived experience may surprise readers steeped in prescriptive writings of the Golden Age, or familiar with the cultural stereotypes of the period. Women's courtship novels corroborate the historian's view that women's subjectivity in early modern Spain embraced a rich and varied array of life-course experiences that extended, in Lou Charnon-Deutsch's words, far "beyond the moment when their kinship definition is changed contractually from daughter or sister to wife" (127). The remaining chapters of this volume are devoted to exploring three areas of female subjectivity "beyond" precept as elaborated in the courtship novels of María de Zayas, Leonor de Meneses and Mariana de Carvajal. Chapter 3 "Agency and Constraint in Courtship Plots," analyzes representations of courtship as sites of contestation between forces that limited female characters' choice (parental constraints and legal restrictions, for example) and societal resources that granted women a degree of agency as they negotiated their social identity (monastic asylum, familial networks, civil law, etc.). Chapter 4, "The Art (and Craft) of Courtesy," explicates "self-fashioning" or strategies of courteous self-presentation as these enhanced female characters' power to achieve matrimonial—or non-matrimonial—ambitions. Chapter 5, "Courtship as Political Allegory," unpacks the political dimensions of courtship for women writers contemplating a dynastic court in crisis, the latter Hapsburg Court of Philip IV.

Notes

1. "Autobiografía" was subsequently republished in *Al balcón* (Valencia: Sempere, n.d. [1913]). Lynn Scott, "Carmen de Burgos: Piecing a Profession: Rewriting Women's Roles" (Ph.D. diss., University of Florida, 1999), 28n16.

2. The best that contemporary authors could do was to address their readership in the most global of terms. Mateo Alemán wrote two prologues to *Guzmán de Alfarache,* one for "el discreto" [the discreet man] and one for "el vulgo" [the vulgar man] (ed. Enrique Miralles García [Barcelona: PPU, 1988]). The noncommittal formula "a los que leyeren" [to the readers] frequently introduces

prologues, but even this is broadened at times to include listeners, in recognition of the ongoing custom of reading aloud to unlettered listeners, according to D. W. Cruickshank ("Literature and the Book Trade in Golden-Age Spain," *Modern Language Notes* 73.4 [1978], 820).

3. Mary Elizabeth Perry, *Ni Espada Rota ni Mujer que Trota*, trans. Margarida Fonrtuny Minguella (Barcelona: Crítica, 1993). The original title in English is *Gender and Disorder in Early Modern Seville*.

4. "Objectified and devalued like so many women in early modern European painting and sculpture, Daphne's transformation into a laurel tree is perceived almost exclusively as Apollo's misfortune" (Yael Even, "Daphne [without Apollo] Reconsidered: Some Disregarded Images of Sexual Pursuit in Italian Renaissance Baroque Art," *Studies in Iconography* 18 [1977], 146).

5. For discussion of thematic and structural similarities as well as mutual indebtedness of drama and narrative of the Golden Age, see Barbara Matulka, *The Feminist Theme in the Drama of the* Siglo de Oro (New York: Columbia University Press, 1936), and Florence Yudin, "The *Novela Corta* as *Comedia*: Lope's *Las Fortunas de Diana*," *Bulletin of Hispanic Studies* 45 (1968), 181-188.

6. In his mock-treatise on dramatic precept, the "Arte nuevo de hacer comedias" [The new art of writing for the theater] of 1613, Lope de Vega recognizes the seventeenth-century theatergoer's taste for cross-dressing: "y si [las actrices] mudaren traje, sea de modo / Que pueda perdonarse, porque suele / El disfraz varonil agradar mucho" [and if the actresses are to cross-dress, let them do so in such a way that what they've done is forgivable, for male garb is often quite pleasing] (Monograph Reprint 2 [Liverpool, England: Bulletin of Hispanic Studies, 1935], 7).

7. The right to perform in public theaters was alternately rescinded and restored to actresses in Spain throughout the sixteenth and seventeenth centuries. See Eric A. Nicholson, "The Theater," in *Renaissance and Enlightenment Paradoxes*, ed. Natalie Zemon Davis and Arlette Farge, 310, in *A History of Women in the West*, Vol. 3, ed. Georges Duby and Michelle Perrot (Cambridge: Harvard University Press, Belknap Press, 1993).

8. Stanton quotes Baldassarre Castiglione, *The Book of the Courtier,* trans. Charles Singleton (New York: Anchor, 1959), 38, 99.

9. Mary Elizabeth Perry tempers this view, insisting that Spain's ongoing wars "preserved a feudal ethos of the warrior." Ironically, she also finds that Spain's ongoing wars "empowered women by corroding patriarchal family structures ("Crisis and Disorder in the World of María de Zayas y Sotomayor," in *María de Zayas: The Dynamics of Discourse*, ed. Amy Williamsen and Judith Whitenack [Cranbury, N.J.: Associated University Press, 1995], 28).

10. Baldassarre Castiglione, *The Book of the Courtier*, trans. George Bull (Baltimore: Penguin, 1967), 211, quoted in Sarah F. Matthews Greico, "The Body, Appearance, and Sexuality," 57, in *Renaissance and Enlightenment*, ed. Zemon and Farge, quoted in *History of Women*, ed. Duby and Perrot, Vol. 3.

11. The first, or priestly narrative of Genesis 1.26, represents their creation as simultaneous: "male and female, created he them," and grants women and men shared sovereignty over the natural world: "let them have dominion over the fish

in the sea" (N. H. Keeble, *The Cultural Identity of Seventeenth-Century Woman: A Reader* [New York: Routledge, 1994], 1).

12. "Es condición averiguada que (cuando Dios formó a Adán y Eva) le cupo menos sabiduría a Eva, por la cual razón dicen los teólogos que se atrevió el demonio a engañarla y no osó tentar al varón, temiendo su mucha sabiduría. La razón desto es que la compostura natural que la mujer tiene en el celebro no es capaz de mucho ingenio ni de mucha sabiduría" [It has been proven that (when God made Adam and Eve) He allotted Eve less wisdom, and it is for this reason that theologians say that the devil dared trick her, and did not attempt such vile temptation with the male, fearing his great wisdom. The reason for this is that the configuration of the female brain does not favor much in the way of ingenuity or wisdom] (Huarte de San Juan, *Examen de Ingenios* [The examination of ingenious men] ed. Guillermo Seres [Madrid: Cátedra, 1989], 25, quoted in María Teresa Cacho, "Misoginia y barroco: Baltasár Gracián" [Mysogyny and baroque: Baltasár Gracián]," in *Literatura y vida cotidiana* [Literature and daily life], Actas de las Cuartas Journadas de Investigación Interdisciplinaria, ed. María Ángeles Durán and José Antonio Rey [Madrid: Universidad Autónoma de Madrid; Zaragoza: Universidad de Zaragoza, 1987], 178).

13. San Juan, *Examen de ingenios*, 180.

14. Others include *El Libre de les dones* [The book of women] (c. 1396) of Francisco Eiximenis (ed. Gracia Lozano Lopez [Madison, Wis.: Hispanic Seminary of Medieval Studies, c1992]) and Christine de Pizan's 1405 *Livre des trois virtus* [The book of the three virtues] (critical edition, notes by Charity Cannon Willard [Paris: H. Champion, 1989]), translated into Portuguese between 1447 and 1455 as *Espelho de Cristina* [Cristina's mirror] (quoted in Tobias Brandenberger, *Literatura de matrimonio (Península Ibérica S. XIV-XVI)* [Marriage literature (Iberian Peninsula, fourteenth to sixteenth centuries)], Hispanica Helvetica 8 [Zaragoza, Spain: Pórtico; Lausanne, Switzerland: Sociedad Suiza de Esudios Hispánicos, 1996], 81-136).

15. Lorenzo Riber, *Obras completas, de Vives* [Complete works of Vives] (Madrid: Aguilar, 1947), 992, quoted in Brandenburger, *Literatura*, 223-224.

16. Vives, who was to become preceptor to Queen Catherine's daughter, Mary, wrote the *Instruction* at the age of thirty, before having married. Erasmus critiqued the text, finding it rather too harsh: "Lo que dices me parece muy bien, sobre todo lo referente al matrimonio. Sin embargo, si quisieras moderar ese fervor, serían más suaves ciertas cosas. En lo del matrimonio te has mostrado duro con las mujeres: espero que serás más blando con la tuya. Y de los afeites, dijiste demasiado" [What you say seems very apt to me, above all when you address the topic of matrimony. However, should you want to moderate your text's zealousness, there are certain things you could tone down. On this subject of matrimony, you've shown yourself to be quite harsh on women; I do hope you're gentler with your own wife. And those things you said about curbing their vanity quite frankly went too far]. (Riber, *Obras*, 173, quoted in Mariló Vigil, "La Importancia de la moda en el Barroco" [The importance of fashion in the baroque], in Durán and Rey, *Vida Cotidiana*, 189).

17. Riber, *Obras*, 996s, quoted in Brandenburger, *Literatura*, 221.

18. Pedro Malon [Fray Melchor] de Chiade, *La conversión de la Magdalena* [The conversion of Mary Magdalene], 3 vols. (Madrid: Ediciones de la lectura, 1930), quoted in Lola Luna, *Leyendo como una Mujer: La imagen de la mujer* [Reading like a woman: The image of the woman] (Barcelona: Anthropos; Seville: Instituto Andaluz de la Mujer, Junta de Andalusía, 1996), 117.

19. Chapter 5, p. 10, quoted in Cacho, "Misoginia," 182.

20. María de Zayas would elaborate upon this metaphor in her *desengaño* [tale of disenchantment], entitled "Estragos que causa el vicio" [The vicissitudes of vice] of 1647. In that tale, d. Gaspar substitutes the pleasure of gazing at his lady's house for that of gazing at the lady herself. However, Zayas adds a third term to the comparison, that of an oyster shell that hides its treasure within: "que ya que no [veía] la perla, se contentaba con ver la caja" [given that he didn't see the pearl, he consoled himself with seeing the shell] (María de Zayas, *Parte Segunda del Sarao y Entretenimiento Honesto [Desengaños Amorosos]* [Second part of the soiree and decorous diversion: Disenchantments of Love], ed. Alicia Yllera [Madrid: Cátedra, 1983], 477).

21. Fray Vicente Mexía, *Saludable instrucción del estado del matrimonio* [Salubrious instruction in the ways of marriage] (Córdoba, Spain: Juan Baptista Escuerdo, 1566), fol. 25, quoted in Vigil, "La Importancia," 192 n22.

22. Gaspar de Astete, *Tratado del gobierno de la familia, y estado de las viudas y doncellas* [Treatise on the how the family shall be governed, and on the status of widows and maidens] 210, quoted in Vigil, "La Importancia," 190.

23. Pedro Galindo,*Verdades morales en que se reprenden y condenan los trajes vanos, superfluos y profanos; con otros vicios y abusos que hoy se usan; mayormente los escotados deshonestos de las mujeres* [Book of moral truths which admonishes and condemns vain, superfluous and profane garb that people of today cloak themselves in; above all, the scandalous necklines of women's dresses] (Madrid: Francisco Sáenz, 1639), 678, fol. 33, quoted in Vigil, "La Importancia," 196-197.

24. *Recopilación de las leyes destos reynos hecha por mandado de la Magestad Catholica Del Rey Don Philippe segundo nuestro señor* [Compilation of the laws of these kingdoms, by mandate of His Catholic Magesty, King Philip II, our lord] Libro octavo, Títuolo 20, Ley 1: "Que pone la pena de los adulteros" [Eighth book, title 20, law 1: "Which assigns the penalty for adultery"], quoted in Melveena McKendrick, *Women and Society in the Spanish Drama of the Golden Age: A Study of the Mujer Varonil* (Cambridge: Cambridge University Press, 1974), 15n1.

25. *Novísima relación* [Most recent royal decrees] book 10, chapter 17, section 8, quoted in Bartolomé Clavero, *Mayorazgo: Propiedad feudal en Castilla (1369-1836)* [Entailment: Feudal property in Castile] (Madrid: Siglo Veintiuno, 1974), 240-241.

26. Pedro Melgarejo, *Compendio de contratos públicos, autos de particiones, ejecutivos y de residencias* [Compendium of public contracts and decrees of partition, both executive and residencial] 1652 (Madrid: Joseph García Lanza, 1758), quoted in Clavero, *Mayorazgo*, 242.

27. D. Leonor de Meneses appears to have become ennobled through marriage. She acquired the title of Countess of Serem through her first marriage, and

that of Countess of Atouguia through her second (Judith Whitenack and Gwyn E. Campbell, introduction to *El desdeñado más firme* [Scorned yet steadfast] by Leonor de Meneses [Potomac, Md.: Scripta Humanistica, 1994], 2-3).

28. According to documents transcribed by Manuel Serrano y Sanz, Doña Baltásara was involved in a legal battle over her Galician mother's inheritance, which the latter had, in turn, inherited from her mother; however at the time of the Royal entitlement, the settlement had not yet been made (*Apuntes para una Biblioteca de Escritoras Españolas desde el año 1401 al 1833* [Notes for a library of Spanish women writers], 2 vols. [Madrid: Sucesores de Rivadeneyra, 1903-1905], I 54-55).

29. Don Rodrigo de Silva offers another instance of a higher title assumed through marriage. De Silva became Duke Consort of Híjar in 1621 upon wedding the Aragonese duchess, doña Isabel Margarita Fernández (IV Duchess of Híjar, Lécera y Aliaga, VI Countess of Belchite and Countess of Valfogona and Guimerá). See Ramón Ezquerra Abadía, *La conspiración del Duque de Híjar (1648)* [The conspiracy of the Duke of Híjar] (Madrid, 1934), 76-79.

30. Hernández Franco cites the case of the Palmero clan, who, by situating successive sons in Church posts, managed to maintain their possessions and prestige within the family (Juan Hernández Franco, ed., *Familia y poder: Sistemas de reproducción social en España [siglos XVI-XVIII]* [Family and power: Systems of social reproduction in Spain (sixteenth to eighteenth centuries)] [Madrid: Temas de Hoy, 1996], 17).

31. As chapter 3 shows, the multi-generational narrative structure of Mariana de Carvajal's "La industria vence desdenes" [Effort vanquishes scorn] relies upon such a "diagonal" transmission of wealth.

32. Mary Gossy's *Untold Stories* and Arenal and Schlau's *Untold Sisters* are two landmarks of Hispanic feminist scholarship. Gossy applies feminist textual analysis to canonical Golden Age texts. Arenal and Schlau annotate and anthologize previously unpublished writings of Spanish nuns.

33. The *Cámara de Gracia y Justicia* [court of religious and secular matters] granted her request, paraphrasing her petition to read "either a knighthood for one of her sons, or a knighthood for whomever marries one of her daughters": "Y que se le haga merced de un auito para uno de sus hijos, o quien casare con una de sus hijas, a su eleccion" (Serrano y Sanz, *Apuntes*, I 242).

34. *Archivo general de la villa de Madrid, archivo de secretaría* [General archives of Madrid, archive of the secretariat], 19-26-5, quoted in Angela Muñoz Fernández, *Acciones e intenciones de mujeres en la vida religiosa de los siglos XVI y XVII* [Actions and intentions of women in the religious life of the sixteenth and seventeenth centuries] (Madrid: Mujeres en Madrid, 1995), 33.

35. "Introduction: Out of Exile," in *Women Writing Culture*, ed. Behar and Gordon (Berkeley and Los Angeles: University of California Press, 1995), 22, quoted in *Constructing Spanish Womanhood: Female Identity in Modern Spain*, ed. Victoria Enders and Pamela Radcliffe (Albany, N.Y.: State University of New York Press, 1999), 1.

36. "De que vi que era imposible ir adonde me matasen por Dios, ordenávamos ser ermitaños; y en una huerta que avía en casa procurávamos, como podíamos, hacer ermitas, puniendo unas pedrecillas, que luego se nos caían, y

ansí no hallávamos remedio en nada para nuestro deseo" [As soon as I saw that it was impossible to go anywhere where I could die a gallant death in the name of God, my brother and I agreed that we should become hermits; and so, in an orchard near our home, we managed (as best we could) to construct hermitages, building them by making piles of stones which invariably fell on us, and so in no measure were any of our religious aspirations fulfilled] (Saint Teresa of Ávila, *Libro de la vida* [Book of my life], ed. Otger Steggink [Madrid: Castalia, 1986], 99).

37. Fray Juan de la Cerda, *Libro llamado vida política de todos los estados de mujeres* [The book known as the political life of all the states of womanhood], (Madrid: Biblioteca Nacional, 1599), Mss 19.212, quoted in Isabel Barbeito Carneiro, *Mujeres de Madrid barroco: Voces testimoniales* [Women of Baroque Madrid: Testimonial voices] (Madrid: Comunidad de Madrid, 1992), 14.

38. Calderón's play *La dama duende* ["The spirit lady"] dramatizes tension between the promogenitor, Juan, and his younger brother, Luis. Luis is depicted as an angry and volatile character, resentful of his elder brother's power. Margaret Greer analyzes their relationship in the context of *mayorazgo* law in "The (Self)-Representation of Control." Juan Ruiz de Alarcón's *comedia, La verdad sospechosa* [The suspicious truth] hinges on the unexpected death of the primogenitor, Gabriel, and the challenge posed by suddenly elevating his carefree younger brother, García, to this special role.

39. Walter Ong, *Interfaces of the Word: Studies in the Evolution of Consciousness and Culture* (Ithaca, N.Y.: Cornell University Press, 1977), quoted in Ruth El Saffar, "The 'I' of the Beholder: Self and Other in Some Golden Age Texts," in *Cultural Authority in Golden Age Spain*, ed. Marina Brownlee and Hans Ulrich Gumbrecht (Baltimore: Johns Hopkins University Press, 1995), 180.

40. For example, the rate of illegitimate births in Talavera de la Reina declined from 5.2 percent in 1550-1599 to 0.9 percent in 1700-1750. María del Carmen González Muñoz, *La población de Talavera de la Reina (Siglos XVI-XX)* [The Population of Talavera de la Reina, from the sixteenth to the twentieth Century] (Toledo: Diputación Provinical, 1974), cited in Sara Nalle, "To Sin in Thought and Deed: Ideas and Actions in Counter-Reformation Spain" (paper presented at the 2nd Seminario de Historia de España, Soria, Spain, July 1992). Mothers during the counter-Reformation campaign against illegitimate births were more likely to abandon these bastard infants. For this reason, natality rates became closely linked to marriage rates during this period. See Henry Kamen, *Spain in the Later Seventeenth Century: 1665-1700* (London: Longmans, 1980), 45.

41. Melibea, the tragic heroine of Fernando de Rojas' *Tragicomedia de Calixto y Melibea*, [Tragi-comedy of Calixto and Melibea] defied her parents in order to pursue an illicit love-affair with Calixto.

42. The great epidemic of 1596-1602 marked a decisive reversal in the prospering demographic growth of the preceding century. The second plague of 1647-1652 was more limited in scope, but also more virulent, causing 200,000 deaths in Andalusia alone (Antonio Domínguez Ortiz, *La sociedad Española en el*

siglo XVII [Spanish society in the seventeenth century], 2 vols. [Madrid: Consejo Superior de Investigaciónes Ceintíficas, 1965], 70-81).

43. The Venetian ambassador, Tiepolo, noted in 1567, "The shortage of men in the provinces is so great that it was considered a great marvel that 14,000 foot were assembled this year to be sent abroad." Translated and quoted in I. A. A. Thompson, *War and Government in Hapsburg Spain 1560-1620* (London: The Athlone Press, 1976), 105-106.

44. Angel Rodríguez Sánchez has shown that recruitment of soldiers exerted a negative impact on marriage-rates in Cáceres in 1571. *Cáceres: población y comportamiento demográficos en el siglo XVI* [Cáceres: Population and demographics in the sixteenth century] (Cáceres, Spain: Aula de Cultura de la Caja de Ahorros y Monte de Piedad, 1977), quoted in Bartolomé Bennassar, *La España del Siglo de Oro* [Golden Age Spain], trans. Pablo Bordonava (Barcelona: Crítica, 1983; Bloomington, Ind.: Indiana University Press, 1932), 64-67.

45. See also Margaret Greer, "The (Self)Representation of Control in *La dama duende*," in *The Golden Age* Comedia*: Text, Theory and Performance*, ed. Charles Ganelin and Howard Mancing (West Lafayette, Ind.: Purdue University Press, 1994), 97.

46. See Lena Sylvania, "Doña María de Zayas y Sotomayor: A Contribution to the Study of Her Works," *Romantic Review* 13 (1922), 197-213, Juan Luis Alborg, *Historia de la literatura Española: época barroca* [History of Spanish literature: baroque epoch] Vol. 2 (Madrid: Gredos, 1967) 500, and Joseph Spieker, "El femenismo como clave estructural en las novelle de Doña María de Zayas" [Feminism as a structural key in the novellas of María de Zayas], *Explicaciones de textos literarios* 6.2 (1978), 153-160.

47. Once she took refuge inside convent walls, it was not unusual for a daughter and her parents soon to become reconciled. Teresa of Ávila's father opposed her profession, as she recounts in her *Life:* "Lo que más se pudo acabar con él fue que después de sus días haría [yo] lo que [yo] quisiese" [It was nearly a mortal blow to him to think that after his death I might do as I wished, after all] (113). However, he learned to accept his stubborn daughter's decision, and, in the face of Teresa's own near-death experience, lived to repent his original opposition: "La pena de mi padre era grande de no me haver dejado confesar" [My father deeply regretted never having permitted me to make my confession] (130). Lope de Vega's daughter, Marcela de San Félix "broke away from home" (Arenal and Schlau, *Untold Sisters*, 235) to enter Orders. In Madre [Mother] Marcela's monastic biography, it is written, "que sus padres la tenían poco amor y que por huir sus molestias se había venido al sagrado como los delinquentes cuando huyen de la Justicia" [her parents showed her scant affection, and in running away from her domestic discomfort, she found her way to the sanctuary of the Church, just like the delinquents fleeing from the long arm of the law do] (quoted in Arenal and Schlau, *Untold Sisters*, 231). Nonetheless, from 1621, when Marcela became a novice, until Lope's death in 1635, her profligate father became a daily visitor at Marcela's convent.

48. Fray Antonio Arbiol, *La religiosa instruida con doctrina de la Sagrada Escritura I* [The religious woman instructed in the doctrine of the Sacred Scriptures I] (1716) 32, quoted in Concha Torres Sánchez, *La clausura femenina en la*

Salamanca del Siglo XVII: Dominicas y Carmelitas Descalzas. [Female enclosure in seventeenth-century Salamanca: Dominicans and Discalced Carmelites] Acta salmanticensia. Estudios históricos y geográficos 73 (Salamanca, Spain: University of Salamanca, 1991), 112.

49. Permissible mealtime readings at the Cistercian convent of Ávila in the years 1489-1492 included the Bible, saints' lives, various patristic writings and the Valencian theologian Francissco Eiximenis's *Vida de Nuestro Señor Jesucristo* [Life of Our Lord, Jesus Christ]. In 1515, the convent of San Francisco de Toledo authorized various New Testament readings, the *Vita Christi,* Contemptus mundi and Domenico Cavalca's *Mirror of the Cross.* See Ronald Surtz, *Writing Women in Late Medieval and Early Modern Spain: The Mothers of Saint Teresa of Ávila* (Philadelphia: University of Pennsylvania Press, 1995), 13.

50. Carmen de Burgos, *El divorcio en España* [Divorce in Spain] (Madrid: Viuda de M. Romero, impresor, 1904), quoted in Lynn Scott, "Carmen de Burgos: Piecing a Profession: Rewriting Women's Roles" (Ph.D. diss., University of Florida, 1999), II, 21n17.

3: Agency and Constraint in Courtship Plots

> AUTOR:　　y así, dejo a todos hoy
> 　　　　　　hacer libres sus papeles;
>
> 　　　　　　(and thus I leave you all today
> 　　　　　　free to interpret your roles your own way)
> —Calderón, *El gran teatro del mundo* [The great theater of the world], 36
>
> si la mitad de los hechos dependen de la arbirariedad de la fortuna, la otra mitad responden a una intervención nuestra dirigida y calculada.
>
> (if one half of that which occurs depends on the arbitrary whims of fortune, the other half responds to our own direct and calculated intervention.)
> —Machiavelli, *El Príncipe* [The Prince][1]

The courting maidens of women's courtship narratives manifest a dawning subjectivity that outstrips the contemporary stereotype of the obedient daughter. In the hands of female novelists, courtship becomes more than a predictable preamble; it is a crucial life-course passage fraught with dangers and challenges for the young women attempting to move beyond the shadow of their parents' threshold. Similarly, marriage in women's courtship plots is no longer a final curtain that cloaks and muffles women's unique needs, but becomes instead a site of self-assertion, agency and identity formation. By resisting the equation of marriage with closure for all and in all cases, by inspecting and dissecting the conditions under which marriage can and cannot vouchsafe happiness, by envisaging its dangers, shortcomings and alternatives, female novelists dismantle the counter-Reformation ideology of *la perfecta casada,* [the perfect wife] and redress their grievances in the new colors of a nascent self.

In chapter 2, early modern courtship were seen to function much like a game that operated outside of the jurisdiction of marriage. In any game one may choose to emphasize play or to focus on score. Courtship plots written by women novelists elect the former approach, attending closely to the play of courtship, to its rules and to infraction of those rules. The reader delights in the "play" of the game rather than in the taking of connubial winnings at novel's end.[2] A jocose poem embedded in Mariana de Carvajal's *Navidades de Madrid* compares courtship to gaming. The second stanza puns that there is no reason for any man to waste his fortune gambling at cards when he could be playing the game of *damas* (ladies/checkers):

> ¡Que haya quien juegue a los naipes,
> habiendo juego de damas!
> pues ¿es mejor que con tantos
> jugar un hombre con tantas? (249)
>
> (Who would waste his time playing cards
> when he could be playing checkers?
> Is it not preferable that a man entertain
> himself with as many pieces as possible?)

In its excerpted form, Carvajal's ladies/checkers conceit seems to cast maidens as passive "pieces" to be moved from square to square for men's recreation. If courtship is understood to be a game, is it a contest which women can actually play and win, or only one to which they are subjected? Fortunately, Carvajal's poem does not appear by itself; an engagement party provides its festive frame. Once the game-plan of the [female] character who recites the poem is understood, her prospects of winning at courtship begin to brighten.

D. Juana, one of eight frame-tale narrators, and who seeks an advantageous match for her daughter, Leonor, recites the verse cited above. Her actions within the novel sharply contradict the message of her poem. Juana's role in the frame-tale is decisive, for it is she who suggests convening a storytelling party during Christmas in order to introduce Leonor to her proprietress's son. After her suggestion receives approval, d. Juana also establishes the "rules of play" of the entertainment: "El primer día de Pascua será la obligada la señora doña Gertrudis; el segundo, el señor don Vicente; el tercero, doña Lucrecia; y el último, el señor don Enrique. Cada uno ha de quedar obligado a contar un suceso la noche que le tocare" [On the first holiday evening, it shall be Lady Gertrudis' turn, on the second, don Vicente's, on the third, Lady Lucrecia's, and lastly, don Enrique's. When the night of your turn comes, each one of you is obliged to tell a story] (17). By exercising initiative and strategically masterminding the courtship game, d. Juana more closely resembles the masculine-gendered checkers-players of her poem than its passive feminine-gendered checkers. The gap between Juana's words and her narrative situation further deepens when the plot of "La industria vence desdenes," [Effort vanquishes scorn] the narrative that she recites on the seventh night of the Christmas party, is recalled. Her novella portrays a son and a daughter who collaborate to save their family name from extinction, a tale of male-female partnership rather than of male control.

The portrait of d. Juana that emerges from these observations is one of autonomy rather than of subjugation in courtship. Yet her poem describes women as checkers, as non-volitional objects. The tension between autonomous and predetermined action to which the damas/checkers metaphor points to two theoretical "stories" that can be told about women's fiction, one story "that speak[s] of the subject's determination" and one "that speak[s] of the subject's ethical, political agency," according to Mieli Steele (108). Nancy Fraser summarizes this tension in the following manner:

> The net result of these conflicting tendencies is the following dilemma: *either* we limn the structural constraints of gender so well that we deny woman any agency *or* we portray women's agency so glowingly that the power of subordination evaporates. Either way, what we often seem to lack is a coherent, integrated, balanced conception of agency, a conception that can accommodate both the power of social constraints and the capacity to act situationally against them. (17, Fraser's emphasis)[3]

Scholars have begun to recognize that the early modern period offers a third kind of story, a dialectical encounter of the first two, in which, "[t]here was inequality, to be sure, but there was also a shifting zone in which women found and used a multitude of strategies outside the roles of inevitable victims or exceptional heroines to make themselves active agents in history" (Davis, Farge 4). D. Juana's appropriation of the checkers metaphor occupies this shifting zone.

D. Juana appeases her male listeners through flattery.[4] By comparing men to powerful players exerting total control over a field of feminine-gendered tokens, she, paradoxically, gains greater control over them. Lulled and gratified at having heard what they wanted to hear, Juana's male listeners fail to notice that Juana (much like Lisis of Zayas's *Desengaños* [Disenchantments]) has enmeshed them in a courtship game of her own devising. In addition to establishing the courtship-as-game conceit, d. Juana's poem serves to warn the alert reader that rhetorical subtlety often colors that game's representation. A plot that initially appears to disenfranchise women may yield an opposite interpretation once other narrative features are considered.

The outcome of courtship is less fundamental to an understanding of women's courtship plots than is the encounter between a volitional female character and her more or less limiting circumstances. Plot unfurls and meaning emerges in crosscurrents of opportunity and restraint rather than in a univocal story either of total repression or of untrammeled self-determination. Thus, courtship plots do not resemble action plots as closely as they resemble what Northrop Frye has characterized as anatomies: "The word 'anatomy' in Burton's title [*Anatomy of Melancholy*] means a dissection or analysis, and . . . we may as well adopt it as a convenient name to replace the cumbersome and in modern times rather misleading 'Menippean satire'" (311, 12). Just as Burton anatomizes the phenomenon of melancholy, and Castiglione's dialogues construct an image of the perfect courtier, women's courtship plots anatomize the shifting zone between the checker and the checker-player, the dialectical interplay of opportunity and constraint faced by courting women. Against a dominant discourse oppressive to women, female novelists launched into circulation alternative stories in which women exercised agency even in the absence of authority.[5]

The primary plotting unit of women's courtship novels may be encapsulated as a literary motif analogous to those that Stith Thompson designed to help classify world folktales,[6] by restating it in this fashion: "Female characters face prospect of marriage." The verb "face" emphasizes encountering challenges, an open-ended process with no definite outcome, rather than merely dispatching them. Additionally, the term "face" is intended to offset the typological impact of the phrase "female characters." Each female subject differentiates herself from her literary sisters by facing her narrative circumstances in a unique manner. Through her distinctive attitudes and strategies of play, she transcends her generic limitations as a "female character" and achieves a degree of distinctiveness not evident at the outset.

Chapters 3 and 4 address the question, "which factors help or hinder women as they face the prospect of courtship?" At least three distinct classes of causality generate plotting variation in baroque women's courtship novels. The first two correspond to socioeconomic circumstances: advantageous conditions that assist women in asserting their will and disadvantageous conditions that deter them. A third cluster of causes predicative of plot variation is made up of behaviors rather than circumstances that enhance women's prospects for winning at courtship. While mastery of these codes of comportment, which I call "courtesy," is also somewhat dependent upon socioeconomic factors (birth and upbringing, for example), the stress is on strategic personal intervention rather than on a set of preexisting conditions. Therefore they will be treated separately.

Although splitting circumstance and behavior into two separate chapters arbitrarily divides plotting elements that coexist within the novels themselves, two benefits justify their separation for analytical purposes. Not only does this schema permit due attention to be paid to two distinct aspects of courtship that have yet to be fully acknowledged and studied (socioeconomic circumstances and strategic behaviors), but it also underscores the correspondence of two complementary literary operations: those of mimesis and instruction.

Mimesis and Instruction

Mimesis or imitation may be thought of as the text's marshalling of references to Spanish Court society to fabricate an artful simulacrum of the implied reader's world. In addition to creating the web of conditions that help or hinder women in courtship these familiar details help to assuage the reader's incredulity and promote greater identification with the characters' socioeconomic predicament. For example, in Carvajal's *Navidades,* we learn that Lucrecia's house in Madrid is "labrada a la malicia," that is, it was exempt from the requirement of housing visiting dignitaries to the Court at the owner's expense (13).[7] The reader is also informed that Lucrecia hosts six boarders. Together, these details concisely position Lucrecia in a socioeconomic niche readily identifiable by the seventeenth-century Spanish reader: that of a noblewoman with multiple property-holdings, who rents rooms in her dwelling at Court to earn extra income. Lucrecia's situation epitomizes the predicament of Spain's cash-poor lower nobility, and her tale promises to interest readers sympathetic to their plight.[8]

Mimesis in the courtship novel corresponds to the rhetorical principal of *probabilitas* or *imitatio.* Like other rhetorical devices, imitation was a tool for attracting the reader, drawing him or her into the text, in this case, by delivering the pleasurable experience of recognition. To cite a famous example, Cervantes's Priest finds the tale of the "Curioso impertinente" [The novel of the curious impertinent] good, but defective because it fails to adhere to the principle of verisimilitude: "—Bien—dijo el cura—me parece esta novela; pero no me puedo persuadir que esto sea verdad; y si es fingido, fingió mal el autor, porque no se puede imaginar que haya marido tan necio, que quiera hacer tan costosa experiencia como Anselmo. Si este caso se pusiera entre un galán y una dama, pudiérase llevar; pero entre marido y mujer, algo tiene del imposible" ["This novel," said the priest, "seems all well and good to me, but I cannot convince myself that it is factual, and if it is false, its author falsified badly, as it is simply unimaginable that a husband could be so foolish as to want to undertake an experiment as costly as Anselmo's. If this case involved a beau and his belle, perhaps one could believe it, but between a husband and his wife, well, something about it smacks of the impossible"] (I.35 p. 304).[9] Segregating the representation of circumstance from that of self-fashioning behaviors brings more fully to view the significance of mimesis as a strategy for inducing the reader's identification with the text.

The courtship novel also exhibits an instructive impulse, which moves in the opposite direction than mimesis. While imitation draws the reader toward the text through recognition, the instructive current moves from text outward toward the reader through example. The behavior of successful fictional characters works in much the same manner as moral conduct operates in parable: both serve as exempla or didactic models that may imprint good customs upon the receptive reader. As Boscán writes in his prologue to the Spanish edition of *El cortesano,* [The courtier] the didactic purpose of courtly models is to demonstrate: "cuál sea (a mi parecer) la forma de cortesanía más convenible a un gentil cortesano que ande en una corte para que pueda y sepa perfetamente servir a un príncipe . . . y que, en fin, merezca ser llamado perfeto cortesano, así que cosa ninguna no le falte" [that which is, in my opinion, the form of courtliness that is most advisable for a young man of good breeding who presents himself at court, so that he may perfectly serve his prince and so that, finally, he may merit the moniker of "perfect subject," for then he will never want for anything] (23, 24). Put another way, while circumstantial or custombristic detail is novelistic art imitating life, courtesy models invite life to imitate art. The Spanish aristocrat who reads courtship novels may be expected both to see him or herself reflected therein, and to refashion his or her actions in the likeness of textual models of courtesy.

Nowhere is the functional reciprocity of mimesis and instruction more evident than in the frame-tale of María de Zayas's *Desengaños amorosos.* [Disenchantments of love] Not only does Lisis insist that the narratives recited at her storytelling soirée be true (mimetic)— "que los que refiriesen fuesen casos verdaderos" [that the stories told be true stories] (118)— she also demands that they instruct through the negative example of the cautionary tale. Isabel Fajardo, the first storyteller or disenchanter, explains the didactic function of the betrayal tale she is about to recite in this manner, "Para que escarmentando en mí, no haya tantas perdidas y tan pocas escarmentadas" [So that, learning a lesson from my example, there cease to be so many dishonored women and so few reformed ones] (125). Examples of courtesy (or, in the case of the *Desengaños,* discourtesy) permit the reader to transform his or her life without repeating the same mistakes.

By separating the anatomizing impulse of courtship novels into two areas, that of circumstance and that of exemplary behavior, the texts' mimetic and instructive operations are seen more clearly as they work to attract, motivate and train the implied reader to court effectively. The present chapter traces the web of circumstances—family, marriage, inheritance, friendship, church and state—which women's courtship novels enlist to augment or to diminish their female characters' agency in courtship. Chapter 2 already identified many of these historically available resources and impediments, it is their appropriation as a recourse of plot that merits attention here. Chapter 4, in turn, foregrounds those interactive rituals which I am calling courtesy, that allow daughters to negotiate the transition from their parents' home to an alternate means of sustenance.

Circumstances Favorable To Women

Five clusters of conditions assist maidens facing the prospect of marriage in María de Zayas's *Desengaños amorosos,* [Disenchantments of love] Leonor de Meneses's *Desdeñado más firme,* [Scorned yet steadfast] and Mariana de Carvajal's *Navidades de Madrid.* [Christmastide in Madrid] The first grouping, subtitled "socioeconomic agency," specifies variations in the characters' options as as they shift from the status of daughter to wife, widow, orphan, etc. As these transitions unfold, such factors such as inheritance, parental ambition and the designs of half- or stepsiblings are shown to affect the protagonists' prospects for social ascent and well being. Noble birth, honor or dishonor and the intervention or loss of parental protection further augment women's agency in courtship. A second grouping of favorable circumstances, entitled "cooperation," analyzes the positive impact of friends, relatives and servants who assist maidens to negotiate the transition away from their parents' or guardians' care. A third section, "The kindness of strangers," enumerates social and legal resources and cases of woman-to-woman assistance. Disorder is shown to serve female characters' courtship ambitions often enough to merit a fourth subheading of its own, that of "chaos." Turmoil symptomizes that patriarchy has lost a measure of control. Female characters may move more freely in such situations, often benefiting from a temporary relaxation of social restriction. Finally, women's courtship plots also grant supernatural protection to imperiled maidens, albeit rarely. These instances are examined in a fifth section, "supernatural interventions."

Although physical appearance represents another important circumstantial factor, beauty is so universally ascribed to the courting women of these fictions that in truth it can scarcely be considered a differentiating asset. To the contrary, beauty often precipitates young women's misfortunes. For this reason, I have classified physical appearance as an impediment to women's agency in courtship rather than as a resource.

Socioeconomic Agency

Women's courtship fictions credit three socioeconomic phenomena—family, wealth and pedigree—with helping to redress the imbalance of power between the sexes during courtship, and even with ceding the advantage to women at times. The female principal of the courtship novel is commonly a virgin daughter living at home under the vigilance of parents or guardians. Her access to potential suitors and the selection of her spouse rest largely in their hands. In the second half of Carvajal's "La Venus de Ferrara," this arrangement works well for Venus. Her parents, the Duke and Duchess of Ferrara invite suitors to compete formally in a series of public spectacles for their daughter's hand in marriage, permitting Venus to select her spouse freely from among them "había de ser el escogido aquel [pretendiente] a quien ella se inclinara" [the chosen one would have to be the suitor to whom she was most inclined] (32).

The degree of autonomy that young women are granted while living under familial control is truly surprising. As the following pair of examples illustrates, parental absence or inattention facilitates their freedom of movement. In Carvajal's "La dicha de Doristea," [Doristea's good fortune] Doristea enjoys more power and fewer restrictions than is beneficial. Orphaned and living under her elderly aunt's care, Doristea decides to elope with her secret suitor. At the appointed hour, she has only to gather her jewels and flee with him. Although the short-term consequences of her risky behavior are grave, she is saved from harm and restored to honor by the end of the tale.

Even the most apparently restrictive circumstances grant their female "captives" great latitude of movement. When Venus's mother, Floripa, was trying to catch the eye of Venus's father in the first half of "La Venus de Ferrara," she appeared to be oppressed by excessive parental control. As a youth, Floripa was locked in a tower guarded by twenty men while her father served in distant wars. Nonetheless, she too enjoyed great autonomy in her father's absence. Normally, novelistic convention would demand that such a damsel be "rescued" by the husband-to-be. Floripa, however, orchestrates her own liberation. With the aid of the family steward, she escapes to her cousin, the Duke of Ferrara's castle, where he (belatedly) falls in love with her. Both Doristea and Floripa avail themselves of the absence or inattention of their guardians, Doristea exploiting her wealth and the cooperation of her suitor, and Floripa engaging the services of a family servant to help her resist parental authority.

Parents and guardians are shown to provide their daughters a certain amount of security and leverage during courtship. As noted in chapter 1, Blanca of Zayas's "Mal presagio casar lejos" [Only disaster awaits a bride far from home] revels in a glorious two-year courtship under her brother's protection (*Desengaños* 347). However, Blanca's fortunes reverse after marriage when she departs for her husband's estate in Flanders. There her husband falls back under the influence of his fiercely anti-Spanish father, and the two men conspire to destroy what is left of Blanca's health and life.

Wealth is less a resource than one might imagine in women's courtship fiction. When Carvajal's Doristea takes jewels and money to elope with Claudio in "La dicha de Doristea" or when Zayas's Isabel Fajardo uses it to finance her pursuit of Manuel in "La esclava de su amante," [Her lover's slave girl] their high-rolling adventures founder: Doristea is betrayed and Isabel returns from Sicily without

Manuel. Carvajal's twins, Pedro and Jacinta of "La industria vence desdenes," treat wealth as a resource for collaborative gain rather than a pretext for sibling rivalry. Their parents had wished to use the meager resources of their estate to send both children into Orders. However, this would have produced the effect of extinguishing the family name. Instead, after the parents die, Pedro relinquishes his portion of the bequest to dower his sister. He becomes wealthy and powerful as a painter, and Jacinta bears a child that he will later take under his wing. As a result of her brother's generosity, Jacinta's destiny is altered: rather than join a convent choir, her life's work becomes that of bringing up a son worthy of their lineage.

In precarious diplomatic situations, however, wealth empowers women. For example, it is essential that the fugitive Princess Beatriz dress royally in Zayas's "La perseguida triunfante." Her bejeweled gown serves as a mute letter of introduction at each new Court to which she flees, assuring that she will be well received. Arriving in remotest Germany, she is hailed by a passing gentleman who addresses her thus: "Hermosísima señora: admirada estoy de ver en una parte tan lejos de poblado y sola una mujer *de tanta belleza y rico adorno*" [Lovliest lady, I am stunned to see a woman *of such beauty and sumptuous dress* alone in a place so remote and uninhabited] (432, my emphasis). When later, still royally clad, she is thrown in among rustic shepherds, the King of Germany spots her, "tan hermosa y bien aderezada con vestido de tanto riqueza" [so beautiful and finely bedecked in such a priceless dress] (447). Puzzled to see such a noble lady surrounded by rubes, His Highness inquires of her, and she is once again raised to the highest of stations.

In Carvajal's "El esclavo de su esclavo," [His slave's slave] wealth oils the wheels of diplomacy between Algiers and Barcelona, to women's great advantage. Audalia, the pasha instrumental in rescuing captive Matilde and Christian-sympathizer, Tarifa, from Algiers, makes sure before the women board the vessel that will carry them to their literal and figurative salvation that he had "metido aquella noche de secreto en la galeota toda su riqueza" [that night he secretly smuggled all his wealth onto the galleon] (102). Once safe on Christian soil, Tarifa (now baptized) orchestrates an ostentatious and costly spectacle to affirm publicly her gratitude to the Virgin of Monserrat. This concrete dramatization of faith reassures her Christian hosts of the sincerity of her conversion and paves the way for her integration into Catalonian society: "Previniéronse cuatro lámparas de cuatro mil ducados cada una, ricas telas para frontales y ornamentos, y dos mil ducados para el aumento de la caridad que se da a los muchos peregrinos que visitan aquel santuario" [and thus four lamps worth four thousand ducats each and rich fabric for altar cloths and embellishments were prepared, and two thousand ducats were added to the charity fund set aside for the many pilgrims who visit that sanctuary]

(103). Meanwhile, Matilde's father and mother have ascended to the rank of Count and Countess of Barcelona. Overjoyed to reunite with their lost daughter, the grateful parents invest the resources at their disposal to appease the King of Algiers for the loss of his prize captive. They send a letter of friendship to the king accompanied by a boatload of freshly clothed Algerian captives, royal rainments for the Sultana, one hundred horses draped in brocade and four thousand gold coins (104). The King of Algiers accepts this generous peace offering and, for the sake of his love for Matilde, desists from further reprisals against Barcelona.

In the absence of influential parents or significant economic support, pedigree can be a trump card that wins the courtship game for women. An impoverished orphan, Beatriz, in Carvajal's "La industria vence desdenes," competes against the rich but plebian d. Leonor for dashing Jacinto's favor. Although some characters are swayed by Leonor's wealth, "Si su tío tratara de casarle [a Jacinto], mejor era para doña Leonor, que tiene dote suficiente" [If his uncle were to attempt to marry Jacinto off, so much the better for Lady Leonor, who at least had a sufficient dowry] (149), the poorer Beatriz prevails strictly on the grounds of breeding, as Jacinto's uncle and protector delicately insinuates, "Doña Leonor, aunque es rica, no es a mi propósito" [Lady Leonor, although rich, simply will not do] (172).

The best hand to be dealt in courtship is wealth, cooperative parents plus pedigree. Venus of "La Venus de Ferrara" embodies this winning combination of assets. Her doting and protective parents offer Venus, who is heiress to a dukedom, the right to participate in selection of her spouse. But Venus's good fortune does not merely put a face to her mother, Floripa's earlier success in marrying the duke. Venus's marriage plot is exceptional in its own right, lending the narrative its name. Furthermore, of the twenty-one plots under consideration in this study, Venus's stands out as the only one in which *favorable* courtship conditions rather than unfavorable ones generate narrative tension.[10]

The novelty of Venus's situation lies precisely in having everything on her side. Her security during courtship negotiations is symbolized by the balcony from which she views her tournament of suitors: "llegado el día de las fiestas, pidieron los príncipes licencia para entrar en palacio a ver pasar a Venus desde su cuarto a la sala donde estaban los balcones. Fueles concedida" [when the day of the festivities had arrived, the princes asked to be allowed to enter the palace in order to see Venus as she passed from her chamber to the salon where the balconies were. Their request was granted] (33) as well as by the disguise she wears, permitting her to behave "con más desenfado" [with greater ease and self-assurance] (33). Her suitors prize her not only for her inheritance and lineage, but for her own personal charms: "era tan rara su belleza que hacía muchas ventajas a la de Floripa, su madre" [her beauty was so singular that it far surpassed that of her mother, Floripa] (32). However, Floripa fears that there are those among her daughter's suitors who care more for the dukedom than for the young duchess whose possession unlocks its gates. To test the suitors' sincerity, Floripa sets in motion an elaborate masquerade in which Venus switches roles and costumes with her own lady-in-waiting: "[Floripa] tenía determinado de dar a entender que [otra dama] era Venus, para hacer experiencia de la voluntad de los pretendientes" [Floripa had resolved to lead the suitors to believe that another young lady was Venus, in order to better judge their intentions] (33). The knight authentically inclined toward Venus for her own merits will prove himself worthy of her hand in marriage by his willingness to sacrifice a dukedom for the sake of a woman he believes to be her servant. Other testing strategies (to be discussed in chapter 5) differ from Venus's contest in that they compensate for a bride-to-be's weakness in courtship. Venus's strength represents an exceptional best-case scenario: the luxury to probe for true love.[11]

Cooperation

In the examples above, the maiden figure's credentials—her wealth, social standing and relation to parents or guardians—set the scene for a more or less traumatic passage from one life-stage to the next, traditionally from singlehood through courtship to marriage, but possibly to conventual reclusion, confirmed singlehood or ongoing uncertainty. As maidens embark upon this life-course transition, another resource that courtship novels invoke to reinforce their position is the cooperation, both intentional and unwitting, of relatives, friends and allies. Parents can be highly instrumental in courtship, as in the case of Floripa including her daughter in the process of selecting her spouse, or highly uncooperative, as in Floripa's own case, where her absentee father had imprisoned her in a tower. But relatives extend many other forms of assistance to young women during courtship, as well.

Octavia takes for granted that relatives will help her if she needs them in Zayas's "La más infame venganza." [Vengeance most foul] After Carlos persuades her that her future father-in-law is angry, Octavia's first impulse is to "ocultarme en la casa de algún deudo mío" [hide out in the home of one of my relatives] (186). Usually, however, the relative that comes to a woman's aid is a parent or guardian. Parental assistance takes the form of judiciously balancing the offensive and defensive demands of courtship, for example, offsetting the need for modesty with that of visibility. In the framing tale of the *Navidades de Madrid,* Juana keeps her daughter Leonor in strict reclusion. But this outward show of protectiveness belies Juana's unequivocal matrimonial ambitions for her daughter. Well aware that her proprietress's son, d. Antonio had just inherited his father's fortune of thirty thousand ducats, Juana skillfully plants the seeds of interest in this match. First she speaks warmly of Antonio within earshot of Leonor: "su madre, hablando con las amigas que la visitaban, celebraba las bizarras partes de don Antonio, dando a entender se tendría por dichosa de ver a su hija tan bien empleada . . . aunque no lo decía a tiempo que estuviera [ésta] delante" [her mother, chatting with her confidantes who had come to visit her, praised Antonio's more dashing and gallant qualities, insinuating that she would consider herself fortunate to see Leonor so well-matched . . . though she would not say such things in her daughter's presence] (15, 16). Then, Juana acts aggressively to fend off other suitors such as Enrique, the Vizcayan: "Respondió Doña Juana que no trataba de casarla hasta concluir con un pleito que tenía, y esperaba la merced de un hábito; y aparte de estas cosas, no la casaría con forastero, por que no se la quitara de los ojos al mejor tiempo" [Lady Juana replied that her daughter could not be wed until a certain petition she had before the Court was heard and settled, and that she was awaiting recompense from the Church as well, and, besides all these matters, she would never allow her daughter to marry a foreigner who would do nothing but snatch her daughter away from her] (15). Finally, by allowing herself to be talked into bringing Leonor out of reclusion to participate in the Christmas soirée, Juana coaxes the young pair's courtship forward without appearing to do anything of the sort:[12] "Prometo a vuestras mercedes—respondió d. Juana—que le dejo [en su cuarto] por darle gusto, porque es tan encogida que me enfada algunas veces; mas no por eso dejaré de servirlas. Voy por ella, porque no vendrá [a la fiesta] aunque la envíe a llamar" ["I promise you, my honored guests," replied Lady Juana, "that I only allow her to stay in her room because she wants to, for she is so bashful that, at times, she tries even my patience; this, however, is not a valid excuse for me to disappoint Your Graces with her absence. I will go and fetch her, because she'll not come to the party of her own accord even if I am the one who summons her"] (18).

Relatives' accidental or unwitting aid represents another frequent source of help in courtship. The title of Carvajal's "Quién bien obra siempre acierta" [Kindness always pays] alludes to Esperanza's rescue by her future brother-in-law even before he knows her identity. In Leonor de Meneses's *El desdeñado más firme* [Scorned yet steadfast], d. Felipe unintentionally saves his daughter and niece from a bothersome suitor by disqualifying d. César from the list. D. Felipe rejects him, partially because he finds him attempting to talk to his daughter through a window at night, but mostly in favor of other more lucrative matches. In a similar vein, Princess Lisena receives the unintended aid of her father in "Amar sin saber a quién." [Her mystery lover] When Lisena's father remarries, the new stepmother resents the esteem in which Lisena's subject hold her. To win the people's loyalty, the new queen must produce an heir before Lisena does so. Lisena, well aware of the predicament in which she finds herself, and not wishing to provoke a civil war, asks her father's leave to hold her own leisure court on a nearby island: "Padre y señor, yo quiero pedirle a vuestra Majestad una merced con que me parece que los pesares de la Reina se templarán. Ya vuestra Majestad sabe que yo gusto de ir a La Isla; allí viviré contenta, considerando su quietud" [Most honored father, I would like to ask Your Majesty for a favor that I believe will assuage the troubles of our queen. Your Majesty already knows how much I enjoy going to the Island—there I will live contentedly, contemplating its tranquility] (190). In the tranquil rusticity of the island haven, a perseverant suitor gradually wins Lisena's admiration and consent to wed, something that had proven impossible in the formal confines of Lisena's father's Court. However, not until news reaches the island that the queen has born a son do Lisena and her "rustic lover" formalize an engagement.

A perverse variation on the motif of unwitting aid from relatives occupies the frame tale of Zayas's *Desengaños amorosos,* in which Lisis manages to manipulate her mother and cousin into helping her wreak vengeance upon her unfaithful former suitor, Juan. It will be recalled that the *Desengaños* opens with Lisis recovering from a life-threatening illness to face the prospect of an unwanted engagement to d. Diego. Once recovered, Lisis docilely agrees to the match, asking only her mother Laura's permission to host an engagement party. Laura is delighted to oblige: "Mucho se alegró su madre con la fiesta que quería hacer Lisis" [Hearing about the party that Lisis wanted to give made her mother very happy] (118). What Laura does not anticipate is that the entertainment that her daughter proposes, the recitation of *desengaños* [tales of disillusionment], will have the effect of dissuading her guests from marriage altogether, and justify her daughter's decision to break off her engagements to Diego as a result.

Lisis can summon no enthusiasm for Diego because the man she truly loved, Juan, abandoned her for her cousin, Lisarda. But Lisis will enjoy sweet revenge by using Lisarda to hurt Juan. By novel's end, readers are ready to recognize this stratagem of revenge-by-proxy when it arises at the close of the frame tale because a similar episode artfully embedded within "La más infame venganza" has prepared them for such a twist. In that *desengaño,* Carlos abandons Octavia in favor of Camila. Having retired to a convent, Octavia summons her brother, Juan, to avenge her dishonor. Instead of simply challenging Carlos to a duel, Juan embarks on a more diabolical plan: he decides to dishonor Carlos by seducing his wife:[13] "Y fue que [Juan] propuso quitarle a Carlos el honor con Camila como él [Carlos] se le había quitado a él con Octavia" [And so it was that Juan set out to dishonor

Carlos through Camilla, just as Carlos had dishonored him through Octavia] (190). After failing to conquer Camila by cunning, the avenging brother rapes her in her own bed, declaring, "Haga la fuerza lo que no ha podido la astucia" [Let force succeed where cunning failed] (193). In this fashion, Camila becomes the unwitting instrument by which Juan visits dishonor upon Carlos.

Analogously, Lisarda of Zayas's frame tale becomes an instrument of Lisis's effort to avenge Juan's unfaithfulness. Just as Camila had resisted Juan's efforts to seduce her in "La más infame venganza," Lisarda had resisted participating in Lisis's *desengaños* party: "Más por cumplir con la obligación que por ofenderle hago esto" [It is in order to fulfill my obligation rather than to offend you that I do this] (171). Lisarda's reluctance to recite a tale of male treachery stems from her loyalty to Lisis's former suitor, her new admirer, Juan. Lisarda would prefer not to recite a story confirming that men are wicked and ruthless with Juan in the audience, but decorum prevails, and she summons a spectacular *desengaño* starring a character whose name is also Juan: "La más infame venganza." In this manner, Zayas plants a delicious irony: Lisarda naively recounts a revenge plot foretelling the very operation that will enmesh her in Lisis's effort to punish Juan. For after listening to nine disenchanting tales, Lisarda voluntarily cancels her engagement to Juan, little suspecting that this is the very outcome that Lisis had contrived to bring about. While her counterpart Camila had been intruded upon by a rapist, Lisarda was visited by the rhetorical seduction of Lisis's storytelling party. In the end, she believes that it is her own idea that she abandons Juan, when Lisis has actually manipulated her into snubbing him on her behalf. This rejection crowns a double revenge plot by third parties in which behind-the-scenes actors (Juan and Lisis) puppeteer Camila and Lisarda in order to avenge their respective honor. That is, Juan punishes Carlos by dishonoring Camila; Lisis punishes Juan by imperceptibly convincing her cousin Lisarda to snub him. The persuasive power of the storytelling party also grants Lisis license to abandon d. Diego in favor of conventual reclusion. As a result, even after Juan is free of Lisarda, he cannot attempt a rapprochement with her.

Camila's rape does not result in pregnancy, but it does lead to a protracted swelling of her stomach when Carlos poisons her in retaliation for shaming him. Lisarda receives a lighter sentence: several months after leaving Juan, she weds a wealthy foreigner.[14] Lisis's ultimate revenge comes when Juan, finding himself rejected and alone, dies of madness in full cogniscence of his own guilty share in his demise: "A pocos meses se casó Lisarda con un caballero forastero, muy rico, dejando mal contento a don Juan, el cual confesaba que, por ser desleal a Lisis, le había dado Lisarda el pago que merecía, de lo que le sobrevino una peligrosa enfermedad, y de ella un frenesí, con que acabó la vida" [Only a few months later, Lisarda married a very wealthy foreign gentleman, much to the displeasure of Juan, who conceded that, because he had been disloyal to Lisis, Lisarda had given him his just desserts; in this state a dangerous illness overcame him, which gave way to fits of frenzy which ended his life] (510). Perhaps the strongest testimony that Juan's destruction rather than Lisis's own escape from Diego was the "point" of the *desengaños* party, and that Lisis manipulated both her mother and her cousin in order to achieve the desired revenge, is that narrative ceases abruptly with Juan's death. The sentence immediately following the citation above reads, "Yo he llegado al fin de mi entretenido sarao"[I have come to the end of my entertaining soiree] (510).

The Kindness of Strangers

Gallantry, female solidarity, the Church and civil law represent a third cluster of courtship resources moblized to empower female characters in women's courtship plots. Although, like a literary tombstone, Cervantes's *Don Quijote* marks the sepulcher of the Age of Chivalry, women's courtship novels continue to portray male characters as gallantly protecting women. Passing strangers rescue Doristea of "La dicha de Doristea" [Doristea's good fortune] and, as noted above, Esperanza of "Quién bien obra siempre acierta." [Kindness always pays] In Zayas's "Estragos que causa el vicio" [The vicisstitudes of vice], d. Gaspar rushes to the aid of an injured female figure whose cries move him to pity even before he recognizes that she is his beloved Florentina. An Algerian pasha rescues a captured Spanish princess in "El esclavo de su esclavo." [His slave's slave] In "El verdugo de su esposa" [His wife's executioner], Roseleta's husband, who, in accordance with literary convention might well have blamed his wife, instead defends her against an impertinent friend's advances.[15] Carlos Félix of Meneses's *Desdeñado* desists from his pretensions and abandons the field when so commanded by his lady instead of continuing to importune her against her will. In all of these instances, male characters extend help to female characters in distress, without regard for their own reward.

Perhaps just as common as gallantry, however, are acts of female solidarity that augment women's agency during courtship. A salient example of this form of assistance occurs in "La dicha de Doristea." Doristea is dishonored when d. Claudio, with whom she elopes, betrays her and tries to take her life. A passing gentleman, d. Carlos, rescues Doristea, who must now hide her identity from him lest her dishonor become public in Seville. Meanwhile, Carlos is content to keep her in a luxurious secret chamber in his father's house until such time as she return his favors: "Yo pienso obligaros, de suerte que mis finezas os merezcan el favor que espero recibir" [I intend to oblige you in such a way that my refinement and courtesy merit the favors I expect to receive from you] (54). His motives are suspect, however, since he has not told his father about her. Worse, the widow charged with her care, d. Laura, has sided with Carlos: "Mal hiciera vuesa merced—dijo d. Laura—en no pagarla [deuda], y me espanto de ver sus desdenes cuando son tantas las finezas del señor d. Carlos" ["You would be ill-advised, milady," said Lady Laura, "to not repay your debt, and I am horrified by the scornful way I see you treat Carlos, whose excellence and breeding are so evident"] (59). Doristea turns for advice to d. Inés, an influential nun, who acts decisively to help her troubled friend. Her plan is to shelter Doristea in the convent until Carlos learns (by letter) of Doristea's noble lineage. If Carlos does not intend to marry her, she will remain in the convent and take vows; if he does, he will fetch her to be his wife, thereby erasing the stain caused by the Claudio escapade: "Amiga mía . . . en estando acá dentro [de las murallas del convento] dile a don Carlos tu calidad, que si te quiere con amor verdadero no dudo de que se case contigo. Y si fuere apetito, te hallarás honrada sin que triunfe de tí. Yo diré a la señora priora en secreto todo lo que me dices, para que no tengan a liviandad dejar la religión, si acaso sucede tan en favor tuyo como yo deseo" [My friend, during your stay inside these convent walls, tell Carlos of your worth, and if he truly loves you, I do not doubt that he will marry you. And if his intentions were fueled only by lust, you will preserve your honor, as he will not have triumphed over you. I will secretly tell the prioress everything you tell me, so that they will not think you fickle should you decide to leave the order: should, perchance, everything turn out well for you, as I hope it will] (60). With the help of the prioress and d. Inés, Doristea threads her way through the labyrinth of courtship to safety and social reintegration.

Two additional examples of female solidarity may be cited. First, Inés of Zayas's "La inocencia castigada" has been immured alive for six years when a neighboring widow hears her cries through the wall. The widow consults with her landlady, and the two neighbors contact the authorities to free Inés and detain her captors. Second, in Mariana de Carvajal's "El amante venturoso" [The lucky lover], woman-to-woman aid ends an eight-month stalemate in the courtship of Teodora and Carlos. Teodora's best friend, Margarita, is Carlos's sister. Margarita lends her assistance as intermediary, facilitating an exchange of letters that breaks the impasse: "No se descuidó Margarita de aliviar las penas de su hermano" [Margarita did not fail to assuage her brother's suffering] (81).

Institutions of authority, both secular and ecclesiastic, are also shown to extend "the kindness of strangers" to imperiled women. D. Inés, of "La inocencia castigada," cited above, benefits from civil intervention at three junctures in the course of her misfortunes. First, she calls upon a magistrate to frame d. Diego in the act of harassing her:

"Inés envió a llamar al Corregidor. Y venido, le puso en parte donde pudiese oír lo que pasaba, diciéndole convenía a su honor que fuese testigo y juez de un caso de mucha gravedad" [Inés sent for the magistrate. Upon his arrival, she placed him so that he could hear everything that went on, telling him that her very honor depended on his being witness and judge in a case of the utmost gravity] (274). Later, when Diego is found guilty of resorting to sorcery to seduce Inés, a magistrate prevents Inés's brother from taking revenge on the two of them then and there: "que fue bien menester la autoridad y presencia del Corregidor para que en ella y en don Diego [el hermano de Inés] no tomase la justa venganza que a su parecer merecían" [the authority and the presence of the Magistrate were necessary, as they prevented Inés' brother from exacting the vengeance against her and Diego that he had deemed deserved] (280). Finally, a combination of civil and Church forces frees Inés after six years of immurement. The neighboring widow and landlady, fearing that local authorities might dismiss their claim of having heard a lady moaning inside their walls, first win the Archbishop's sympathy for their cause. With his imprimatur backing the inquiry, municipal officials quickly mount a "sting" operation on the house in question: "Y porque con su autoridad se diese más crédito al caso, se fue ella y la viuda al Arzobispo . . . el cual, admirado, avisó al Asistente y juntos con todos sus ministros, seglares y eclesiásticos, se fueron a la casa de don Francisco y don Alonso, y, cercándola por todas partes, porque no se escapasen, entraron dentro y prendieron a los dichos" [And because, with his authority, more credence was given to the case, she and the widow went before the Archbishop, who, amazed, alerted his Assistant and all his ministers—both secular and ecclesiastical—and together they went to Francisco and Alonso's house, surrounding it on all sides so that the two could not escape, and then they entered, taking both men into custody] (286).

The incidents above involve only local officials. However, municipal law girds itself with royal backing in order to right the injustices that send Esperanza to the brink of death in Carvajal's "Quién bien obra siempre acierta." In this plot of happy coincidences and rapid reversals of fortune, Esperanza's father, Álvaro, quarrels with Esperanza's fiancé, Luis, subsequently withdrawing his support for Luis's engagement to his daughter. When Álvaro discovers that the courtship is continuing behind his back, he conspires with his bastard son to murder Esperanza and frame Luis for the crime. In this fashion, Leonardo will gain Esperanza's inheritance. The plot fails when chance places Luis's brother in the very spot where Leonardo is about to kill Esperanza, and he rescues her.

However, because both Álvaro and Luis are *veinticuatros,* or city councilors, and because Álvaro's paternal status granted him an advantage over Luis's weaker position as fiancé, extraordinary judiciary measures are required to resolve their dispute. After Luis's brother indicts Álvaro, these measures include besieging Álvaro's house, arresting him by force, threatening his servants with torture to confess what they witnessed, and appealing to the president of Castile for a decision in the case. Once the servants have attested to Esperanza and Luis's innocence, the royal edict is publicized. Instead of beheading, the Crown extends clemency, obliging Álvaro to make peace with Luis, decreeing that his marriage to Esperanza to proceed, and insisting that Álvaro grant liberty to his concubine (Leonardo's mother) and provide her with a suitable spouse: "Hallóse Alváro convencido, y afrentado de que fuese público el trato que tenía con la esclava; y así, le respondió que estaba obediente a su orden. Estimó el Corregidor su prudencia y careándolos a todos, se hicieron las capitulaciones, pena de la vida el que quebrase las amistades" [Álvaro, faced with the embarrassing fact that his relationship with the slave girl had become public knowledge, found that his mind had been made up for him, and therefore he responded that he would accept the Crown's judgment. The Magistrate applauded his prudence and, bringing all the parties face to face, the marriage contract was solemnized, with the threat of a life sentence for anyone who would ever dare to sever these ties of amity] (117).

By contrast, neither civil nor military authority saves Enrique's victims, Mencía and Ana in "El traidor contra su sangre." [Traitor against his own kind] Instead, the law intervenes to punish Enrique and his cohort only after the fact: "Sentenciáronle a degollar, y a Marco Antonio, ahorcar, y otro día salieron a morir" [Enrique was sentenced to death by beheading, and Marco Antonio to death by hanging, and the next day they both went to their deaths] (397). A high-speed sea chase from Naples to Genoa in pursuit of Ana's assassins symbolizes this belatedness of the law. Enrique's apostrophe to Ana's disembodied head, moments before the obligatory removal of his own further underlines women's unprotectedness both at home (Jaén) and afar (Naples). "Ya doña Ana, pago con una vida culpada la que te quité sin culpa. No te puedo dar más satisfacción de la que te doy" [Lady Ana, I now pay with my guilty life for the innocent life I took from you. I cannot give you any more satisfaction than this] (398).

Although these scenes appear to represent the law in an unflattering light, I propose a non-ironic reading that vindicates Spain's military governors in Naples. The evidence for a non-ironic reading is found in four highly-favorable references to historical figures: Of the first, D. Pedro Fernández de Castro, VII Count of Lemos, Viceroy of Naples (386 n6), Zayas writes, "el excelentísimo señor conde de Lemos, don Pedro Fernández de Castro, que era virrey en aquel reino" [the most excellent gentleman, the Count of Lemos, don Pedro Fernández de Castro, who was the viceroy of that realm] (386). Zayas also names his brother, Francisco Ruiz de Castro y de Portugal, who would later become Viceroy of Sicily (393 n13) in connection with bringing Alonso to justice, as well as d. Pedro Téllez de Girón, Duke of Osuna and future Viceroy of Naples (392 n12). Finally, Zayas grants a heroic role to Álvaro de Bazán, general of the fleet of Naples, who: "despachó tras las galeras en un barcón grande, una escuadra de soldados, y por cabo al sargento don Antonio de Lerma, con cartas pidiendo al marqués de Santa Cruz, como general de las galeras, los reos" [sent a sizeable launch out after the galleons with a squadron of soldiers aboard under the command of Sargeant Antonio de Lerma, who had letters asking the Marquis of Santa Cruz, commodore of that fleet of galleons, to hand over the defendants] (396). It is unlikely that Zayas would have named these figures only to condemn their ineptitude; rather, she seems to be congratulating them for their decisive response to a grave breach of public order.[16]

The Church is depicted as an ally of women on many occasions in women's courtship novels. We have already seen how, in Zayas's "La inocencia castigada," two women leverage their complaint to civil authorities by first gaining the support of their archbishop. Carvajal's "La industria vence desdenes" [Effort vanquishes scorn], in which Pedro invests the wealth he earns as a successful ecclesiastic to support his sister and her son, illustrates that having one family member propser in the Church can benefit the entire family, women included. When Pedro ascends to the position of Prelate of Toledo, he brings to Spain with him much needed relief to his destitute twin sister and her son, Jacinto: "Y . . . remitió a su hermana algunas piezas de telas, lienzas y otras cosas; con que estimaron en mucho, por enviarles una libranza de doscientos escudos con que se remediaron muchas cosas que se padecían de puertas adentro por no descaecer de la pública ostentación" [to his sister he sent some bolts of fabric, cord and other things, which they greatly appreciated, as it brought them a promissory note for two hundred escudos, which they used to obtain the many things they lacked in private, behind closed doors, because of having made such an effort to keep up appearances in public] (140). In the second half of the novel, Pedro sets the scene for Jacinto to take an interest in an undowered but noble parishioner named Beatriz. Having assumed the title of Canon of Toledo, Pedro sends for his nephew to come live with him, whereupon he takes great pains to paint him a dazzling picture of Beatriz: "Son madre e hija y . . . son de lo más ilustre de esta ciudad. La madre, señora de valor, prudente y bien entendida; la muchacha será de vuestra edad, grande música y de lás más lindas damas que hay en esta ciudad" [They are mother and daughter, and they are among this city's most distinguished. The mother, a lady of merit, prudent and wise; the girl must be your age, a great musician and one of the lovliest maidens this city has to offer] (143-144). By playing matchmaker to Beatriz and his nephew, Pedro not only encourages Jacinto to make a sound matrimonial choice that will restore his own family's line, but he also resolves Beatriz and Guiomar's financial problems by marrying them into his own family.

Of all the Church's services to women, that of maintaining female religious communities of enclosure is its most far-reaching. Convents frequently figure in the resolution of the twenty-one plots under consideration, offering refuge to imperiled women, and providing an alternative life-path for those who have become disenchanted with the prospect of a wifely vocation. Examples of conventual refuge that have already been cited include Doristea of Carvajal's "La dicha de Doristea," [Doristea's good fortune] who eludes d. Carlos by slipping away to a convent and Esperanza of "Quién bien obra siempre acierta," [Kindness always pays] who enters a convent near Córdoba until her fiancé's name has been cleared and a date for her marriage to him fixed. After her rape at daggerpoint by d. Juan, Camila of "La más infame venganza" [Vengeance most foul] also flees to a convent where she remains for a year. When she returns to her husband's household, she realizes regretfully that she has lost a great measure of security: "y con esta vida bien arrepentida de haber salido del convento, vivió poco más de un año" [and, living this life, thoroughly repenting having ever left the convent, she survived little more than a year] (195).

It is one thing to retreat from enemies to a convent, another to elect freely its enclosure. Yet many of Zayas's young maidens and brides—Inés ("La inocencia castigada"), Beatriz ("La perseguida triunfante"), Isabel ("La esclava de su amante"), Laurela's sisters and mother ("Amar sólo por vencer") and Lisis and her mother of the *Desengaños*' frame-tale—choose conventual reclusion from positions of security. Octavia of Zayas's "La más infame venganza" represents a third pattern. She neither enters Orders under duress nor voluntarily, but rather under false pretenses. By contrasting the good fortune of a vengeful nun with the misfortune of a dead wife, "La más infame venganza" deconstructs counter-Reformation pro-matrimonial propaganda. Octavia's lover, Carlos, it will be recalled, deposits Octavia in a convent, promising to retrieve her shortly for their wedding. Instead, he marries Camila and Octavia remains enclosed, eventually taking the veil. Yet, the omniscient narrator deems her fate fortunate, for in devotion to Christ, she has found an alternative to mortal men's treachery: "Octavia profesó, siendo la más dichosa, pues trocó por el verdadero Esposo el falso y traidor que la engañó y dejó burlada" [Octavia, being the most fortunate, took her vows, and so exchanged a false and treacherous husband who had duped and betrayed her for the one true Husband] (195). Carlos's betrayal yields an unanticipated boon for Octavia, one that contrasts sharply with her rival's fate. For although by conventional measures Camila "wins" and Octavia "loses" Carlos's favor, the long view offers a frightening corrective to this misleading first impression. Ultimately, remaining enclosed grants Octavia greater defensive and offensive power than Camila enjoys in wedlock. In addition to the physical safety it affords, Octavia's inadvertent enclosure allows her to initiate a counter-plot of retaliation, so that even as she recites her daily devotions, her brother out in the secular world is busy fulfilling her wish to be avenged. The aftershocks created by Octavia's ongoing agency within the convent (Camila's rape, Carlos's repudiation and revenge, Camila's death), allow the reader to appreciate the silver lining hidden in Octavia's veil.

Paradoxically, while shedding a flattering light on marriage to Christ, "La más infame venganza" also exposes the ironic register in which much pro-monastic rhetoric is uttered in the *Desengaños* — ironic in light of Sister Octavia's impious machinations. Isabel/Zelima, in closing her autobiographical *desengaño* entitled "La esclava de su amante," [His slave's slave] offers a similarly double-edged paeon to conventual reclusion: "yo, como ya no los he menester [a los hombres], ni me importa que sean fingidos o verdaderos, porque tengo elegido Amante que no me olvidará, y Esposo que no me despreciará . . . te suplico como esclava tuya me concedas la licencia para entregarme a mi divino Esposo, entrándome en religión" [I, having no need whatsoever for men, nor caring if they are sincere or hypocrites, have selected a Lover who will not forsake me, a Husband who will not spurn me—I beg you as your slave that you grant me the permission that will deliver me, by taking my vows, to my Divine Husband] (166, 167). Superficially, Isabel appears to be endorsing the vocation of monasticism. However, within the context of romantic disillusionment through which she arrives at this decision (her betrayal at the hands of d. Manuel), her devout fervor suddenly assumes a more polemical tone. Phrases such as, "No he menester [a los hombres]" [I have no need of men], "ni me importa que [los hombres] sean fingidos o verdaderos" [I care not if they are sincere or hypocrites], "Amante que no me olvidará" [Lover who will not forsake me] and "Esposo que no me despreciará" [Husband who will not spurn me] now resonate with the power of proof, functioning less as praise of the attributes possessed by the Divine Spouse than as indictments of those that mortal spouses lack.

The most unequivocal case for reclusion as an alternative to wedlock occurs in the *Desengaños'* frame-tale. Although initially the frame tale appears to mirror the disempowerment of women reiterated throughout the individual *desengaños,* this redoubling turns out to be illusory. To the contrary, Lisis seizes power by hosting her storytelling soiree. No mere idle entertainment, the *desengaños* dissuade Lisis's female listeners from marriage, and create a consensual community of support for her own decision to spurn Diego in favor of retiring to a convent. Addressing first the women in attendance, Lisis explicates the allegorical connection between the *desengaños* that they had just heard at her *sarao,* and each of their lives: "¿Pensáis ser más dichosas que las referidas en estos desengaños?" [Do you ladies think yourselves any more lucky than those described in these tales?] (508). If secular marriage is categorically risky, it is only reasonable, she explains politely to d. Diego, for her to protect herself from its reach: "Me voy a salvar de los engaños de los hombres" [I am going to save myself from the treachery of men] (509). No one in attendance fails to grasp the link that Lisis has established between fact and fiction; not a single voice rises in protest or reproach. Rather, Lisis's mother, and her former servant, Zelima/Isabel, accompany Lisis into conventual retirement, convinced that reclusion is the wisest choice.

Chaos

At junctures where social controls fail—emergencies or random events—disorder is often shown to grant female characters greater leverage in their dealings with men. For example, in Carvajal's "Amar sin saber a quién," [Her mystery lover] Princess Lisena of Scotland indulges an anonymous servant who plays at courting her, interpreting his attentions as an idle game of gallantry. However, the entertainment takes a decisive turn toward reality following an emergency that allows the mysterious suitor to demonstrate his valor. When, on a holiday outing, Lisena loses her footing and falls into the river that surrounds her island retreat, the "Rustic Lover" valiantly rescues her, taking such brilliant charge of her recovery, that Lisena thinks to herself "¿Quién sino un rey amante pudiera tener tanto valor?" [Who but a royal lover could be so valiant?] (205). Suddenly Lisena sees the "Rustic Lover's" prior courtesies in a new light and she elevates him to the rank of her personal physician. Soon afterward, her secretary verifies that the "Rustic Lover" descends from royalty, and the two are wed.

Chaos need not entail forces of nature such as falling into a river; for Leonor de Meneses, social turmoil also improves women's fortune. Entropy is the equalizing lever in *El desdeñado más firme's* [Scorned yet steadfast] battle of the sexes, entropy created first by appropriating the hoary plotting pattern of the comedy of errors, but then by disappointing the readers' expectations of comicity and return to order. *El desdeñado* presents a degraded variant of the familiar folk motif wherein many suitors vie for the hand of a closely guarded maiden. In Meneses's version, there are five suitors: Carlos Félix, Jacinto, César, Luis and the Marquis and two maidens, cousins, both named Lisis. The redoubling of the women's names sets the scene for considerable confusion, augmented by a series of reversals, changes of heart and missed cues. In the ensuing mayhem, the merits of the suitors, the wishes of the maidens and the designs of their father/uncle, d. Felipe, become hopelessly scrambled.

Officially, the two unmarried women living under d. Felipe's care are undifferentiated: both have excellent pedigree, good dowries, unimpeached reputations and the same name, address and family. Having established the pretext for a familiar comedy of errors plot based on escalating entanglements and mistaken identity, Meneses directs the resultant chaos in two unexpected directions. First, not unlike the old television sitcom, *The Patty Duke Show,* her "identical cousins" respond in opposite ways to the same courtship events. This contrast suggests that women are more individuated and unique than the patriarchal order normally admitted them to be. Furthermore, the two Lises exercise considerable de facto power despite their complete *de jure* lack of authority to influence the outcome of courtship.[17]

The authoritarian Felipe's inability to impose his will over the young women, and the muddles resulting from their both being named Lisis might be expected to produce a farcical effect not unlike that of Moreto's *El lindo don Diego* [The handsome don Diego] or the typical *comedia de enredo.* [comedy of errors] Indeed, visual and verbal gags abound: Lisis trips over her own hoopskirt during a tryst and falls flat on her face awakening the slumbering household; a ribald poem is recited about women's lustiness during menstruation; a suitor courteously proffers his dagger to his enraged lady so that she can the more easily plunge it into his chest, etc. However, Meneses allows all of these scenes to pass without arching a brow. By contrast, when Carvajal's "Rustic Lover" trips in the flush of his promotion to the post of court physician, the occasion becomes a pretext for general merriment:

> Riéronse todos, y don Sancho le dijo:
> —¿Qué es eso, Amador? ¿Así te turbas?
> Miróle diciendo:
> —¡Cuerpo de tal con vos! ¿No queréis que me turbe, si desde criado de Alberto he dado un salto a médico de cámara? (205)

> (They all laughed, and don Sancho said to him:
> "What's this, lover? So easily perturbed?"
> He looked at don Sancho, saying:
> "The hell with you! Why shouldn't I be perturbed, having just made the leap from Alberto's servant to Court Physician?")

Chaos, however, does not engender entertainment or whimsy in *El desdeñado;* rather, it incites frustration, bitterness, violence and death. Moreover, these negative forces are unleashed in the absence of the conventional return to order. The narrative closes with Jacinto dead, Carlos Félix abandoning the field and César wounded and uncertain.

Meanwhile Luis (also wounded but recovering) and the Marquis remain hopeful of wedding two women who do not want them. From the women's perspective, Lisis of Madrid has lost her beloved suitor, Jacinto, and is unwillingly betrothed to Luis, while Lisis of Toledo has been spared one unwanted suitor (César), but faces the prospect of another equally distasteful match with the Marquis. D. Felipe has been obliged on multiple occasions to postpone the weddings and to switch potential sons-in-law. His street and garden have been the site of stabbing, shootings and discovered assignations.

First Felipe must delay the weddings that he has unilaterally ordained when his niece's suitor, César, stabs his daughter's suitor, d. Luis. The duel was fought at night behind d. Felipe's house, neither party realizing that they were courting different women, both named Lisis, at the same address. Felipe's will is further curbed when his hand-picked son-in-law elect, the marquis, declares that he would prefer to marry d. Felipe's niece rather than his daughter, while Felipe's nephew, Luis, asks for the hand of his daughter. This gentlemen's agreement reached, the wedding must again be postponed when Luis guns down his rival, Jacinto, at the garden gate.

Meneses reinforces the sense that Felipe is vulnerable to forces beyond his control by eschewing a framing device that would provide a sense of structure, and by scaling back the interventions of the omniscient narrator. In the absence of these reassuring containments, and in light of the recurring uncertainties of plot, Felipe cuts a pathetic figure. Rather than the solid patrician he fancies himself to be, he emerges as a curiously unstable character, flung to the winds of fortune not unlike the hapless bird of whom Agustín sings in Discourse One. Agustín's *romance* [ballad] concerns a nightingale "que huyendo de la prisión con la liga presa al pie, le enredó en el de un árbol, donde murió" [that died because, while fleeing from its prison with a band still around its foot, the band subsequently became entangled in a tree, where the nightengale perished] (107):

> Contra los hados ¿qué importan
> agenas vozes o avisos?
> Tú el sepulcro te buscaste;
> tú te das la muerte mismo (108).

> (Against the Fates, what good are
> distant voices, distant warnings?
> You searched out your own sepulcher;
> Your death will be by your own hand)

Like Felipe, the bird inhabits a zero-sum universe where the more he tries to escape fate, the more ineluctably his doom approaches.

If turmoil merely unfolded as a temporary lapse into the carnivalesque "corrected" by a return to order in the final scenes, the irony of the reversals would be lost. Instead, the reader is left with a disturbed impression at novel's end. What does it mean that the ostensible patriarch (Felipe) and the perfect courtier (César) fail to control the outcome of events? Why do the maidens remain unwed and what is the significance of this indeterminacy? By resisting the temptations of comicity and closure, *El desdeñado* renders more significant and enduring the misfirings of its peculiar plot.

Despite its negative associations, chaos in *El desdeñado* represents a positive force for female characters, an equalizer in a matrix of power where men have more to lose than women do. Lisis of Toledo's nocturnal stabbing of César is a case in point. In a botched attempt to deliver the deceased Jacinto's effects into the hands of the grieving Lisis of Madrid, César enters d. Felipe's house at night. To avoid being seen by a passing servant, he ducks into a room that turns out to be that of Lisis of Toledo, whom he adores, but who detests him. Finding herself face to face with an armed man in her chamber, Lisis takes César's dagger (which he obligingly offers her), stabs him twice, then hauls his body out the window to preclude the dishonor that its discovery in her room would incur: "presumiendo que César entrara allí a ofenderla . . . [p]orfió con la criada, y entrambas le arrojaron a la calle, bolviendo a cerrar la ventana y guardando entre sí tan importante secreto" [assuming that César had entered her room intending to harm her . . . after some arguing she convinced her maid of this, and between the two of them they flung his body out into the street and closed the window once again, and kept such an important secret to themselves] (148). Here, it is César who fulfills the prophecy of the errant nightingale by offending the woman that he loves. In return, Lisis of Toledo delivers the most denigrating of reproaches: she stabs him and throws his body out the window. César's passivity and entrapment in circumstances beyond his control contrast sharply with Lisis's decisive response to César's intrusion.

Although legal and conventional limits make it impossible for the cousins to oppose their father, guardian or suitor's will in the most significant passage of their life, that of selecting their marriage partner, the ineptitude, rivalry, violence and lack of control exhibited by the men themselves attenuates this constraint. Moreover, at times the women are able to capitalize on the very forces of entanglement that they themselves inspire. A short speech made by Lisis of Madrid in Discourse One concisely illustrates this point, recalling the limitations of reducing women's courtship plots to either the "airtight oppression of patriarchal society" or the "jubilant liberty of the marginalized subject" (Steele 108).

Three characters, Lisis's father, her suitor and her sister contribute to the chaotic courtship situation that Lisis of Madrid faces. Lisis's father's decision to marry her off to d. César when she loves d. Jacinto represents the primary cause of her anguish; second, the suitor, César, is pursuing her by mistake—he really means to pursue the other Lisis, her cousin. Finally, Lisis of Madrid's cousin, Lisis of Toledo, fully cogniscent of César's error, refuses to warn César that he is about to marry the wrong woman—not out of any personal interest in César, whom she roundly detests, but merely to mock him, albeit at her cousin's expense. Thus, Lisis of Madrid is as much a victim of César's ignorance and her cousin's intransigence as she is of her father's venal designs. Her solution, confided below to her cousin, is to launch herself through writing into the exclusively male site of the marriage negotiation. She plans to write a note to undeceive César so that he can take the necessary steps to correct the course of events: "—A ti [prima mía, Lisis de Toledo] te ama [don César], yo soy con quien me padre le casa; él es hombre y lo puede estorbar. Yo, hija, que no puedo dexar de obedecer, ni tampoco es posible olvidar a don Jacinto. No quisiste por un papel tuyo desengañar a César. . . . Mañana determino enbiar una criada que le informe" [You, my cousin Lisis of Toledo, are don César's beloved, but I am the one whose father is making her marry him; César is a man, and he can take matters into his own hands, upsetting these plans. I am only a daughter, unable to do anything but obey, but at the same time I find it impossible to forget don Jacinto. You, for your own reasons, refused to explain the truth to don César . . . But I am determined to send out a servant who will do so tomorrow] (120, 121).

The multiple paradoxes and contradictions that Meneses weaves into Lisis of Madrid's predicament prevent the reader from encountering the expected parable of male domination and female subjugation to an implacable patriarchal law in this scene. Certainly, Lisis of Toledo's double negation, "no puedo dexar de obedecer, ni tampoco . . . olvidar" [I cannot cease to obey, nor can I . . . forget] testifies to a degree of anxiety regarding the limits of women's agency in courtship. However, Lisis of Madrid, by reproaching Lisis of Toledo for her deliberate inaction ("No quisiste . . . desengañar") [You refused . . . to explain the truth], places the blames for a share of her own misery in the hands of a another woman, her obstinate cousin. Furthermore, the marked disparity in the two Lises' attitudes toward César's error (Lisis of Madrid is horrified and mobilized; Lisis of Toledo is indifferent, perhaps even pleased to see César barking up the wrong tree) undermines a reading that would gather all men under the sign of the oppressor and all women under that of the oppressed. Most astonishingly, Lisis of Madrid grasps that d. César, the unwanted suitor himself, could actually serve as her greatest ally. Both Lisis of Madrid and César face an undesired match should their ill-conceived engagement come to fruition; both stand to gain by rerouting the course of events. By informing César of his error, Lisis of Madrid defends her own courtship interests as well as his. Thoughtful collaboration replaces the typological aggressor/prey relationship, and Lisis of Madrid emerges from the chaos with exactly what she needs—the engagement is canceled forthwith.

Supernatural Intervention

Finally, although women's courtship plots rarely recruit the supernatural on behalf of female characters at risk, María de Zayas's "La perseguida triunfante" [The triumph of the fugitive damsel] hands women this advantage. The persecuted Queen Beatriz triumphs against her vindictive brother-in-law with the help of the Virgin Mary, who rescues her repeatedly from Federico's diabolical schemes. Another example of supernatural intervention are the numerous instances of posthumous sanctification of the female body. Although in these instances Divine intervention does not improve women's agency in life, it can infuse their battered, sometimes scattered remains with a trace of sanctity that compensates on a transcendental plane for the unjust circumstances of their worldly death, while projecting a corrective lesson for future generations.

Two female victims receive this posthumous consecration in "El traidor contra su sangre." [Traitor against his own kind] In this bipartite tale, Alonso murders first his tragically eponymous sister, Mencía, and later, his Neapolitan wife, Ana. In the first case, enraged to find that his sister was being courted, he stabs Mencía to death. Nine hours later, when Mencía's suitor arrives at the house, a great thundering occurs and the door opens to his lightest touch. Within, the horrified gentleman views Mencía's body, illuminated by a mysterious light, her wounds still bleeding as freely as if she had just been stabbed. A weak and delicate voice emanates from the corpse, explaining her end at her brother's hand, and urging him to flee for his life. In the second half of the tale, Alonso murders his wife with as little remorse as he had shown for his sister, and stuffs her body down a well. The head, however, he buries in a cave near the seaport. Six months later when Alonso's crimes come to light and justice is served, Ana's unearthed head is found to be incorrupt.[18]

While for the modern reader, posthumous consolations such as those cited above offer cold comfort for the senseless waste of women's lives, seventeenth-century readers versed in hagiographic literature had come to expect such narratives to repay virtue, if not in this life, in the next. In fact, many features of the *Desengaños* invite comparison with Christian martyr narrative. In addition to the supernatural preservation of the victims' bodies, the victim formula itself, the sensationalist ornamentation that sets this collection of novellas apart from others of the period,[19] and the tales' reiterative exaltation of monasticism recall the conventions and motifs of hagiographic discourse. In effect, the absence of the obligatory signs of Grace visited upon the slain might have appeared heterodox in a context that traditionally rewarded martyrdom with eternal glory.[20]

Circumstancial Impediments to Female Agency

In addition to anatomizing sources of succor and sustenance for courting women, women's courtship narratives also embed deterrent factors in their plots. Indeed, the limitations placed on female autonomy are at times shown to be unremitting. Two examples of restricted autonomy that immediately come to mind are those of two of Zayas's most memorable creations, Inés of "La inocencia castigada," [Her innocence punished] and Roseleta of "El verdugo de su esposa." [His wife's executioner] As noted in chapter 1, Inés gives her consent to marry as much to escape her cruel sister-in-law as to gain a husband. Her exercise of freedom consists of no more than selecting the lesser of two evils, or, as we would say in English, of "jumping out of the frying pan and into the fire." In Zayas's imagery, however, the picturesque kitchen humor of the English saying gives way to a darker, more overdetermined vision of human misery: "De manera que antes de dos meses [d. Inés] se halló, por salir de un cautiverio, puesta en otro martirio" [and so, before two months had gone by, Lady Inés found herself, having escaped one captivity, consigned to another sort of martyrdom] (265). (It will be recalled that Inés's martyrdom takes the form of immurement for six years in a chimney fouled by her own excrement.) In "El verdugo de su esposa," Roseleta's husband Pedro mobilizes both Roseleta's frying pan and her fire, her captivity and her martyrdom. In the first extreme, Pedro overvalues Roseleta to such a degree that his bragging lures his best friend to fall in love with her. However, later in the tale, Pedro swings to the other extreme, that of severe mistrust, falling prey to slanderous rumors about his wife. With no outside corroboration to confirm Roseleta's alleged unfaithfulness, Pedro arranges for his wife to be bled to death as though by accident. Either extreme in a husband—excessive trust or excessive mistrust—can drastically reduce the bride's range of choice.

Impediments to female agency that are analyzed below include familial opposition to desired matches, unscrupulous suitors and loss of parental protection through the death or absence of a parent. Beauty restricts women's agency by inciting their suitors' ungoverned passions. Supernatural interventions can also diminish rather than abet women's courtship prospects.

Familial Opposition

Familial opposition to courtship figures as a secondary pretext in numerous courtship plots. For example, Floripa of "La Venus de Ferrara" [The Venus from Ferrara] must escape from her father's tower in order to meet her future husband, the Duke of Ferrara; Doristea of "La dicha de Doristea" [Doristea's good fortune] elopes; Jacinta and Pedro's parents in "La industria vence desdenes" [Effort vanquishes scorn] ordain that the twins enter Orders rather than wed; and Count Rodulfo of "El esclavo de su esclavo"[His slave's slave] opposes his sister Blanca's marriage to Félix Centellas for political reasons. However, as Juan Luis Vives complained in his *Instruction of a Christian Woman,* marrying a dowry rather than marrying a wife can only lead to misery (*Instruction* XVIII, 198). When venality and patriarchal courtship practices combine with the presence of a strong-willed daughter, conflict dominates and shapes the courtship plot.

Leonor de Meneses mobilizes the motif of generational strife based on greed in *El desdeñado más firme*. [Scorned yet steadfast] D. Felipe, Lisis of Madrid's father and Lisis of Toledo's uncle, epitomizes parental control over courtship. Not only does Felipe fail to consult with his daughter, Lisis, in the choice of her spouse—"Consultó a sus deudos don Felipe el casamiento de Lisis" [Don Felipe consulted his relatives about Lisis's prospects for marriage] (125)—he does not even advise her directly when he rearranges her match: "Con ella no hizo su padre la ordinaria ceremonia de practicárselo; a la otra Lisis [her cousin] lo dixo, y se vino a entender della"[21] [Lisis's father did not even take the customary step of informing her of her engagement; he did, however, tell the other Lisis about it, and it was from her cousin that his daughter finally heard the news of her own impending marriage] (125, 126). D. Felipe opposes his daughter, Lisis's choice of Jacinto as her suitor, and equally opposes his niece Lisis's desire to remain unwed. Félix's motive for restricting his daughter and niece's choice in courtship is pecuniary; under the influence of his relatives, he seeks the most lucrative match "y ellos . . . les propusieron conveniencias y no afectos" [and they proposed that Lisis marry for money and not for love] (125).

Often, competition for limited resources within the family motivates conflict in women's courtship plots. Carvajal's novella, "Quién bien obra siempre acierta,"[Kindness always pays][22] typifies the motif of an ambitious parent who favor's his son's inheritance rights over his daughter's. Álvaro, the opposing parent, wishes to legitimate his bastard son Leonardo by eliminating his daughter and legal heir, Esperanza. Álvaro conspires with Leonardo to frame Esperanza's fiancé, Luis, for murdering her. Fortunately, as delineated earlier in this chapter, Luis's brother rescues Esperanza and brings her father and half-brother to justice. A cruel father partial to his son also victimizes two women in Zayas's "El traidor contra su sangre." [Traitor against his own kind] D. Pedro favors his son Alonso's claim to the family's inheritance over that of his daughter, Mencía. Pedro instructs Alonso to do away with the competing sister "deseoso de que toda la hacienda la gozase don Alonso" [for Pedro was anxious that Alonso possess the entire estate] (372). After murdering Mencía, Alonso flees to Italy where he secretly weds a poor but noble Neapolitan woman, d. Ana de Añasco. When news of Alonsos's clandestine marriage to an impoverished woman reaches Pedro's ears, however, he flies into a rage:

> cuando lo supo, loco de enojo, le escribió una carta muy pesada, diciéndole en ella que ni se nombrase su hijo ni le tuviese por padre, pues cuando entendió que le diera por nuera una gran señora de aquel reino, que engrandeciera su casa de calidad y riqueza, añadiendo renta a su renta, se había casado con una pobre mujer, que antes servía de afrenta a su linaje que de honor. (391)

> (when Pedro found out, insane with rage, he wrote his son Alonso a very disagreeable letter in which he told Alonso that he was no longer his son, and Alonso should no longer consider him his father, for Pedro had been led to believe that the woman who was to be his daughter-in-law was a great lady in her kingdom who increase the stature of his house with her wealth and status, adding to his income, when, in reality, Alonso had married a poor woman who would be an affront rather than an asset to his lineage.)

D. Pedro asserts that he would rather squander his entire fortune at gambling than see d. Ana de Añasco enjoy any of his wealth. Pedro's threats soon turn Alonso against his new bride, whom he murders by decapitation. As noted above, however, the law catches up with Alonso, whereupon he and his crony are condemned and executed. Upon receiving written notice of his son's crime and punishment, d. Pedro brusquely retorts, "Más quiero tener un hijo degollado que mal casado" [I would rather see my son's throat slit from ear to ear than see him marry badly] (398).[23]

Pedro's indifference to his son's death coupled with his maniacal resistance to the prospect of misalliance, begins to reveal the true nature of his partiality toward Alonso over Mencía. Whereas Mencía's dowry would have sapped the family's economic resources, Pedro calculated that Alonso's marriage could enhance them. Moreover, by wedding a woman of higher pedigree, Alonso could ennoble his offspring, thereby adding luster to future generations that bore Pedro's family name. When Alonso failed to fulfill his father's ambitions, he forfeited Pedro's approval. The tale ends on an ironic note: d. Pedro unexpectedly dies, and his fortune reverts to d. Ana de Añasco's surviving son.

While Mencía and Ana of "El traidor contra su sangre" [Traitor against his own kind] sacrificed their lives to the perception that women deplete the family's coffers, female characters who enrich their relatives also incur danger. In "Estragos que causa el vicio," [The vicissisitudes of vice] for example, an uncle finds his estate greatly increased when he becomes protector and executor to two orphaned nieces. To marry them off would represent a financial loss: "Magdalena [se determinó] de casarse sin la voluntad de su tío, conociendo en él la poca que mostraba en darle estado, temoroso de perder la comodidad con que con nuestra buena y lucida haciendo pasaba. Y así gustara más que fuéramos religiosas" [Magdalena was determined to marry without the consent of her uncle, as she knew that he was scarce inclined to grant it to her, for he feared losing the luxury that our splendid estate provided him. Given the circumstances, he would have preferred that we become nuns] (486). The uncle's reluctance to marry Magdalena to Dionis results in a hazardous protraction of their courtship. Exposed to this ongoing drama, Magdalena's adoptive sister, Florentina, falls in love with Dionis. This triangle, forged in the competition for resources between a poor protector and his wealthier charges, leads to tragedy when Dionis and Florentina join forces to betray Magdalena.[24]

Finally, not all competition for resources within the family is intergenerational. "La más infame venganza" [Vengeance most foul] takes as the departure point for female subjugation a brother who squanders his elder sister's inheritance on gaming and women. Juan imprisons Octavia in the house to keep her from spending any money: "Y para que ella no gastase nada, la tenía tan encerrada y necesitada de todo, que aunque él no la tuviera así, ella misma se quitara de los ojos de todos, por no parecer en menos porte que el que traía en vida de su padres" [And so that she might not spend even a penny of her own money, he kept her locked up tight and in such dire straits that even if he had not shut her away, she would have hidden herself voluntarily, to keep everyone from seeing the deplorable state she was in, so different from the privilege and luxury she had known when her parents were alive] (179). Affined relations such as sisters-in-law may also resent the presence of a marriageable maiden in their household. In "La inocencia castigada," [Her innocence punished] Zayas does not explain why Inés's sister-in-law oppresses Inés, but she does indicate that Inés lived in her house as her brother's dependent. In the day-to-day running of the household, and on account of the dowry that she would require for marriage, Inés indeed competed with her sister-in-law for her husband's resources, and could easily become an object of jealousy and maltreatment for that motive.[25] When a match presents itself for Inés that stations her advantageously without costing dearly in dowry, both brother and sister-in-law are inclined to believe "que aquella dicha venía sólo del cielo" [that that bit of luck had been purely Heaven-sent] (265).

Unscrupulous Suitors

Unscrupulous suitors pose a serious threat to women during courtship. Manuel of María de Zayas's "La esclava de su amante," Carlos of her "La más infame" [Vengeance] and d. Claudio of Mariana de Carvajal's "La dicha de Doristea" [Doristea's good fortune] enact the familiar motif of seducing a maiden with false promises of matrimony, but other hazards abound as well. For example, as shown earlier, although d. Carlos rescues Doristea from the murderous designs of d. Claudio, Carlos himself soon threatens Doristea's honor with his increasingly bold importuning. Rivals can also restrict a maiden's agency in courtship, as the violent antics of Narcisa's Milanese suitors, Duke Arnaldo and Count Leonido in Carvajal's "Celos vengan desprecios" [Jealousy avenges disdain] attest. Dissatisfied with Narcisa's ongoing disdain, Arnaldo and Leonido shift from requesting Narcisa's favor, to demanding it, to attempting to claim it by force. Their escalating assaults take the form of threats, intrusions and finally, an armed ambush and attempted rape:

> En esto llegó el coche, y arrojándose los seis hombres a él, los tres llegaron al estribo, para que el gentilhombre se apeara, amenazándole de que le darían muerte si daba voces. Yo los otros tres hicieron lo mismo con el cochero, llevándolos asidos a lo espeso de los árboles. Llegóse el Duque, diciendo:
> —De esta suerte he de vencer vuestra curel tiranía, pues gozando vuestra hermosura, os obligaré a que me deis la mano." (129)

(At that moment, the carriage arrived, and six men threw themselves at it; three of them got to the running board, forcing the manservant to climb down from it by threatening to kill him if he uttered a word. The other three attackers did the same thing to the coachman, and both captives were taken deep into the woods. The Duke approached, saying: "This is the way you force me to overthrow your cruel tyranny, for by fully enjoying your beauty, I will oblige you to grant me your hand in marriage.")

Fortunately, a third suitor, d. Duarte, rescues Narcisa.

Rivalry can lead to other negative consequences as well. In *El desdeñado más firme*, for example, Lisis of Madrid loses her lover, d. Jacinto, when her (unwanted) fiancé, d. Luis, shoots him down. Luis arrogantly defends his action before Lisis, claiming that he prefers displeasing her to having Jacinto dishonor him: "Ya, ingratíssima Lisis, no tendré que sentir zelos, aunque tenga desprecios que llorar. Quexoso estará tu gusto de mi atrevimiento, mas mi honor no supo dissimular a los de don Jacinto" [Now, most ungrateful Lisis, I shan't have to be jealous any more, although your scorn has been enough to make a grown man cry. Your delicate sensibilities will be offended by my daring, but don Jacinto's shameful deeds were such an affront to my honor that I could not let them go unpunished] (142). María de Zayas concocts the most flamboyantly unscrupulous suitor to be found in the twenty-one plots under consideration in the person of Esteban of "Amar sólo por vencer" [Loving only to conquer], whose cross-dressing strategies of seduction are elaborated under the heading of "beauty," below.

Loss of Parental Protection

Loss of parental protection often accompanies exogamy, that is, marriage that obliges the bride to move far from home. Exogamy implicitly causes women's vulnerability in both "Mal presagio casar lejos" [Only disaster awaits a bride far from home] and "La perseguida triunfante." [The triumph of the fugitive damsel] In the former, a Spanish wife is targeted for abuse by her Flemish father-in-law and husband; in the latter, the very act of escorting Princess Beatriz from England to Hungary touches off a chain of events that leaves the foreign bride stranded far from sympathetic allies.

"Mal presagio casar lejos," as the title implies, warns that the bride whom marriage obliges to leave behind her family and travel to a remote country, sacrifices the security and protection that proximate relatives can afford. Worse, her person, her body, becomes a synechdocal site for reprisals by Spain's political enemies. One by one, Blanca witnesses the sad fates of her elder sisters who wed afar. Her eldest sister, d. Mayor, marries a Portuguese man who stabs her to death "por la poca simpatía que la nación portuguesa tiene con las damas castellanas" [because of the Portugese nation's disdain for Castillian ladies] (338). Blanca's next sister, Leonor, weds another of Spain's traditional enemies, an Italian, who strangles her with her own tresses and poisons their only child. Blanca's turn arrives in the person of a Flemish prince, proposed to her in marriage "por conveniencias a la real corona y gusto de su hermano" [to the advantage of the Crown and to her brother's delight] (339). The suitor's nationality indeed portends ill, for Catholic Spain and the Protestant Low Countries had waged war against each other for nearly a century by the year that Zayas published her *Desengaños amorosos* in 1647. As soon as Blanca's idyllic two-year courtship culminates in marriage, the young groom tires of pleasing his new wife. Not until the couple is safely removed from Blanca's brother's purview, however, does the prince reveal his contempt: "como ya estaba en posesión [de d. Blanca] se iba cansando de los gustos que en esperanza le habían agradado; mas disimulaba a la cuenta *hasta sacarla del poder de su hermano*" [now that Lady Blanca was firmly in his grasp, all the little niceties that he showed her, instead of pleasing him as they had before, began to become progressively more tiresome; but he kept his feelings hidden *until he had effectively removed her from her brother's sphere of influence*] (349, my emphasis). Back in Flanders, the prince neglects and maltreats his wife, eventually murdering her by a method that infuses her name with newfound meaning: the prince and his father bleed Blanca to death, leaving her as pallid as her name foretells.

Zayas foregrounds the deleterious effects of marrying afar with two final literary flourishes. First, she has Spanish troops arrive in Flanders to avenge Blanca's maltreatment too late to rescue her (364, 365), and second, she demonstrates that future generations learn from Blanca's fate that daughters fare better under endogamy than exogamy. When Blanca's surviving sister returns safely to Spain, she weds her offspring, "con un deudo muy cercano de doña Blanca" [to a very close relative of Lady Blanca's] (365).

"La perseguida triunfante" [The triumph of the fugitive damsel] also rehearses a disastrous tale of exogamy. Although d. Beatriz's travails receive fuller treatment below under the heading of "supernatural impediments," it is noteworthy that the English princess's agency is gravely reduced upon moving from her father's Court to that of her Hungarian groom, Ludovico. When her brother-in-law tries to seduce her, Beatriz's first line of defense is to call upon the only person at her disposal to protect her, her childhood governess: "ordenó al aya que la había criado y había venido de Inglaterra con ella, asistiéndola, que ni de día ni de noche se apartase de ella. Mandó que durmiese en la misma cámara " [she ordered that her governess, who had raised her and who had come with her from England to serve her, not leave her side even for a moment, commanding that the governess sleep in the same room with her] (418). This precaution and the many others of which Beatriz avails herself, fail to neutralize her brother-in-law's destructive provocations, and it is only through divine intervention that the foreign princess gains the leverage necessary to choose between reaffirming or renouncing her matrimonial bonds.

Beauty

Beauty is a pretext for plot, an incitement which the virtuous Christian man resists through exercise of free will, but which many men fail to control. Beauty in women's courtship plots does not automatically brand all women as seductresses, but it does necessitate that the beautiful maiden who wishes to steer her courtship safely to port act with unflagging prudence, caution and even disdain. The compensatory behaviors that attractive maidens such as Beatriz of Carvajal's "La industria vence desdenes" [Effort vanquishes scorn] or Teodora of Carvajal's "El amante venturoso" [The lucky lover] deploy are analyzed in chapter 4 under the rubric of courtesy. Here, beauty is approached as a factor that limits women's autonomy in courtship by arousing dangerous passions.

Being beautiful to behold, while necessary, is by no means a sufficient guarantor of success in courtship. As Lisarda remarks in her preamble to the second *desengaño,* "ya no es dote la hermosura" [beauty is no kind of dowry] (176). Beauty cannot save the four lovely orphans of "Mal presagio casar lejos" from harm, prompting the narrator, d. Luisa, to remark: "de cada una se pudiera contar un desengaño, pues ni les sirvió la hermosura, la virtud, el entendimiento, la real sangre, ni la inocencia para que no fuesen víctimas sacrificadas en las aras de la desgracia" [every one of them could have been the subject of a tale of disenchantment, for neither their beauty, their virtue, their intelligence, their royal blood, nor their innocence could keep them from being slaughtered, sacrificial lambs on misfortune's altar] (338).

At best, attractiveness is a mixed blessing that brings misfortune to women in proportion to itself, as seen in the following pair of passages excerpted from the *Desengaños*: "porque fuese esta señora (Roseleta) como bella desgraciada" [for this lady was as wretched as she was beautiful] (202) and "hermosa es fuerza que [Mencía] lo sea, porque había de ser desgraciada" [perforce Mencía was beautiful, for she was destined to meet with misfortune] (372). Often, beauty is depicted as an outright curse, inducing misfortune at first sight, as the passages below, drawn from "Amar sólo por vencer" and "La inocencia castigada" respectively attest: "[La bella Laurela] no se pudo esconder de los ojos de la desdicha" [Lovely Laurela could not shield herself from misfortune's prying eyes] (295), and "su esposo [el de Inés] hacía la estimación de ella que merecía su valor y hermosura; por ésta le vino la desgracia porque siempre la belleza anda en pasos de ella" [Inés's husband had deemed her worthy of her merit and beauty; it was because of the latter that misfortune, always nipping at beauty's heels, found her] (266).

Predatory men girded with ingenuity continually threaten marriageable maidens in women's courtship plots, no matter how well-guarded or virtuous the maidens may be. Although examples of the "dangerous beauty" motif abound, one final proof-text will suffice to illustrate this point. Laurela of "Amar sólo por vencer" [Loving only to conquer] epitomizes the maiden whose beauty provokes disaster. Laurela attracts Esteban's attention during an outing by coach in the company of her mother. That single visual encounter obsesses Esteban, who sets out to conquer Laurela. Failing by conventional means, Esteban eventually manages to install himself in Laurela's household disguised as a female servant, where he quickly wins Laurela's affection, and ill-conceived love.

Supernatural Impediments

Supernatural powers contribute to the subjugation of women in three novellas of the *Desengaños:* "La perseguida triunfante"(satanic doctor), "El verdugo de su esposa" (revived corpse) and "La inocencia castigada" (voodoo-doll). The lengthiest of the *desengaños* in Zayas's collection, "La perseguida triunfante" also relies most heavily on the intervention of supernatural beings in human affairs. Plot unfolds as an epic Faustian battle for the soul of the king's brother. The forces of good condense around the person of Beatriz, the medieval English princess mentioned above, brought to Hungary to wed King Ladislao. Unfortunately, the task of escorting her across Europe is delegated to Federico, the king's brother, who falls in love with his future sister-in-law. When Beatriz traps the impertinent prince in a cage to keep him from dishonoring himself and her, Federico retaliates by denouncing her as unfaithful to Ladislao. Federico pursues Beatriz with the aid of an evil doctor who can see across time and space, mix magic potions and even make himself invisible. Eventually, as noted above, Beatriz, aided by the Virgin Mary, prevails, and Federico's nefarious schemes are brought to light. Federico repents, Beatriz takes the veil, her mortified husband Ladislao becomes a Benedictine monk, and Federico, after marrying Beatriz's younger sister, succeeds his brother to the Hungarian throne.

The Virgin does not always aid women. In Zayas's "El verdugo de su esposa," [His wife's executioner] she intervenes to defend an unscrupulous man. In a tale that begins like Cervantes's "El curioso impertinente" and ends like Calderón's *El médico de su honra*[26] [The physician of his honor], Juan responds to his best friend Pedro's praise of Pedro's new bride, Roseleta, by falling in love with her. Juan's efforts to seduce Roseleta are thwarted when she confides in Pedro that Juan is harassing her. In a twist of plot that will sound familiar to readers of *Don Quijote,* Pedro and Roseleta conspire to frame Juan; Roseleta invites Juan for a tryst at their country house where Pedro lies in wait for him. En route to the assignation, however,

Juan stops at a shrine to the Virgin Mary, who, further down the road, intercedes in the form of a talking corpse to rescue him from Pedro's ambush. This miracle causes Juan to repent, confess his crime to his friend and retreat to monastic orders. But although the Holy Mother's initiative saves Juan from perdition and also causes him to desist from his persecution of Roseleta, the young bride might have been better off without this miracle. In the second half of the novel, Pedro is tricked into believing that Juan and Roseleta actually did have an affair. His response, in true Calderonian fashion, is to have his wife bled to death, creating the appearance of medical mishap rather than foul play. Because "El verdugo" (like "El traidor de su sangre") blends two distinct plots into one, it becomes impossible to blame the Virgin, who dominates the first half, for the events that her action unleashes in the second. Her participation belongs to a plot that might have closed in "happily ever after" fashion, with Pedro and Roseleta's reconciliation were it not for the frame-tale's stipulation that each *desengaño* affirm men's perfidy. Hence, while Juan's reformation and the triumph of Marian grace it represents is permanent, Roseleta's victory is short-lived.

Finally, in "La inocencia castigada," [Her innocence punished] the supernatural vanquishes the virtue of a valiant female character. This tale rehearses an important theological question and literary leitmotif of the period: that of culpability where agency is impaired, for example by madness or sorcery. Book I, chapter 46 of *Don Quijote* presents an early instance of the insanity plea. Recall that the *cuadrilleros* [squadron of Inquisition deputies] finally decides not to arrest d. Quijote for having liberated the galley-slaves because they adjudge him to be crazy. After witnessing his lunatic insistence that a shaving basin is really the Helmet of Mambrino, they agree with the priest on the futility of hauling d. Quijote before a judge—the case would be thrown out of court on the grounds that the addled knight had acted without benefit of free will. Similarly, in "La inocenica castigada," when magic overcomes Inés's defenses, she is exculpated on the grounds that sorcery had deprived her of the freedom to resist seduction.[27]

Inés's nemesis, Diego, obtains a magical candle fashioned in Inés's likeness. When lit, the candle transforms the normally chaste and retiring Inés into a compliant zombie who shows up in Diego's bed whenever he wishes. One evening after dark, a magistrate follows the scantily-clad Inés as she heads to Diego's house. Once apprised of the candle and its spell, the magistrate immediately declares the apparently indecent woman innocent of any wrongdoing. That a legal system normally hostile to women sympathizes with a blatantly prodigal female may strike the reader as extraordinary. However, Inés's brother, who also witnesses her entrancement and believes she is faking it in order to avoid punishment for her affair takes matters into his own hands to effect Inés's required demise. Inés's brother, aided by his wife and Inés's husband, kidnaps Inés and removes her to Seville, where the cruel trio immure her for six years.

In Zayas's *Desengaños*, the supernatural complicates and extends a reiterative plot in which human malice causes women's downfall, but does not itself deprive women of their agency. Even the spell-bound Inés recovers her freedom in "La inocencia castigada," only to lose it again at the hands of her family. At the same time, the Virgin Mary is instrumental in saving the souls of Juan ("El verdugo") and Federico ("La perseguida"). In this sense, Zayas depicts the Virgin as perhaps a greater ally of men than of women, for she graces two of them with eternal reward.

Conclusion

In opposition to the dominant discourse, courtship novels generously delineate a set of institutional and communitarian resources by which maidens may maximize their range of choice in courtship. When the socioeconomic deck is stacked against them, women are shown to receive help from one another, from relatives, friends and from institutions such as civil law and the Church. This is not to say, however, that female protagonists are not embattled, nor that they always achieve their courtship goals, whatever those might be. To the contrary, women's courtship plots, particularly María de Zayas's, also anatomize a set of factors that challenge women as they struggle to position themselves within society. Courtship narratives written by women associate female oppression at home with patterns of competition for resources within the family, while they depict misfortune away from home as stemming from the practice of exogamy, which isolates women from their family and places them at the mercy of their foes. After marriage, severe over-attention (sexual predation, torture, murder), and severe under-attention (neglect or abandonment) alike afflict young brides. Beauty that awakens uncontrolled desire, and supernatural interventions favorable to men's designs are portrayed as potentially constrictive of female characters' optative horizons as well.

I have intentionally separated the preceding indagation into circumstantial factors that affect the balance of power between women and men in courtship from the inquiry that follows. Chapter 4,"The Art (and Craft) of Courtesy" elucidates the role of interactive rituals or courtesy in the courtship game. Mastery of complex courtesy codes can decisively fortify women's position in courtship. Indeed, switching from the checkers metaphor with which this chapter opened to comparing courtship to a game of cards, courtesy in women's courtship plots may be conceived of as the elite woman's trump card, a set of interactive strategies that allow her to prevail even when the patriarchal deck is stacked against her.

Notes

1. Nicolás Maquiavelo, *El príncipe*, 11a edición (Madrid: Espasa-Calpe, 1967), quoted in José Antonio Maravall, *El mundo social de* La Celestina [The social world of *La Celestina*] (Madrid: Gredos, 1976),143.

2. To think of courtship as a game in women's courtship plots also squares with the postulations of proponents of *écriture féminine*, who characterize women's writing by its non-goal-directed playfulness, its *jouissance*. For Elaine Marks and Isabelle de Courtivron, "Women's jouissance carries with it the notion of fluidity, diffusion, duration. It is a kind of potlatch in the world of orgasm, a giving, expending, dispensing of pleasure *without concern about ends or closure*" (*New French Feminisms* [Amherst, Mass.: University of Massachusetts Press; Boston: Harvester, 1980], 36; my emphasis).

3. On one hand, it has been fashionable to assume that patriarchy was more firmly entrenched in earlier periods and that consequently we can discern an evolutionary movement from bondage toward female liberation in the history of women's literature. See Elaine Showalter, "Feminist Criticism in the Wilderness", *Critical Inquiry* 8.2 (winter 1981): 179-205; *A Literature of Their Own* (Princeton, N.J.: Princeton University Press, 1981). However, Margaret Ezell rejects this model on the grounds that it condemns early modern literature to the role of servile precursor for later manifestations of feminism: "The theoretical model of women's literary studies as a field rests upon the assumption that women before 1700 either were effectively silenced or constituted an evolutionary model of 'female literature' an early 'imitative' phase, contained and co-opted in patriarchal discourse" (*Writing Women's Literary History* [Baltimore: Johns Hopkins University Press, 1993], 4).

Ironically, the opposite tendency, that of overprivileging woman's volition by attributing to her acts of heroic resistance and subversion at every turn of the text, offers an equally distorted paradigm by underestimating forces of patriarchal oppression.

4. For Ruth El Saffar, preoccupation with the maiden and her control in the *comedia* [Golden Age drama] symptomizes anxiety about the power of the mother. With reference to male authors, she writes: "Fear of mother power underlies the efforts at dominance and control so central to Golden Age drama in general, which is why the action so often focuses on the feminine figure least capable of defending herself, the young maiden. To win the battle that stifles her rebellion, as in, for example, Shakespeare's *The Taming of the Shrew*, is to offer the audience an image of order and reason winning over chaos" ("The 'I' of the Beholder: Self and Other in Some Golden Age Texts," in *Cultural Authority in Golden Age Spain*, ed. Marina Brownlee and Hans Ulrich Gumbrecht [Baltimore: Johns Hopkins University Press, 1995], 187).

5. Constance Jordan advocates guarding the distinction between "power" and "authority" when discussing Renaissance women. Power she defines as a capacity to secure obedience while authority suggests a political or social title to do so. Renaissance women often exerted power unofficially, making it easy to miscalculate the extent of their agency (*Renaissance Feminism: Literary Texts and Political Models* [Ithaca, N.Y.: Cornell University Press, 1990], 3-4).

6. With reference to folktales, Stith Thompson defines motif as "those details out of which full-fledged narratives are composed. It is these simple elements which can form a common basis for a systematic arrangement of the whole body of traditional literature" (*Motif-Index of Folk Literature*, 6 vols. [Bloomington, Ind.: Indiana Univeristy Press, 1966], 2).

7. Mariana de Carvajal y Saavdra, *Navidades de Madrid y noches entretenidas en ocho novelas* [Christmastide in Madrid and nights of amusement in eight novels] (1663), ed. Catherine Soriano (Madrid: Clásicos Madrileños, 1993), n.1.

8. I am indebted to Richard Kagan for his insights into Carvajal's position at Court, as reflected or refracted in the figure of Lucrecia.

9. Robert J. Clements and Joseph Gibaldi sketch the transmission of teachings on verisimilitude from Cicero and Quintilian to Renaissance novelists (*Anatomy of the Novella: The European Tale Collection from Boccaccio and Chaucer to Cervantes* [New York: New York University Press, 1977], 17). See also Edward C. Riley, *Cervantes's Theory of the Novel* (Oxford: Clarendon, 1962), and Bernard Weinberg, *A History of Literary Criticism in the Renaissance*, 2 vols. (Chicago: University of Chicago Press, 1961).

10. Technically, these conditions occupy only part of the intergenerational tale of Floripa and Venus's courtships.

11. Surely Venus's liberty to select the best partner from among a field of excellent contenders represents the desiring female subject's dream-come-true. This element of female fantasy fulfillment accounts for the idealized fairy-tale atmosphere of the story, with its castles and guards, tournaments, detailed descriptions of horsemen and their livery, etc.

12. This delicate interplay of diffidence and ambition will be analyzed in chapter 4. Here, as in the case of gallantry, the line between cooperation and courtesy becomes somewhat arbitrary. The purpose of separating the two is to emphasize in the present chapter features of the social landscape to which women could turn for help, and in chapter 4, behaviors that the character herself could adopt to optimize her position during courtship.

13. The better to foreground the parallelism between Lisarda's situation and Camila's, Zayas has Lisarda narrate this tale.

14. Or does she? The risks inherent in exogamy are explicated in "Mal presagio casar lejos" [Only disaster awaits a bride far from home] and "La perseguida triunfante" [The triumph of the fugitive damsel], leaving Lisarda's ultimate felicity very much in question.

15. D. Mencía of Pedro Calderón de la Barca's uxorcide drama, *El médico de su honra* [The physician of his honor] is bled to death by her husband (ed. D.W. Cruikshank [Madrid: Cátedra, 1981]).

16. Margaret Greer observes that Zayas makes reference to the Count of Lemos's wife as "mi señora" [my lady], which, as Greer conjectures, may "suggest some personal relationship" (*Desiring Readers: María de Zayas Tells Baroque Tales of Love and the Cruelty of Men* [University Park, Pa: Pennsylvania State University Press, in press], 334).

17. See note 5.

18. Likewise, the bled body of d. Blanca remains undecomposed for four years in "Mal presagio casar lejos": "También, sacaron el cuerpo de doña Blanca para traerle a España, que estaba tan lindo como si entonces acabara de morir (señal de la gloria que goza el alma)" [Also, they took the body of Lady Blanca with them, in order to bring it back to Spain, and the corpse was still so lovely that it appeared recently deceased (a sign of a soul that has gone to its heavenly rest)] (Calderón de la Barca, *El médico*, 365).

19. For Patricia Grieve, "The hagiographic model permitted Zayas a tremendous amount of artistic liberty within the circumscribed conventions of that genre and the novella form" ("Embroidering with Saintly Threads: María de Zayas Challenges Cervantes and the Church," *Renaissance Quarterly* 44.1 [1991], 104).

20. Grieve discerns a subversive message in Zayas's juxtaposition of martyrdom and marriage: "women should reject the secular martyrdom sanctioned by society's view of civilized behavior—marriage—and seek refuge in the communities of women afforded by the convents" ("Embroidering" 104).

21. Both d. Felipe's daughter and his niece are named Lisis in Leonor de Meneses's *El desdeñado más firme* [Scorned yet steadfast] (1665) (ed. Judith Whitenack and Gwyn E. Campbell [Potomac, Md.: Scripta Humanistica, 1994]). This curious narrative feature is addressed more fully below under heading "Circumstances Favorable to Women," in the section entitled "Chaos."

22. Familial opposition to courtship figures as a secondary pretext in numerous plots. We recall that Floripa of "La Venus de Ferrara" [The Venus from Ferrara] escapes from her father's tower in order to initiate courtship, that Doristea of "La dicha de Doristea" [Doristea's good fortune] eludes her elderly aunt in order to follow d. Claudio, that Jacinta and Pedro's parents in "La industria vence desdenes" [Effort vanquishes scorn] ordain that the twins enter orders rather than wed, and that Count Rodulfo of "El esclavo de su esclavo" [His slave's slave] opposes his sister Blanca's marriage to Félix Centellas, fearful that such a match could undermine his sovereignty over Catalunya.

23. D. Pedro is in the midst of gambling at cards when he receives the news of Alonso's death. For insightful analysis of d. Pedro's card game, see Greer, *Desiring Readers*, 330-332.

24. For Margaret Greer, Florentina is the "enemy within" her adoptive sister, Magdalena's house (*Desiring Readers* 354). However, rather than posit sister-sister rivalry as an obstacle to female empowerment, I continue to view Florentina and Magdalena's emnity as a secondary consequence of their prolonged stay under their covetous uncle's roof.

25. Margaret Greer recognizes that "considerations related to her dowry" presented a potential economic threat to Ángela's brother, Juan, in Calderón's *La*

dama duende [The spirit lady] ("The [Self]Representation of Control in *La dama duende*," in *The Golden Age Comedia: Text, Theory and Performance*, ed. Charles Ganelin and Howard Mancing [West Lafayette, Ind.: Purdue University Press, 1994], 93). She writes, "providing a dowry could severely strain a noble family's resources and even liquidate a fortune." For Greer, Zayas's "Estragos" and "Traidor" exemplify the "covetousness" resulting from the financial drain of providing a dowry ("(Self)Representation" 98-99).

26. 1605 and c. 1637, respectively.

27. "En tanto que don Quijote esto decía, estaba persuadiendo el cura a los cuadrilleros como don Quijote era falto de juicio, como lo veían por sus obras y por sus palabras, y que no tenían para qué llevar aquel negocio adelante, pues aunque le prendiesen y llevasen, luego le habían de dejar por loco" [And as don Quijote was saying this, the priest was persuading the Inquisition's squadron of deputies that because don Quijote was out of his mind, as they could observe from his actions and his words, they did not have to pursue the business of his arrest any futher, for even if they were to seize him and drag him away, they would have to abandon their case later, because he was mad]. Miguel de Cervantes, *El ingenioso Hidalgo Don Quijote de la Mancha* [The ingenious Hidalgo Don Quijote of la Mancha], ed. Salvador Fajardo and James Parr (Asheville, N.C.: Pegasus, 1998), I, 525. According to María Helena Sánchez Ortega, sorcerers and sorceresses were prosecuted by the Inquisition "for their deviation from one of the fundamental dogmas of the Catholic Church, the exercise of free will" ("Sorcery and Eroticism in Love Magic," in *Cultural Encounters: The Impact of the Inquisition in Spain and the New World*, ed. Mary Elizabeth Perry and Anne Cruz [Berkeley and Los Angeles: University of California Press, 1991], 59). The extent to which Melibea can be held responsible for either her seduction or her suicide in Rojas's *Tragicomedia de Calixto y Melibea* revolves around interpretation of the *philocaptio* theme—whether and to what extent Celestina's love potion deprived her of her native free will. See "La magia, tema integral de 'La celestina'" in Peter E. Russell, *Temas de* La Celestina *y Otro Estudios* [Themes in *La Celestina* and other Studies] (Barcelona: Ariel, 1978), 243-276. See also "La idea de la fortuna y la visión mecánica del mundo. El papel de la magia" in Maravall, *Mundo,* 134-152, and Elizabeth Sánchez, "Magia en *La Celestina*," *Hispanic Review* 46.4 (autumn 1979), 481-494.

4: The Art (and Craft) of Courtesy

> Arte para ser dichoso. [N]o hay más dicha ni más desdicha que prudencia, o imprudencia (Gracián, *Oráculo manual,* máxima 21. 64).
>
> [The art of being lucky. [T]here are no such things as good luck or bad luck, only prudence or imprudence] ("The Oracle", Maxim 21. Tr. Walton 65).

Women's courtship novels imitate as well as instruct. Chapter 3 underscored the imitative impulse evident in women's courtship novels, their enlistment of the sometimes empowering yet often obstructive institutional landscape of the Hapsburg Court to favor young maidens facing the prospect of wedlock. However, in addition to utilizing such institutional expedients as family networks, ecclesiastical support and legal channels, female characters often gain a measure of autonomy in courtship by practicing the art of courtesy, the polite interactions that the courtier mobilizes to impress others with his or her social worth. Within this sphere of individual "self-fashioning," to borrow Stephen Greenblatt's phrase, women's courtship plots fulfill an instructive function, demonstrating how to project an effective public mask through ritual displays of courtesy. Since courtesy manuals of the day tended to gender the ideal courtier[1] as male,[2] it is useful to observe that in women's courtship plots the reverse is true. Courtship novels counterbalanced the message that only men stood to benefit by mastering the art of self-fashioning, teaching women through fictional example that courtesy could also empower them as they negotiated the important life-course passage of courtship. The present chapter aims to elucidate the lessons in the art and craft of courtesy encoded within women's courtship plots.

Renaissance courtesy guides codified the art of ritualized social interaction for male and female readers alike. In his introductory sonnet to Gracián Dantisco's courtesy guide, the *Galateo español* [Spanish Galateo], Gálvez de Montalvo compares training in the art of courteous action to the air needed to hold up the wing of nobility:

> Nadie nace instruido ni enseñado,
> porque el buen natural, sin el consejo,
> lo mismo es que sin el aire el ala.
>   El más vazío quedará colmado
> si lo ofrescieren este claro espejo,
> Galateo y Gracían, de gracia y gala. (101)

(No one is born well-informed, nor well-educated,
for natural goodness, without a guiding hand,
is as limp as a wing without air to lift it
Even the emptiest vessel will end up replete
if it is offered in this faultless mirror of yours,
Galateo and Gracian, a glimpse of grace and elegance.)

Novelists Mariana de Carvajal, Leonor de Meneses and María de Zayas ratify Gálvez de Montalvo's metaphor, granting wing to the courtship aspirations of discreet female characters who master refined "airs," while thwarting the efforts of indiscreet characters in courtship. In order to analyze effectively the impact of courteous interaction on the outcome of women's courtship plots, it is first necessary to define what was meant by courtesy in the seventeenth century. I then outline the historical process by which courtesy came to supplant military prowess as a channel of social elevation in Renaissance society. This shift is crucial to an understanding of the rise of women's courtship fictions, for it granted women access to a new vector of social ascent that feudal society lacked: that of polite interaction. Next, as a point of comparison, it is useful to delineate the courtesy practices elaborated by contemporary courtesy manuals, emblem books and allegorical drama. Finally, turning from the preceptive discourse of conduct literature to the fictional discourse of courtship novels, I identify similar courtesy practices as they affect female agency in María de Zayas's *Desengaños amorosos* [Disenchantments of love], Leonor de Meneses's *El desdeñado más firme* [Scorned yet steadfast] and Mariana de Carvajal's *Navidades de Madrid* [Christmastide in Madrid].

Women's courtship novels, by modeling effective masking strategies and inversely, by exemplifying unsuccessful interactive behaviors, assume the didactic function of training female readers at Court in the art and craft of courtesy. This statement may at first cause surprise by positing a linkage between two genres normally thought of as separate, that of conduct manuals and that of the ostensibly escapist genre of recreational fiction (see chapter 1).[3] However, the simultaneous rise of both of these genres, their similar aims and the coincidence of their readership evidence that courtesy guides and courtship novels represent related responses to a single contemporary social formation: the rise of the absolutist courts of Renaissance Europe.

As in all the great courts of early modern Europe, a complex code of social interactions governed life at the Hapsburg Court of Madrid. A corresponding spate of courtesy literature, beginning with Castiglione's *The Book of the Courtier*, promised to initiate readers into the intricacies of *politesse*. Juan Boscán's 1534 adaptation of Castiglione's *Courtier* underwent nine reprintings from 1534 to 1634 (Boscán 1). Other Spanish courtesy guidebooks included musician

Luis Milán's 1561 portrait of the Venetian court entitled *El cortesano*, [The courtier], Cristóbal de Villalón's idealization of the university professor, *El scholástico*[4] [The academician] and Gracián Dantisco's 1583 adaptation of Giovanni della Casa's *Galateo*, which he entitled the *Galateo español* [Spanish Galateo]. In the meantime, more than 157 romances of chivalry were published in Spain between 1501 and 1550 (Burke 17). That Charles V complimented papal nuncio Baltasar de Castiglione for being one of the best knights in the world ("uno de los mejores caballeros del mundo") (Burke 23) not only demonstrates that Castiglione's courtesy guide, *The Book of the Courtier*, earned its author the distinction of being called a chivalric knight, but also suggests that adventures of chivalry themselves were read as paradigms of civility.

While the modern novel would eventually come to be a primarily mimetic construct which attempted to imitate reality, the early modern novel continued to draw inspiration from exemplary and epic forms, which invited readers to imitate the actions of their (male) heroes. According to Francisco de Lugo y Dávila, author of the 1622 *Teatro popular*, while prose "poems" do imitate men's deeds, men also imitate fiction in their deeds:

> El fin que tienen estos poemas, como ya apunté, es poner á los ojos del entendimiento un espejo en que hacen reflexión los sucesos humanos para que el hombre de la suerte que en el cristal se compone á sí, mirándose en los varios casos que abrazan y representan las novelas, componga sus acciones, imitando lo bueno y huyendo lo malo. (26)

> (The end result of these poems, as I already mentioned, is that they put a mirror before the mind's eye of the reader that reveals the events of human life in such a way any man predisposed to contemplating himself in its glass, gazing upon himself reflected in the various aspects of life represented in and embraced by the novels, will configure his actions accordingly, imitating that which is good, and avoiding that which is bad.)

In a similar vein, Cervantes's Canon of *Don Quijote* Book I, famously attests that the beauty of fiction lies in permitting the novelist to unfold "todas aquellas acciones que pueden hacer perfecto a un varón ilustre, ahora poniéndose en uno solo, ahora dividiéndolas en muchos" [all those actions that could make an illustrious male perfect; at one moment placing them all in one character, dividing them between many at the next] (398). These citations from Lugo y Dávila *Teatro popular* and Cervantes' *Don Quijote* manifest a common faith in the novel's capacity to model right conduct.

The seventeenth century presents an even clearer case for understanding recreactional fiction as a paradigm of proper comportment. Baltásar Gracián dominated the courtesy genre in Spain with *El héroe* [The hero] (1637), *El discreto* [The discreet gentleman] (1646), *El oráculo manual* [The oracle] (1647), *El político* [The politician] (1640) and the *Agudeza y arte de ingenio* [Cleverness and the art of ingenuity] (1648). In these preceptive writings, Gracián emphasizes the value of constructing a likeable public persona, a work of art that he called "The Eminent Man," through speech and interactive behavior. When he crossed over from preceptive literature into fiction with *El criticón* [The master critic], published in installments under a series of pseudonyms between 1651-1656, Gracián retained the same message. Although bleak, *El criticón*'s allegorical journey allows mankind one redemptive outlet, the Island of Immortality, reached only by the *chalupa de arte,* the Life Raft of Art, equipped with wisdom, ingeniousness and moral purpose (vol. 3, chapter xii, 996). While *El criticón* is not a courtship novel, it demonstrates once again recreational fiction's ability to exemplify courtly conduct.

Castiglione and Gracián's readership coincided with the population to whom courtship novels appealed. Courtesy guide readers in Spain during the sixteenth and seventeenth centuries included not only noblemen, but also "new men" such as the Fuggers, a central European mercantilist dynasty elevated to noble status through their financial assistance to the Spanish Crown. Peter Burke speculates that these upstarts "might be assumed to have needed the *Courtier* most and to have used it as a guide to good behavior and impression management" (145). Courtship novel consumers were likewise patrons and clients, nobles and aspirants to noble status, males and females, vying with one another for privileges, concessions and opportunities (Ife 1-11). Both genres, the courtesy guide and the courtship novel taught these readers effective strategies for ascending the social pyramid, while also charting the dangers and pitfalls awaiting the unwary courtier. However, courtship novels written by women writers focused particularly upon those strategies that aristocratic women would require as they faced the prospect of courtship.

The idea that courtship novels taught their readers modes of social interaction is not entirely new. As early as 1926, Edwin Place had noted the kinship between novels of courtship and the didactic novel (20). Fifty years later, María del Pilar Palomo would come to insist upon a direct line of descent from *The Book of the Courtier* to the Spanish novella collections and their readers. In *La novela cortesana (forma y estructura)* [The courtly novel (form and structure)] (1976) she writes: "Las colecciones renacentistas se destinan a un entretenimiento y adiestramiento sociales; lo que debe destacar en ellas es el ingenio, y van a ser, en sí, una práctica de cultos hombres renacentistas, y destinadas, por tanto, a una sociedad de aspiración cortesana" [The Renaissance collections are meant for social training and entertainment; what should stand out in them is their ingenuity, and, consequently, they end up being, in and of themselves, a practice of cultured Renaissance men, and therefore meant for that sector of society which aspired to nobility] (55).[5] Carrying Palomo's argument from the domain of the male reader to that of the female reader, the present chapter aims to establish that women's courtship plots "are meant for social training and entertainment" of specifically female readers as they faced the prospect of courtship.

Courtesy

Courteous behaviors are interactive rituals governed consensually by rules of conduct. According to Erving Goffman, interactive rituals, by virtue of their universal acceptance within a given culture, "transform both action and inaction into expression, and whether the individual abides by the rules or breaks them, something significant is likely to be communicated" (51). That which courteous or discourteous comportment communicates within Court society is pedigree, the alleged virtue or inner worth possessed by pure-blooded aristocrats. *Politesse* was thought to externalize or enact social worth. To prove this point, Castiglione's El Manífico Julián argues that Queen Isabel of Spain earned her subjects' loyalty not by sheer strength, but through the virtue evident in her actions:

> y puesto que la fama desta señora [Isabela la Católica] en toda parte sea muy grande, los que con ella vivieron . . . afirman haber esta fama procedido totalmente de su virtud y de sus grandes hechos. Y el que quisiere considerar sus cosas, fácilmente conocerá ser la verdad ésta: porque dexando infinitas hazañas suyas que darían desto buen testigo y podrían agora decirse si fuese este nuestro principal propósito, no hay quien no sepa que cuando ella comenzó a reinar halló la mayor parte de Castilla en poder de los grandes, pero ella se dió tan *buena maña* y tuvo *tal seso* en cobrallo todo tan justamente que los mismos despojados de los estados que se habían usurpado y que tenían ya por suyos, le quedaron aficionados en todo estremo y muy contentos de dexar lo que poseían. (Boscán, Book III, 261, 262, my emphasis)[6]

> (and given that the renown of this lady [Queen Isabella] is very great throughout the land, those that lived in her presence . . . affirm that the source of her fame was her virtue and great deeds. And whosoever might wish to ponder such things will easily recognize the following truth: in leaving behind innumerable heroic exploits that would faithfully bear

witness to her greatness, it can now be said that if this were our self-same principle goal [we could do no better than to imitate her], for there is not a single person who does not know that when she began her reign, Queen Isabella found the majority of Castille in the hands of the Grandees; but she confronted this situation with *such astuteness* and *good judgment* that the selfsame aristocrats whose lands and possessions she usurped and took charge of ended up not only extremely fond of her, but utterly willing to give up all that they owned.)

Even though the Castilian aristocracy lost lands and possessions to the Catholic Queen, her *seso,* or good judgment, as well as her *maña,* or astuteness, mollified the disenfranchised nobility and even earned their gratitude.

The dedication to Mariana de Carvajal's 1663 novel collection, the *Navidades de Madrid* similarly insists that courteous action is itself the truest test of pedigree. There, the author of the dedication, possibly Carvajal herself, or her publisher, Gregorio Rodríguez, praises the work's dedicatee, Count von Pötting for his ability to earn his peers' respect through valorous actions rather than merely relying on his illustrious lineage: "Grande es V. Exc. por la exaltación de su Casa, pero *por sus acciones ilustres* se ha grangeado tantos títulos y renombres, que no caben en las hojas de los volúmenes de la Retórica" [Of course Your Excellency is great because of the exaltation of your House, but *it is because of your illustrious actions* that you have won for yourself so many titles and so much acclaim that to recount all of them, all the pages of all the volumes of the Rhetoric would be insufficient] (3, my emphasis). Noble birth is estimable, but even more praiseworthy is the fact that the count has succeeded in translating his inherited potential for virtue into action.

Courtesy displays such as Queen Isabel's *buena maña,* [astuteness], or the *Navidades'* dedication, while superficially cordial, were actually competitive performances credited with converting the actor's genealogical merit into measurable semiotic codes. Much as Johan Huizinga has written of Chinese politeness contests, the early modern European courtier's displays of gentility could either win him honor or dishonor, depending upon their perceived artfulness:

> Competition for honour may also take, as in China, an inverted form by turning into a contest in politeness. The special word for this—*jang*—means literally "to yield to another," hence one demolishes one's adversary by superior manners, making way for him or giving him precedence. The courtesy-match . . . is to be met with all over the world. We might call it an inverted boasting-match, since the reason for this display of civility to others lies in an intense regard for one's own honour. (66)

The words "competition" and "match" connote the pitched conflict characteristic of chivalry in the etymological sense of equestrian prowess. The European manifestation of these "inverted boasting matches," however, came to rely less on military skills and increasingly to depend upon mastery of a set of performative and discursive competencies that detractors called "feminine" precisely because women could and did excel at them.

Gentrification of the Warrior

As mentioned in chapter 2 courtesy began to supplement and even supplant martial achievement as a vehicle of social convection in Spain with the definitive consolidation of the Hapsburg Court in Madrid after 1607. Women benefited from this resituating of the theater of power from battlefield to Court because, although women had been excluded from the former, they were (literally) at home in the latter. Once the king was installed at a fixed location, those wishing to win his favor were compelled to station themselves in his proximity. Honor, projecting the right image, played a vital role in maintaining and improving one's position in this pyramid of "ambition and privilege" (Whigham). To remain in good social standing it was not sufficient to be a good Catholic, a loyal subject and a gentleman of means ("hombre de bien"); one also had to earn a reputation for living an aristocratic lifestyle ("vivir noblemente").[7]

North of the Pyrenees, at Louis XIV's Versailles, the courtier's struggle to enhance his reputation was understood, according to Elizabeth Goldsmith, as "a kind of military campaign, for which the gentleman trained by learning defensive and offensive tactics" (18). In Spain, Baltasar Gracián was responsible for "rethinking the public space as a battlefield in which to pursue power and individual success" (Castillo 203). At the Hapsburg Court, the existence of a special architectural space consecrated to women's social activity suggests that conditions similar to those documented in French salon society also prevailed in Madrid. That feminine space was the *estrado* [salon], defined by the *Diccionario de Autoridades* as an orientalized platform or, by extension, room, reserved for aristocratic women's entertainment:

> [Estrado] El conjunto de alhajas que sirve para cubrir y adornar el lugar o pieza en que se sientan las señoras para recibir las visitas, que se compone de alfombra o tapicete, almohada, taburetes o sillas baxas. Vale también el lugar o sala cubierta con la alfombra y demás alhajas del estrado, donde se sientan las mugeres y reciben las visitas.

([*Estrado*] The inventory of precious objects which serve to cover and adorn the place or room where ladies sit to receive their visitors, which is comprised of a rug or Persian carpet, pillows, stools, or low chairs. The term is also used to refer to the place or room adorned by the rug and the *objets d'art,* where women sit and receive their visitors.)

Both the *estrado* in Spain and the salon of seventeenth-century France functioned as a self-conscious stage or "théâtre de la conversation des femmes" [theater for women's conversation] (Goldsmith 20), where courtesy displays determined a shifting hierarchy of privilege and prestige. The same conditions appear to have prevailed in Italy, for Castiglione incites the courtier to refine his musical talents among women: "Será mejor y converná mucho más si fuere entre mujeres; porque en esto la presencia y vista dellas suelen ablandar y enternecer los corazones de los que están presentes, y los hacen más aparejados a que en ellos más hondamente penetre la suavidad de la música y aun levantan el espíritu de quien la hace." [It would be better and much more suitable if it were done among women; because the feminine gaze and presence usually soften and touch the hearts of those around them, causing everyone to be more predisposed to allow the sweetness of the music to penetrate their souls more deeply, and even serving to exalt the spirit of the one who performs before them] (Book II 124). That poet Ana Caro and novelist Leonor de Meneses dedicated certain works to women rather than to men[8] and that Nicholás Antonio appends forty-nine women writers to his 1684 bibliography of Hispanic writers (Luna 28-40), attests that women and men shared the cultural stage in Golden Age Spain. It is also noteworthy that women did not strut for one another alone. In 1623, for example, female poet Cristobalina Fernández Alarcón of Antequera won first prize in a poetry contest judged by Góngora (Luna 83).

Women's real economic and estamental power, combined with their relative authority in matters of courtly protocol and culture, mingled to create the empowering conditions fictionalized in many women's courtship narratives. Courtesy codes constituted a semiotic arsenal in the pitched battle for self-promotion at Court, a battle that Cristobalina Fernández Alarcón of Antequera triumphantly demonstrated that women could win. However, the ongoing displacement of the "masculine" attribute of military prowess by the "feminine" value of courtly manners elicited mixed response from contemporary Spanish observers. At one extreme, Quevedo, in his "Epístola satírica y censoria" ["Censorious and satirical epistle"] disparages the courtier who exchanges his sword for the harmless spectacles of Court: "¡Qué cosa es ver un infanzón de España / abreviado en la silla a la gineta / y gastar un caballo en una caña . . . ejercite sus fuerzas el mancebo / en frentes de escuadrones, no en la frente / del útil bruto l'asta del acebo" [What a sorry sight it is to see a strapping Spanish infantryman trussed up in some silly saddle and wasting a fine horse in some perverse jousting match . . . young man, expend your forces and the brute strength of your lance at the head of military squadrons, not on the heads of fighting cocks] (130-137). In the hands of dramatist Andrés de Claramonte, on the other hand, the gentrification of the warrior becomes a richly ironic medium for exploring questions of honor and virtue. In Claramonte's 1638 drama, *El valiente negro en Flandes,* [The brave Ebon in Flanders] a black character named Juan de Mérida ascends from the status of unranked volunteer to that of captain. Although Juan earns his military stripes on the battlefield, in order to collect his honors, he must return to the capital and submit to the rigors of courtly protocol. Act 3 depicts Juan "midiendo / losa a losa" [measuring / stone by stone] the halls and patios of Court, (III vv 2055, 2056, p. 251) awaiting an audience with the king. Decked out in a plumed hat, his titanic frame squeezed into ridiculous breeches, Juan suffers the jeers and taunts of other courtiers also waiting to catch the king's eye. Having never engaged in live combat, these preening brats fart and sneeze derisively at the giant in their midst: "Vive Dios, que ya me enfada / la corte, donde estoy viendo / A ejércitos los hermosos / causando y haciendo gestos" [For the love of God! Now I am offended by this court, where I must witness the spectacle of the beautiful people doing what they do best: making faces and breaking wind] (III vv 2042-2045, pp. 250, 251). Only after Juan de Mérida submits to this courtly i(or)deal does the king authorize the generous allowances, rewards and titles that the warrior deserves.

It is significant in the context of the feminization of criteria for social ascent at Court that Claramonte's Juan de Mérida should attain his greatest honor not at the foot of the king, but at the hand of a woman, that of d. Juana, who offered hers to him in marriage: "Pues si ha de ser / ya el casarme por tu cuenta / y el cielo te ha dado honor / que ha igualado en mi nobleza, / que ha igualado en mi nobleza, / de negro quiero que subas / a dueño" [Then if it is to be that I marry you for who you are, because the honor that heaven has endowed you with has found its match in my nobility, then from mere negro it is my desire that you ascend, becoming my master] (III vv 2623-1628, pp. 284, 285). As chapter 2 demonstrated, Spanish women's capacity to inherit and bequeath titles and inheritances placed them in a position analogous to that of d. Juana, from which they could ennoble or enrich the men who married them.

The following pages elucidate the empowering role that the art and craft of courtesy play in Carvajal, Zayas and Meneses's courtship fictions. The "art" of courtesy can be thought of as the cultivation of gentility in speech, appearance and action in order to fashion a pleasing and effective public image, while the "craft" of courtesy refers to the shrewd adaptation of one's persona to shifting circumstances. Together, the phrase "art and craft of courtesy" evokes the playful, mobile quality of baroque masking, the skill and canniness that enable female and male characters to reshape themselves as events demand in order to realize their courtship goals.

Discretion: A Habit of Practical Intellect

In order to historicize both artful display and crafty deployment of courtesy, I shall begin by introducing the term "discretion." The rich and polyvalent meanings associated with this usage in contemporary conduct literature make of discretion a supple organizing signifier for investigating the art and craft of courtesy in women's courtship novels. *Discreción* [discretion] in the seventeenth century referred to a set of varying, sometimes contradictory qualities of polite interaction that are probably unfamiliar to readers of today. Before the instrumentality of discreet behaviors for resolving conflicts in women's courtship plots can be seen, a working knowledge of this cluster of interactive principles must be acquired. Discretion enhanced the reputation of the aristocrat in all interactions and informed her or his appraisals of the social worth of others. Returning to Gálvez de Montalvo's dedicatory sonnet to the *Galateo español,* the poet compares Gracián Dantisco to a perfect key for unlocking the doors of discretion. By passing through that "door" (by reading the *Galateo español*) the courtier learns to transform himself from ignoramus to man of prudence, from oaf to gentleman:

> Pues al ignorante hazes prudente,
> al más grossero tornas cortesano
> pones en perfeción al que no sabe.
> Publícate por luz toda la gente
> y espejo en que se mira el mundo ufano
> Gracián, de discreción perfecta llave. (103)

> (You are the one who makes the ignoramus wise,
> you turn the biggest buffoon into a courtly genteman,
> you make even the least-learned perfect.
> Allow others to recognize you for the guiding light
> and mirror that you are, showing this vain and boastful world,
> Gracián, the perfect key to discretion.)

In 1579, Damasio de Frías published the *Diálogo de la discreción* [Dialogue on discretion], in which he compiles etymological, historical, literary and religious usage of the word *discreción*. The closest Latin synonym for the word *discreto* is *prudens*; indeed King Philip II was known as "El prudente" [The prudent one] (Domínguez Ortiz I, 282). Baltasar de Gracián entitled his 1647 courtesy guide *Oráculo manual y arte de prudencia,* which Walton renders into English as *The Oracle: A Manual of the Art of Discretion.* The meanings of the two terms, prudence and discretion, are very similar, both being tied to the classical ideal of the "mean" or *aurea mediocritas,* that is, the middle ground between extremes, where right action abides. Prudence not only guides the courtier along a path of moderation; it also enables him, in Boscán's reworking of Castiglione, to make sound judgments: "De todas éstas [virtudes] es después guía la prudencia, la cual consiste en un cierto juicio de saber bien elegir" [Prudence is the key to all of these [virtues] and it consists of a certain wisdom in knowing how to choose well] (IV, 334). Sebastián de Covarrubias's 1611 *Tesoro de la lengua castellana* [Thesaurus of the Castilian language] likewise links discretion to the faculty of judgement or discernment. The dictionary states: "Vale vulgarmente distinguir una cosa de otra y hazer juycio dellas; de aquí se dixo discreto al hombre cuerdo y de buen seso"[9] [The ability to distinguish one thing from another and to make judgments about these things is commonly referred to as "discretion"; it was because of this initial usage that the wise and sensible man came to be called "discreet"].

Emblem books of the period such as Bernardino de Daza Pinciano's Spanish adaptation of Alciati's Emblems give modern readers a glimpse of the conceptual range covered by the term discretion. Daza Pinciano's adaptation includes eleven emblems related to prudence. "Que las doncellas han de ser muy guardadas" [Watch over maidens with consummate care] and "La vigilencia y la guarda" [Vigilence and safekeeping] interpret prudence as a form of modesty that defends against vice. Three emblems—"Que los prudentes se refrenan del vino" [Prudent people drink in moderation], "Bibir templadamente y no creer de ligero" [Live abstemiously and avoid thinking rashly] and "Que se ha de considerarse lo que se obra" [Consider your actions carefully]—advocate temperance in drink and deed. "Que todo se deve hazer con sazón" [All things must be done opportunely] and "El prudente sin elocuencia" [The prudent man who lacked eloquence] praise the exercise of tact and propriety. "El engañador assido" [The persistent trickster] teaches the virtue of caution. "Que con consejo se vencen los más fuertes y engañadores" [Even the strongest and most deceptive enemies are vanquished by good advice] and "La grama" [Grass] applaud tactical prudence. Finally, "Los prudentes" [The prudent ones] credits the man possessed of both foresight and hindsight.

The Spanish adjective *recatado* [circumspect, modest] pulls together several connotations of prudence emblematized by Daza Pinciano. In Cervantes's *Don Quijote, recatado* can mean variously forewarned, careful, modest or honest (Fajarda, Parr 973). Frequently, *recato* [modesty, demureness, reserve, restraint] describes women who guard themselves from men: "Guardábala su padre, y guardábase ella; que no hay candados, guardas ni cerraduras que mejor guarden a una doncella que las del recato propio" [Her father watched over her, and she protected herself as well, for there are no padlocks, guards or hasps that can protect a maiden better than self-restraint] (416). For Baltasar Gracián, caution is the antidote for prying curiosity: "Compite la detención del recato con la atención del advertido" [The reserve of caution combats the watchfulness of the curious] (*Oráculo manual*, Maxim 98. Tr. Walton 120, 121).

Damasio de Frías acknowledges the polysemy of *discreción* without attempting to reduce the term to a single meaning. The closest he comes to synthesizing its varied connotations and usage is to characterize *discreción* as a habit of practical intellect:

> El obrar . . . es de la voluntad; pero el cómo y el cuándo no sino del entendimiento. Porque no es otra cosa discreción que un hábito del entendimiento práctico mediante el cual obramos en las cosas cuándo y cómo, dónde y con quién, y con las demás circunstancias que debemos. Y este hábito, como tan universal que es, participan dél los demás hábitos morales y aun especulativos todos, según que cada uno se ejercita y pone por obra. (Parker, 220)

> (Actions are a question of will, but how and when one acts is a question of understanding. Discretion is nothing but a habit that stems from practical knowledge which allows us to undertake actions when and how we should, where and with whom we should, bearing all other appropriate circumstances in mind. And in this habit, as universal as it is, are found all other moral habits and perhaps even all speculative habits, depending on the way each person exercises and puts into action the discretion he possesses.)

Frías distinguishes between the intention to act ("voluntad") and the pragmatic operations involved in selecting the most expedient course of action ("cuándo y cómo, dónde y con quién" [when and how, where and with whom]). Discretion chooses the best game plan by taking variable tastes into account. As Maxim 101 of Baltasar Gracián's *Oráculo manual* teaches, "No hay defecto sin afecto, ni se ha de desconfiar porque no agraden las cosas a alguno, que no faltarán otros que las aprecien" [There is no failing which is not somebody's pet; nor need we lose hope because things as they are may displease some people, for there will be no lack of others to appreciate them] (122, 123. Tr. Walton). Not only can this faculty of discrimination help overcome adversity, but Gracián even trusts discretion to reverse fate, as he writes in Maxim 167, "el discreto de todo sale con vitoria, hasta de las estrellas" [The prudent man emerges victorious over everything, even the stars] (176, 177. Tr. Walton).

Calderón de la Barca's allegorical passion play (*auto sacramental*) *No hay más fortuna que Dios* [God is all the good fortune you need] mirrors many of Daza Pinciano, Frías, Castiglione and Gracián's observations regarding the power of discreet action. Calderón insists that, while discretion itself is not a virtue, the fulfillment of all virtue depends upon this quality. The character Fortune proclaims on behalf of discretion:

> Yo soy el alma de todas
> las perfecciones, supuesto
> que no hay virtud que sin mí
> logre su merecimiento:
> pues no siendo virtud, soy
> quien modera sus extremos,
> para que su elevación
> subsista siendo yo el medio;
> y si esto, Poder, no basta
> para haberte dicho en esto
> que soy la Discreción, hablen
> las experiencias, pues vemos
> que sin Discreción no hay
> virtud que no corra riesgo,
> pues virtud sin Discreción
> si no es vicio corre a serlo. (vv 838-853. In Parker 227)

> (I am the soul of all that is perfect,
> given that there is no virtue that, without me,
> can achieve its fullest potential:
> though I am not virtue itself, I am
> the one who tempers its extremes,
> so that its loftiness may endure
> by my being its mean;
> and, Power, if my having told you
> that I am Discretion does not suffice,
> then let experience speak, and then we will see
> that without Discretion there is no
> virtue that is not at risk,
> for virtue without Discretion
> is only vice about to happen.)

Excess transforms even the noblest trait into vice. For Calderón, discretion is a necessary accompaniment and precondition for goodness because it prevents overindulgence. Furthermore, recalling Covarrubias's definition, Calderón's Discretion governs the discernment of good and evil: "del Mal y el Bien / en mí está el conocimiento / por más que los disimule / la Malicia de los tiempos" [the knowledge of Good and Evil is in me, despite Maliciousness' best efforts to muddy the difference between them] (vv 854-859. In Parker 227). However, once discretion has been unhinged from moral ends it edges toward malice, impropriety and astuteness. This is the sense of Berganza's query in Cervantes's "The Dog's Colloquy"; "¿Quién hizo a esta mala vieja tan discreta y tan mala? . . . . ¿Cómo peca tan de malicia no escusándose la ignorancia?" [Who made this evil old woman so discreet and so wicked? How could she fall prey to such spite, not to mention ignorance?] (II 344).

The diverse properties of discretion may be divided into two broad classes. Belonging to the first are those features of discretion corresponding to the art of courtesy. These are social skills observable in judgement, speech and performance. Belonging to the second class are crafty maneuvers that confound direct observation, and which help the courtier to project a flawless public facade. The marriageable maidens of women's courtship fictions mobilize both of these facets of polite interaction to empower themselves in courtship, and in so doing, model for their readers the art and craft of courtesy. However, while discretion forms a common thread in Zayas, Carvajal and Meneses's courtship plots, remarkable differences in the treatment of this trope are also evident. In the following section, I foreground those observable and concealed facets of discretion that help to resolve courtship conflicts in María de Zayas's *Desengaños amorosos,* Mariana de Carvajal's *Navidades de Madrid* and Leonor de Meneses's *El desdeñado más firme*. These observations, in turn, can lead us to see with greater clarity the distinct lessons in courtesy that each courtship novels propounds.

Observable Facets of Discretion: The Art of Courtesy

Observable facets of discretion that reinforce women's position in courtship include discernment, moderation, pragmatism, modesty, propriety and caution. Beginning with discernment, I demonstrate that each of these facets of discretion exerts a decisive, but hitherto unrecognized effect on plot outcome.

Discretion operates as a cultivated (learned) property governing the decision-making processes entailed in courtship and marriage transactions. Characters mobilize this discerning aspect of discretion when judging people, performances and the disposition of finances, as for example where Blanca revels in her Flemish suitor's gallantry in Zayas's "Mal presagio casar lejos" [Only disaster awaits a bride far from home] (more fully elaborated in chapter 3), or where Doña Juana of Carvajal's frame tale defers her daughter Leonor's marriage in order to optimize her prospects. In the first instance, Blanca permits the niceties of courtship to bedazzle her into forgetting her elder sisters' grim fates at the hands of foreigners. Her discretion impaired, Blanca mistakes the theatrics of courtship under her brother's vigilance for the truth that her sisters' experience had evidenced: once removed from her family's sphere of influence, a bride falls completely under the her husband's power. After marriage, Blanca's disenchantment and ultimate destruction at the hands of her husband and father-in-law amounts to a return to her senses, but not a return to the relative freedom she had enjoyed during courtship. Discretion without power cannot empower, a lesson for which young Blanca pays with her life.

Carvajal's frame-tale character, d. Juana, who prudently waits to marry off Leonor until she has augmented her daughter's eligibility with a knighthood, also exercises discernment: "Respondió doña Juana que no trataba de casarla hasta concluir con un pleito que tenía, y esperaba la merced de un hábito" [Lady Juana replied that her daughter could not be wed until a certain legal claim she was pursuing was settled in her favor and she received her expected knighthood entitlement papers"] (15). By keeping Leonor's options open until her credentials improve, Juana parlays her daughter into an advantageous engagement with their noble proprietress's son and primogenitor, Antonio.

In addition to discernment, corollary qualities of discretion— moderation, pragmatism, modesty, propriety and caution—are also shown to affect female agency in courtship. Through negative example, María de Zayas's "Amar sólo por vencer" [Loving only to conquer] teaches the virtue of moderation in courtship. According to Matilde, the narrator of "Amar sólo por vencer," the purpose of her narrative is "para que sirva a las damas de desengaño, para no fiarse de lo bien fingidos engaños de los cautelosos amantes, que no les dura la voluntad más de hasta vencerlas" [to disabuse these ladies of their lofty notions about love, so that they will not be taken in by cagey casanovas with their fraudulent romances that last only as long as it takes to separate a maiden from her virginity] (331). She characterizes the victim of her tale, Laurela, as "mal leída en desengaños" [poorly versed in disenchantments], needy of a guidebook such as Zayas's to supplement her inexperience. Ironically, it is Laurela's nemesis, Esteban, speaking in drag as the maid, Estefanía, who admonishes women to tread a middle path between extremes of disdain and favor:

"ni han de ser las damas tan desdeñosas que tropiecen en crueles, ni tan desenvueltas que caigan en desestimación" [women must not be so disdainful as to stumble into cruel behavior, nor should they be so brazen that they bring contempt upon themselves] (318). Laurela does not ignore this advice; indeed she declares herself the enemy of extremes, "no soy amiga de prodigios" [I'm no fan of prodigies] (318). However, "Amar" demonstrates that Laurela's inexperience, the "canidez de [su] inocencia" [the absolute naiveté of her innocence] (323), leads her to behave immoderately, indiscreetly. If only Laurela had received the benefit of reading Zayas's volume before Esteban espied her, Matilde implies, the forewarned maiden could have forestalled disgrace.

Often, multiple aspects of discreet behavior may be seen to affect courtship within a single plot. Mariana de Carvajal's novella, "La dicha de Doristea" [Doristea's good forutne] both illustrates the negative consequences of indiscretion, and shows the merits and rewards that discretion assures for men and women alike. The narrative begins with Doristea defying her guardian's will and placing herself in the hands of her vengeful suitor, don Claudio. However, after undergoing rigorous experiential schooling in various aspects of the art of discretion, including prudence, propriety and modesty, Doristea regains her proper place in society. Exposure to Doristea's object lesson in turn impacts the frame tale's community of listeners. Antonio finds in the thematics of discretion a pretext for flirting with Leonor, causing Enrique to switch his courtship aspirations from Leonor to Lupercia.[10]

"La dicha de Doristea" opens with Doristea's kidnapping and near murder at the hands of her false suitor, don Claudio. When d. Carlos rescues Doristea from Claudio, he exercises propriety, seeking an opportune moment to discuss Doristea's plight with her: "Arrojóse Doristea a sus pies, agradeciéndole la vida y honra que le debía y el *discreto* Cavallero le dijo: —No es tiempo de responderos que importa apartarnos deste sitio. Y sin decir más, tomó la maleta" [Doristea threw herself at his feet, thanking him for saving her life and her honor, and the *discreet* knight answered her: "Now is not the time to discuss your situation; we must be gone from here." And without another word, he picked up her suitcase] (50, emphasis added). For his part, d. Carlos singles out two qualities which he esteems in Doristea: her beauty and her discretion, her other virtues serving only to confirm his devotion. When she requests a harp to play music for him, Carlos responds, "No bastaba para rendirme a tu belleza y *discreción* sin el tener otras habilidades para enriquecerme más" [As if your beauty and *discretion* hadn't captivated me already, you show me still other talents in order to win me over, a feat you'd already accomplished] (55, emphasis added). Doristea has correspondingly fallen in love with her protector. She sings him a poem allegorically elaborating the paradoxical tension between adoration and discretion: "El mirar por el decoro, / es confusión del sentido, / pues quiero dar al olvido, / aquello mismo que adoro" [Being ever-mindful of decorum is a contradiction in terms, for to do so, would be to cast aside the person I adore] (56). As an eminent and recently deceived noblewoman of Seville, Doristea determines to steer a middle path, to "mirar por el decoro," [be ever-mindful of decorum]; hence she resolves not to reveal her identity to Carlos immediately. On the other hand, she still hopes to reserve the possibility of an honorable engagement to d. Carlos. Unfortunately, d. Carlos, unaware that he has rescued a great noblewoman, begins to ask his mysterious guest for favors unworthy of her pedigree.

Doristea's tutelage in the art of discretion continues when her friend d. Inés offers her conventual refuge from the increasingly impatient d. Carlos: "Parecióle bien a Doristea *la prudencia* de su amiga y respondió hiziera lo que le pareciera conveniente" [Doristea approved of her friend's *prudence* and replied that she would do whatever Lady Inés deemed best] (60, emphasis added). Doristea escapes to the convent, where she dispatches to Carlos a letter disclosing her identity to him. Delighted to learn that his beautiful charge is also an eligible marriage prospect, Carlos asks his father's permission to marry Doristea. Upon hearing that his son had delivered a noblewoman from peril, protected her secretly in his house and now wished to request her hand in marriage, Carlos's father applauds his son's prudence: "Espantado me tiene lo que me decís, posible es creerlo por la satisfacción que tengo de que sóis *prudente*" [Your story has me horrified, and the only thing that allows me to believe it is the satisfaction I take in knowing that you are *prudent*] (63, emphasis added). The two are wed and Doristea's disgrace is transformed into honor.

The frame-tale recapitulates "La dicha de Doristea"'s manifest faith in the power of discretion. As the listeners single out Doristea's *recato* for applause. D. Antonio compares Doristea's modesty unfavorably to that of his dinner-companion, d. Leonor:

> —Señores, aunque vuesas mercedes tienen razón de alabar esta dama, no escusaré decir que nació del temor que tuvo al suceso de Claudio. Aténgome al *recato* de mi señora Doña Leonor, pues en dos años que habemos gozado de tan honrada vezindad, ha sido menester que mi madre enviude para merecer verla en esta sala, que si Doristea se guardó de Don Carlos fue temiendo no ser desgraciada. (67, emphasis added)

> ("Ladies and gentlemen, though you are correct in praising this lady, I must point out that her admirable behavior was born only of the fear

that the episode with Claudio provoked in her. I'll stand by my lady Doña Leonor's inherent *modesty*, because in the two years that we have lived under the same roof, only the occaision of my father's death was enough to put us in the same room together; if Doristea kept her distance from Don Carlos, she did so only because she feared she would be disgraced.")

Doristea only exercised modesty out of necessity, Antonio argues, while Leonor, free from imminent danger, has remained invisible in the house for two years. This exaggerated display of modesty impels Antonio to praise Leonor, a bold courtship gesture that amounts to a declaration of matrimonial intent.

Meanwhile, another frame-tale listener exercises that facet of discretion that assesses changing conditions and proceeds accordingly. One of the unmarried noblemen attending Lucrecia's Christmas party is d. Enrique. Although he had originally hoped to court Leonor, Antonio's praise of Leonor, cited above, preempts him. Jealous and confused, Enrique takes counsel with Antonio's mother, Lucrecia, who suggests that he court d. Lupercia instead. Enrique at once yields to her advice: "Pareciole al *discreto* vizcaíno eran palabras de cuidado y perdida la esperanza del casamiento que deseaba, no quiso perder la ocasión" [For the *discreet* Basque gentleman, her words carried a great deal of weight, and having lost all hope for a happy marriage with his first choice for a bride, he decided to seize this second opportunity for wedded bliss] (68, emphasis added). Whereas Antonio admires in Leonor a facet of discretion akin to modesty, Enrique's ability to transform an apparent defeat into victory by redirecting his courtship toward the more readily available Lupercia recalls Baltasar Gracián's strategic pragmatism: "Pero el discreto luego ve lo que se ha de hazer tarde o temprano, y execútalo con gusto y con reputación" [But the sensible man immediately sees what he will have to do, sooner or later, and he does it willingly, and in a way which redounds to his credit] (Maxim 268, 252, 253. Tr. Walton).

A final lesson underscored in Carvajal and Zayas's fictional discourse is the worthlessness of physical attractiveness unembellished by *recato* [modesty, honesty]. In the *Navidades*'s frame tale, Antonio inclines toward Leonor for "su hermosura y honestidad" [her beauty and honesty] (15); beauty unaccompanied by honesty, however, awakens only lust, not love, and certainly not the resolution to marry. Here, a proof-text can be found in Zayas's "Estragos que causa el vicio" [The vicissistudes of vice], in which d. Gaspar courts the youngest of four sisters, "si no de lo más acendrado en calidad, por lo menos de lo más lindo que para sazonar el gusto pudo hallar" [who, though not of the most refined quality possible, was at least pretty enough to whet his appetite]. The lady admits don Gaspar into her chambers at night, leaving Gaspar "si no enamorado, a lo menos agradado" [if not besotted, at least sated] (472). When d. Gaspar finds a corpse near the lady's rooms, he instantly associates the taint of death and dishonor with his wanton companion, interpreting the encounter as a warning to desist from his nightly visits: "juzgó que era aviso de Dios que se apartase de casa donde tales riesgos había . . . y más con mujeres que tienen por renta el vicio y por caudal el deleite" [he took this as a warning from on high to abandon this house where so much danger lurked, where the danger was augmented by these women who make vice their wherewithal and the pleasures of the flesh their currency] (474-475).

Zayas's 1647 *Desengaños amorosos*, by tracking the perils of indiscretion, and Carvajal's 1663 *Navidades de Madrid,* by teaching the efficacy of discretion, mobilize ritual interactions of courtesy to empower female characters (and their readers) in courtship. Such is not the case of Leonor de Meneses, whose 1655 *Desdeñado más firme* chronologically, structurally and ideologically resists the textual commitment to discretion evident in Zayas and Carvajal.

Indiscretion represents a dominant plotting pattern of Meneses's *Desdeñado*. For example, instead of depicting the spurned lover as a patient and faithful strategist (Carvajal's d. Duarte of "Zelos vengan desprecios" [Jealousy avenges disdain]) , or as a malicious instigator (Zayas's d. Esteban of "Amar sólo por vencer" [Loving only to conquer]), Meneses overwhelms and bewilders a suitor named don Jacinto with the mercurial vicissitudes of courtship. After d. Felipe selects another suitor to wed his daughter, Lisis, Jacinto allows emotions to cloud his actions: "estava retirado en una quinta suya, passando en ella harto mal: temores de dexado, zelos de su competidor, y ausencia de Lisis" [he was in seclusion at his country estate, and having quite a bad time of it, for he was suffering simultaneously from fear of rejection, the jealousy that his rival inspired in him, and Lisis' absence] (131). Isolated, deluded and irate, Jacinto composes for Lisis a self-indulgent poem of "quexas" [complaints] (134) condemning the blameless maiden for her father's decision (134). Jacinto's indiscretion provokes others, for Lisis responds to his unfounded attack with equal unreason: "No sintió los zelos que pudiera porque se acordaba sólo de su agravio. Y cúlpese a las mujeres tener poca razón" [He wasn't as jealous as he could have been, for he was thinking obsessively only of the extent to which he had been wronged. And he blamed women, all women, with their lack of reason, for his malaise] (135). Throughout the *Desdeñado,* tangled causal loops of impropriety, bungling and unreason soon snarl all participants in a grand courtship folly that is more fully explicated in chapter 5.

Subtler Manifestations of Discretion: The Craft of Courtesy

"No ser tenido por hombre de artificio, aunque no se pueda ya vivir sin él" [Do not be regarded as a crafty person, although it may be no longer possible to live without craft], admonishes Baltasar de Gracián in his "Manual of the Art of Discretion," the *Oráculo manual* (Maxim 219. Tr. Walton 216, 217) As Gracián's Maxim 219 attests, many discreet performances are calculated to remain self-concealing. Four aspects of discretion that elude direct perception are circumspection, adaptiveness, dissimulation and grace. This section begins with a review of the courtesy literature devoted to these self-concealing modes of discreet action, followed by an analysis of the empowering role that these strategies play within the causal economy of women's courtship fictions.

Particularly in masquerade, where the courtier is called upon, in Boscán's words, to "know how to choose well," *saber bien elegir* (IV, 334), circumspection, adaptiveness, dissimulation and grace expedite the achievement of desired courtship goals. Two-headed Janus, credited with the ability to anticipate the future while recalling the past, symbolizes circumspection in Alciati's Emblems as well as Daza Pinciano's above-mentioned Spanish adaptation, *Los emblemas de Alciati en rhimas españolas*. The month of January takes Janus's name because the two-faced god was thought to look back on the old year as well as forward to the new. Daza Pinciano translates *circumspectum hominem* as *hombre prevenido* [the forewarned man]: "Jano, bifronte, que conoces bien las cosas pasadas y por venir, y que contemplas lo de detrás y ves lo de delante: ¿por qué te pintan con tantos ojos y rostros? ¿Acaso no es porque esta imagen simboliza al hombre prevenido" [Janus, with your two faces, you who knows well all that has occurred and all that is to come, and who comtemplates both that which is behind you, and that which lays ahead, why do they paint your image with so many eyes and faces? Mustn't it be because such a portrait symbolizes the forewarned man?] (Sebastián 50).

The negative connotation of "two-facedness" also troubled theorists of the period; nevertheless, circumspection played a respected role in early modern statecraft. According to Covarrubias, the prudent prince must imitate Janus: "Imítenle pues, quantos goviernan si quiera para que se vea que es más natural efecto de la prudencia que de la traición el tener un hombre dos caras" [Imitate him then, all those who govern, and perchance you will realize that a man's having two faces is more a result of prudence than betrayal]. Glossing Alciati's symbology, Diego López would later write "Y assí tratando de la prudencia viene bien la pintura de Iano, el qual fue un hombre muy prudente y sagaz, lo cual muestra el título *Prudentes,* como si dixera que deven ser semejantes a Iano, y acordarse de las cosas passadas para proveer a las futuras, lo qual deven hazer los buenos Reyes, tomando exemplo de Iano" [Since we are on the subject of prudence, we must mention the portraits of Janus, a man who was both sage and prudent, as the title *The prudent ones* illustrates, as though it were saying that one ought to fashion oneself after Janus' image, taking the past into account in order to predict the future; this is what good kings, modeling themselves after Janus, ought to do] (Sebastián 50).[11] For Gracián, thinking ahead ("Pensar anticipado") ensures success: "Toda la vida ha de ser pensar para acertar el rumbo; el reconsejo y providencia dan arbitrio de vivir anticipado" [All our life long we must think things out in order to hit upon the right course (to take); consideration and foresight supply the judgement which enables us to live in advance] (*Oráculo manual,* Maxim 151, Tr. Walton 162, 163).

An ever-changing world limits the utility of circumspection; as Miser Federico of Castiglione's *The Book of the Courtier* concedes, "realmente sería imposible imaginar todos los casos que pueden ofrecerse" [it really would be impossible to forsee all the cases that could potentially arise] (Book II 124). Therefore, the courtier must supplement circumspection with adaptability. Miser Federico continues, "Y así, si el Cortesano fuere buen juez de sí mismo, sabrá bien conformarse con los tiempos" [And thus, if the Courtier is a good judge of his own character, he will know how to adapt himself to the times] (Book II 124). Gracián delivers similar advice in Maxim 288 of the *Oráculo manual,* "Vivir a la ocasión [Live as the occasion demands]: "No vaya por generalidades en el vivir . . . el sabio sabe que el norte de la prudencia consiste en portarse a la ocasión" [Do not run your life on general principles. . . . The wise man . . . knows that the first rule of prudence demands that he should behave as the occasion demands] (Tr. Walton 268, 269). Gracián's Maxim 58, "Saberse atemperar" [Adapt yourself to your company] explains that adaptiveness permits conservation of effort and resources: "No se ha de mostrar igualmente entendido con todos; ni se han de emplear más fuerzas de las que son menester. No haya desperdicios ni de saber, ni de valer. No echa a la presa el buen cetrero más rapiña de la que ha menester para darle caza" [You should not display the same degree of intelligence to every one; nor should you use more effort than is necessary. There should be no waste of either knowledge or worth. The good falconer does not release more birds than are needed for the chase] (*Oráculo manual,* Tr. Walton 90, 91).

Changing circumstances demand that the courtier correspondingly adjust his or her projected image or "figurative mask" (Rebhorn, 14) in a self-concealing process known as dissimulation. The art of dissimulation comes closer to evasion than to deception, as Gracián's Maxim 73 "Saber usar del desliz. Es el desempeño de los cuerdos" [Know how to be evasive. That is how wise men get themselves out of difficulties] suggests (*Oráculo manual,*Tr. Walton 102, 103). Castiglione warns the courtier not to lie about his abilities (II, 156-164), enjoining him to shape his mask to reflect qualities he really possesses (II 139-155), Elsewhere in the *Oráculo manual,* Gracián compares dissimulation with the discretion of the card player who does not reveal the hand that he has been dealt: "El más plático saber consiste en disimular. Lleva riesgo de perder el que juega a juego descubierto. . . . No le sepa el gusto" [The most practical kind of wisdom consists in dissimulation. The player who shows his hand risks losing the game. . . . Do not allow your inclinations to be known] (Maxim 98 "Cifrar la voluntad" [Conceal your purpose], Tr. Walton 120, 121).

Finally, the courtier fashions himself or herself into a work of art by wearing a mask of effortlessness in all courtly accomplishments from singing and dancing to conversing, to joking, to storytelling. According to Castiglione, the purpose of this "sweet neglect," in Ben Jonson's phrase (Burke 72), is to inspire wonder of everyone yet to wonder at none: "Pero en fin, digo que sería bien que supiese nuestro Cortesano tan perfetamente lo que ha de saber, que todo lo que hiciese y dixiese fuese hecho y dicho fácilmente y sin trabajo, tanto que todos se maravillasen dél y él de nadie" [In short, I say that it would be best that our Courtier know with such perfection that which he must know, so that his every word is said with ease, and his every action is done without effort, so that everyone will marvel at him, and he will marvel at no one] (Book II 155). The effortless grace that the courtier exudes is considered the truest mark of nobility.

Castiglione calls this unaffected grace *grazia* or *sprezzatura* in the *Cortegiano*. However, Boscán resists this terminology in his Castilian adaptation, the *Libro del Cortesano*, preferring the etymologically related *desprecio* [haughtiness, scorn], or the term *descuido* [nonchalance]:

> e per dir forse una nova parole, usar in ogni cosa una certa sprezzatura che nasconda l'arte, e dimostri, ciò che si fa e si dice, venir fatto senza fatica e quasi senza pensarvi. (*Il cortegiano* I, 22)

> usando en toda cosa un cierto *desprecio* o *descuido,* con el cual se encubra el arte y se muestre que todo lo que se hace y se dice, se viene hecho de suyo sin fatiga y casi sin habello pensado. (I, 5. In Morreale, "Castiglione" 163, emphasis added)

> (employing at all times a certain *haughtiness* or *nonchalance* which allows one to mask one's artfulness and which shows that everything one says and does comes out without toilsome effort, almost without having even consciously thought of it.)

In his courtesy guide, *El héroe* [The hero], dedicated to the memory of King Ferdinand the Catholic, Gracián names this *indecible gallardía* [indescribable gallantry] *despejo* [self-confidence], praising it above all other courtly attributes: "el despejo es 'alma de toda prenda'. "Es un realce de los mismos realces. . . . Las demás prendas adornan la naturaleza, pero el despejo realza las mismas prendas" [Ease of manner is at the heart of all talent. It is the most splendid of splendors . . . All other talents are merely superficial embellishments of one's own nature, but this ease, this self-confidence, actually heightens and enhances the talents one already has] (141).

The masterfully circumspect, adaptive, dissimulating and graceful courtier integrates these attributes so skillfully into his or her courtly performance that the onlooker remains unaware of the exertion taking place. Just as the vision of a swan gliding across a pond causes the observer to forget the furious paddling occurring beneath the surface of the water, the elegant nonchalance affected by the courtier blinds his or her audience to the complex operations involved in composing and projecting the pleasing spectacle before them. The novelistic challenge of textualizing this cluster of crafty behaviors which, by definition, defy direct observation, was solved by recourse to elaborate masking and testing scenarios, plots that granted access to the view "beneath the surface of the pond" while still conveying the superficial effect of effortlessness to their readers. In the following section, the four self-concealing courtship strategies noted above: circumspection, adaptability to change, dissimulation and that easy bearing that Boscán termed *descuido,* are seen to augment female characters' agency in women's courtship narratives.

The familiar folk motifs of disguise and the testing of suitors' loyalty resurface in Carvajal, Zayas and Meneses's courtship novels as pretexts for dramatizing the unseen craft of courtesy.[12] For example, Mariana de Carvajal's "La industria vence desdenes" [Effort vanquishes scorn] unspools a protracted drama of masking and testing that highlights the efficacy (and dangers) of circumspection. The narrative contrasts Jacinto's behavior toward an unwanted marriage prospect, Leonor, with the very different mask that he wears in the presence of Beatriz, whose favor he seeks. However, in order for the courtier to achieve a seamless transition from one mask to another he or she is obliged to remain attentive both to the old role and to the new. Like Janus, at the point of transition, the mind must remain open simultaneously to past and future. Unfortunately for Jacinto, as we shall see, Beatriz catches him in the act of changing masks, exposing his two-facedness to derision.

When rich but plebian Leonor offers Jacinto a carnation, he accepts the token, wearing a mask of noncommittal politeness: "Para hallarme favorecido, este basta" [It is enough simply to find myself so favored by you] (156). Nonetheless, even as Jacinto accepts the carnation from Leonor, he calculates a future reappropriation of the flower for the purpose of wooing Beatriz. Shortly thereafter, Jacinto changes masks to represent himself as Beatriz's ardent suitor. In this role, Jacinto bestows upon Beatriz the same flower he had just received from Leonor. Since Beatriz had seen Jacinto accept the flower from her rival's hand, however, his plan backfires: "le puso Don Jacinto el clavel en los rizos de la espalda [de Beatriz]; [ella] volvió la mano y quitándole le hizo pedazos y lo arrojó" [D. Jacinto placed the carnation in the curls at the nape of Beatrice's neck, but she reached back and, snatching the blossom out of her hair, tore it to pieces and flung them at him] (156). The delicate dance of circumspection repeats itself when Leonor, hoping to elicit Jacinto's sympathy, sings a pastoral lament about a spurned shepherd, alluding to Jacinto himself, snubbed by Beatriz. Yet Jacinto again subverts Leonor's intended meaning. Rather than allow Leonor to manipulate him into agreeing that the spurned shepherd deserves pity (which would amount to a complaint about Beatriz's rejection of him) Jacinto instead expresses envy that the shepherd in Leonor's poem was privileged to express his pain directly to his lady. Again Jacinto beams Leonor a witty and noncommittal face, while projecting to Beatriz the generous and forgiving image of a suitor anticipating reconciliation with his cruel mistress: "lejos de presumir su daño [Jacinto] quiso valerse de la referida letra diciéndola: —Mi señora Doña Leonor, ¡dichoso Lisardo pues merece que su pastora sienta sus males!" [far from making a show of his suffering, Jacinto decided to turn the lady's lament to his advantage, saying, "my dear Lady Leonor, how very fortunate this shepard Lisardo was, for he was able to provoke the empathy of his beloved shepardess!"] (165-166). Jacinto, accepting a carnation from one woman while intending to present it to another, or responding to Leonor's *letra* [lament] in terms which veil his affection for Beatriz, looks simultaneously to the past and future.

Jacinto and Beatriz both attempt to beguile one another in courtship by assuming Janus's double visage. Beatriz, who harbors sincere affection for Jacinto, remains hyper-conscious of her own poverty relative to her rival's wealth. Therefore she views Jacinto's favors circumspectly, fearing that his intentions toward her are less than honorable, and repels his advances at every turn. Jacinto's most mendacious gesture is to bait Beatriz into confessing her affection by actively courting her rival.[13] The ruse works, and although Beatriz accuses Jacinto of being "un hombre . . . mudable y falso" [a false and fickle man] (170), Jacinto rejoices at finally having glimpsed the passion hidden behind Beatriz's facade of disinterest: "Quedó tan loco de haber conseguido su empresa dando mil besos al papel, se determinó de apretar la cuerda para que saltara de una vez" [Delirious with joy at his ruse having achieved its goal, he kissed the paper a thousand times, and swore to reel her into his net once and for all] (170). Jacinto ultimately repairs his two-faced image and wins Beatriz's confidence. When the two are wed, Carvajal's omniscient narrator applauds the fact that Beatriz's powers of circumspection equal those of her new spouse: "Vivió casada largo tiempo con su amante esposo tan gustosa cuanto *prevenida* de no darle ocasión a que renovara los passados zelos" [And so she lived for many years in wedded bliss with the man who was both husband and lover to her, and she being sufficiently *forewarned* so as not to rekindle their past jealousies] (176, emphasis added).

Circumspection also occupies a privileged place in the novelistic discourse of María de Zayas's *Desengaños amorosos*. The *casos verdaderos* [true stories] (118) that each female guest recites at Lisis's storytelling soirée look backward in time to past disenchantments "para que las damas se avisen de los engaños y cautelas de los hombres" [so that the ladies are forwarned against the treachery and cunning of men]. Armed with precaution learned from others' misfortune, Lisis's first storyteller, Isabel/Zelima, hopes that her female listeners will gain the foresight necessary to prevent and even vindicate future affront. She fantasizes that those who hear her recite her *desengaño* [cautionary tale], "La esclava de su amante" [Her lover's slave girl], "antes de que ellos [los hombres] tengan tiempo de tratarlas [a las damas] mal, ellas les dan con la ceniza en la cara" [will blind men's eyes with cinders before men have a chance to treat these women badly] (124). Indeed, Isabel/Zelima's two names celebrate the circumspection that she has acquired through the experience of enslavement. The Moorish name Zelima symbolizes her past subjugation to Manuel, while queenly Isabel, the name that she reappropriates through the act of narrating her *desengaño*, gazes into a future informed by that experience, a future crowned by dignity, security, autonomy and female companionship.

Adaptiveness to changing circumstances comprises the second discretionary craft seized upon by female characters as they face the prospect of marriage in women's courtship narratives. Adaptiveness becomes evident only against a cumulative backdrop of episodes that test the courtier's powers of accommodation. The perilous changes of fortune that characterize Carvajal's byzantine-style fourth novella, "Del esclavo de su esclavo" [His slave's slave] compel Audalia, Xarifa, Matilde, Feliciano and Félix to prove their adeptness at negotiating a dizzying sequence of complications (see chapter 3). The plaque commemorating restoration of order in "Del esclavo de su esclavo" draws attention to the Algerian prince Audalia's capacity to adapt to captivity and to freedom without abandoning the aristocratic ideal of loyalty: "Cante la Fama inmortal / de la firmeza que alabo, /

que fue Esclavo de su Esclavo, / Audalia, por ser leal" [Let the voice of eternal reknown sing of the constancy that I now commend, that of Audalia who, wearing loyalty as his crown, consented to be the slave of his slave] (104).

At the other extreme, adaptiveness unguided by inner constancy produces mutability and caprice. Discourse One of Leonor de Meneses's *El Desdeñado más firme* introduces readers to its would-be hero, d. César, as he swings heedlessly from the sight of one beautiful woman to another: "Vio de la otra parte . . . una dama, que lo ayroso del talle le obligó a apearse para poder llegar a hablarla, si bien al ponerlo en execución se le atravessó delante un coche con quatro damas, una de ellas de tan ayroso bizarría que haziéndole olvidar el primer intento, le llevó la suspensión" [He saw, coming from the opposite direction, a lady who cut such a stunningly elegant figure that it obliged him to dismount in order to attempt to speak with her, and as he was doing so, a carriage passed in front of him carrying four young ladies, and one of them displayed such jaunty verve that he gazed at her in wonderment, the very sight of her having made him forget what he had just set out to do] (72). Shortly thereafter, Lisis of Toledo announces to César that men's mutability makes them all odious to her: "—Ni conozco esse don Carlos, ni intento hazer ningún hombre dichoso; los que no aman son ignorantes; los que aman pueden olvidar; los que olvidan son infames" [I don't even know this d. Carlos, nor do I intend to bestow my favors on any man; men who don't love are ignorant, those who do love are capable of forgetting, and those who actually do forget are loathsome] (84). Lisis of Toledo's distaste for men's inconstancy prefigures the machinations of her capricious suitors and fickle guardian, which, combined with repeated confusions of identity, collude to test even the most patient reader's adaptability to narrative permutation.

Although dissimulation is a courtly asset, it frequently degrades into deceit. As Zayas's frame-tale protagonist, Lisis, remonstrates to her male listeners "[H]aréis más transformaciones que Prometeo por traer una mujer a vuestra voluntad" [You men transform yourselves more than Prometheus in order to get a woman to succumb to your will] (331, 332). In the heat of her invective, Lisis has confused Prometheus with Proteus,[14] yet one nevertheless understands that the objects of Lisis's ire are not only adaptive men, but especially duplicitous ones. Lisis continues, "[D]aisla luego mal pago, faltando lo que prometisteis, y lo peor es que faltáis a Dios, a quien habéis hecho la promesa [de matrimonio]" [Once you have your lady, her affections are ill-rewarded, for you go back on your word, avoiding the marriage you had promised her, and the worst thing is that in breaking your promise of marriage, you fail in your duty to God, the One who heard your pledge] (333). A moral element (faltáis a Dios) separates courteous shape-shifting from discourteous fraud. Three cases, drawn from Carvajal's novellas, "Celos vengan desprecios," and "La dicha de Doristea," and from Zayas's *desengaño*, "Amar sólo por vencer" clarify for their readers this distinction between dissimulation and duplicity.

As noted in chapter 3, in Carvajal's "Celos vengan desprecios," the Spanish gentleman, d. Duarte, disguises himself as a gardener the better to serve Narcisa and protect her against her marauding Milanese suitors, Duke Arnaldo and Count Leonido. The arrogant Duke, convinced that "nadie había de gozar su hermosura si no era él, porque todos sus amantes eran unos pobres escuderos indignos de merecerla" [he alone and no one else would possess her beauty, since all of her suitors were nothing but poor pages unworthy of her affections] (120) and his equally ruthless rival, the count, who "no se descuidaba en vengar sus desprecios, hablando mal de la honesta dama con intento de deslucir su honor" [tirelessly avenged himself of her scorn, spreading falsehoods about the honest damsel in order to sully her reputation] (120), embittered Narcisa's life and strengthened her resolve not to marry either one. By contrast, d. Duarte wished only to serve Narcisa at a respectful distance and not offend her: "Sólo temía no enfadarla, mirando que se daba por ofendida de los que la servían" [He took care so as not to offend her, observing that she had indeed taken umbrage at the actions of those suitors who preceeded him] (120). Duarte's concealment in the guise of a gardener represents courtly dissimulation at its best, for it serves the purpose of winning favor without causing harm.

Carvajal's "La dicha de Doristea" and Zayas's "Amar sólo por vencer" link deceitful dissimulation to base pedigree. Claudio of "La dicha" tries to marry Doristea in order to sustain his gambling habit. When Doristea's aunt rebuffs his proposal, Claudio poses as Doristea's devoted suitor, intending only to rob her, and avenge the affront: "Quedó tan ofendido [por la repulsa de la tía] que propuso vengar su agravio. Y pareciéndole que el mejor camino sería galantear a la honesta doncella, lo puso por obra, sirviéndola con tan enamoradas demostraciones que ganó en su pecho el lugar que no merecía" [The whole business left him so offended that he swore to avenge the insult. And because it seemed to him that the best way to do this would be to court the chaste damsel, he undertook this task, serving her with such convincingly amorous displays of affection that he earned a place for himself in her heart that he did not deserve] (47). As d. Carlos rescues Doristea from Claudio's grip, he reproves the latter's betrayal of the aristocratic code, "—A un villano no hay para qué tratarle con respeto" [There is no need to treat a villain with respect]. With his remark, Carlos symbolically divests Claudio of his noble rank prior to gunning him down (50).

Whereas Carvajal's d. Carlos verbally repudiates Claudio's noble status, Zayas withholds noble status altogether from Esteban, the duplicitous suitor of "Amar sólo por vencer." Esteban, it will be recalled, assumes two false roles, first that of the maidservant "Estefanía," and later that of an enamored gentleman of Burgos (319) in his quest to seduce Laurela "sin más acuerdo que por cumplir con la sensualidad del apetito" [his only goal being to sate his lustful appetite] (324). Zayas seems to explain Esteban's immoral dissimulation by recourse to his non-noble identity, that of a carpenter's son.

Courting involves participants in a "highly complex, almost choreographed routine of proposal and response" (Bates 13). Carvajal ubiquitously links success in courtship not only to mastery of the art and craft of courtesy delineated up to this point, but particularly to their effortless blending into a convincing and totalized performance. In the *Navidades*, the terms *bizarría* [gallantry], *donaire* [charm], *desenvoltura* [ease], *gracia,* [grace], *brío* [verve] and *despejo* [confidence] convey this subtle ease of carriage, this ineffable yet unmistakable quality of grace which only the discerning aristocrat can both manifest and detect. The competition between Beatriz and Leonor for Jacinto's favor in "La industria vence desdenes" epitomizes this self-selecting dynamic.

As observed above, action in "La industria" revolves around Jacinto, who is challenged to choose a wife from among two available women, Leonor and Beatriz. Leonor, whose wealth far surpasses Beatriz's, nonetheless lacks her rival's pedigree. Their mismatch in social rank quickly becomes evident in the disparity between the two women's social grace. Leonor sings poorly: "Tomó [el instrumento] deseosa de parecerle bien al que ya la tenía sin sosiego. Aunque no le sucedió como pensaba por cantar unas coplillas algo licenciosas porque a Don Jacinto le pareció tan mal, cuanto no se puede encarecer" [She took up her instrument, anxious to make a good showing, since the man she was crazy about was watching. Things, however, did not turn out as she had planned, for she sang a few licentious little verses that made such a horrible impression on d. Jacinto that she sank irremediably in his estimation] (149). Her dancing proves to be even worse than her singing: "tocó el referido son y bailándolo los dos fueron tantos los ademanes de la viuda, que le pareció mucho peor que en las pasadas coplillas" [the appropriate musical strains were struck up, and, as the two danced to their rhythm, the widow's posturing was so exaggerated that her dancing made Leonor even less attractive to him than her singing already had] (157).

Jacinto recoils from what he immediately perceives to be Leonor's freakish posturing. Although he says nothing, he later parodies Leonor's miserable attempts to pass herself off as a noblewoman, by inviting the slave-girl, Antonia, to dance a "baile mandingo a lo Negro" [mandingo dance in the African style] with him: "traído el adufe lo bailaron con tantos gestos y ademanes que hizo el mancebo remedando a su Negra, que ya les dolían los cuerpos de risa" [a Moorish tambourine was produced, and they both commenced to dance with such an extravagance of gesturing and posturing—the impish young man imitating his negress—that everyone's bodies ached with laughter] (158). The physical gestures of Leonor's dance ("fueron tantos los ademanes" [the widow's posturing was so exaggerated]) juxtaposed against those of Antonia's ("con tantos gestos y ademanes" [extravagance of gesturing and posturing]) disclose the women's social inferiority, their shared inability to incite admiration through courtly performance. Instead, they become objects of ridicule.

Antonia is a black slavewoman and, as such, poses no threat to Jacinto or his social order. Leonor is white, wealthy, free. If not for one factor, discretion, she might be taken for a noblewoman. In courtship and courtly performance, a certain awkwardness, which true nobility instantly detects, betrays the secret of her base parentage. As Jacinto prances around with "su Negra" [his negress] in his arms, he exposes the unseen danger of contamination Leonor poses. For both himself and his audience, their caper ritualistically dispels the possibility of actually falling into the embrace of a low-born partner. Leonor's tell-tale clumsiness is transferred to Antonia, who contains it in its rightful social sphere, and the threats of upward mobility and social infiltration dissolve in waves of laughter.

Jacinto ultimately chooses the noble woman over her wealthier non-noble competitor by contrasting the grace inherent in the two women's courtly performances. A similar pattern informs all of Carvajal's novellas. For instance, Floripa's advisors in "La Venus de Ferrara" incline toward a man they believe to be the Duke of Módena's footman, rather than toward the Duke himself because the former carries himself with such grace: "Vueltos a Palacio los Grandes, les preguntó Floripa qué persona tenía el Duque. Respondieron, que a no traer consigo un Privado y deudo suyo, no era el Duque de malas partes; mas no tenía que ver con Laureano porque se aventajaba con la *bizarría*" [When the Grandees had returned to the palace, Floripa asked them what they had thought of the Duke. They replied that, short of bringing back a confidante or relative of his to attest to his character, they could only say that though there was nothing truly wrong with him, he couldn't hold a candle to Laureano, whose *gallantry* far surpassed the Duke's] (33, emphasis added). The Duke of Ferrara in the same tale recognizes in the peasant girl at his birthday party someone worthy of pursuit because of her disarming speech: "Gustoso del simple *donaire,* quitándose de la pretina una gruesa vuelta de cadena, se la dio" [Her straightforward charm beguiled him, and, taking a thick bracelet from the pouch at his waist, he gave it to her] (25, emphasis added).

Donaire cannot be hidden from the discerning eye, yet members of the nobility do not always succeed in actualizing this inborn grace. As Claudio's attempt on Doristea's life, mentioned above, reminds us, nobility is not immune from pettiness, miscreance and criminality. For Carvajal, Zayas and Meneses, the unhinging of discretion from pedigree carries different connotations. In the *Navidades,* as in Gálvez de Montalvo's introductory sonnet to the *Galateo español*, cited above, breeding functions *in potentia* requiring cultivation and practice for its full realization. This caveat explains the existence of nobly-born villains in the *Navidades* (Claudio of "La dicha de Doristea," Esperanza's father in "Quién bien obra" and Jacinta's gambling husband in "La industria vence desdenes") who betray their presumed inherent virtue with evil deeds. Inconsistency among the nobility also creates the possibility of competition among peers in courtship. All of Venus's suitors in "La Venus de Ferrara" are nobly-born, but only one is worthy of Venus's hand in marriage. The same is true of Narcisa's Italian suitors in "Zelos vengan desprecios," and Lisena's suitors in "Amar sin saber a quién" ["Loving an unknown lover"].

If nobility falls short at times of its potential for *despejo,* Carvajal absolutely bars the lower-born from possessing such refinements. The author imposes this law from the outset by excluding non-aristocratic characters from her narratives. Merchants, thieves, bankers, gypsies, and fortune-seekers are absent from Carvajal's cities and courts. Absent too is the Golden Age's personification of ambivalence toward upward mobility, the figure of the striving *pícaro* [rogue]. The closed doors of Lucrecia's *estrado* [salon] symbolize this hermetic space, in which, "retirado de la calle" [secluded from the street] and "libre de la murmuración de los vecinos" [free from the neighbors' gossip] (17) the storytelling festivities take place:

> Y cerraremos la puerta a que no haya unas excusas melindrosas que suelen ser feos lunares en los divertimientos. . . . Con que desde luego quedamos todos los circumstantes obligados a sacar en público nuestras habilidades y donairosas gracias, sin que haya quien se pueda excusar, porque será hacer una ofensa . . . y un agravio a todos los circumstantes que, habiendo intervenido en el pacto y concierto, haya quien falte a lo prometido. (228, 229)

> (And we'll lock the door so that no one will have to make any of those fussy, prudish excuses not to participate that usually cast a pall over merry gatherings such as ours. Of course all of us, everyone present, will thus be obliged to put our choicest talents and most charming wit

on display, and no one must ask to be spared his or her turn, for to do so would be an offense and an insult to all those present who, having participated as planned, find that someone can wriggle out of his or her turn at the last minute.)

Lucrecia's guests deem this pact of exclusivity a "buena y prudente disposición" [good and prudent arrangement] (229), concurring that the presence of persons of unknown quality would hinder their recreation.[15]

Contrasting starkly with the *Navidades*'s celebration of the sorting and courting mechanism of courtly grace, Zayas portrays few noblemen behaving nobly, and few noblewomen who possess the critical acumen required to forestall maleficence. Consequently, it behooves women to drop their chivalric illusions and, instead, to anticipate the worst from men. By exposing the proclivity of aristocratic men to abuse the privileges of their rank, Zayas's text arms her readers with the circumspection necessary to defend against men's wiles. Only Zayas's frame-tale narrator, Lisis, partially vitiates this glum view, for Lisis successfully outmaneuvers and eludes her unfaithful lover, d. Juan (see chapter 3), while appearing to do nothing of the sort. So seamlessly does Lisis conceal her vengeful archplot from her cousin Lisarda, her mother, Laura, her suitor, d. Diego, and from the target of her intrigue, d. Juan, that modern critics have been slow to credit Lisis with the crafty effortlessness that facilitates her ultimate triumph.

In Leonor de Meneses's courtship folly, the *Desdeñado más firme*, grace is the missing cipher that confounds d. Felipe's calculations as he tries without success to marry off his daughter and his niece. Much like Carlos Félix, who, in Discourse One, discreetly bows out of the narrative at Lisis's request, effortlessness turns its back on those who need it most, yielding to ponderous and ineffectual courtship gestures that lead nowhere. Curiously charmless, the *Desdeñado*'s plot allows gallantry and courage to swamp in storms of unreason that appear to obstruct rather than facilitate an apprenticeship in courtesy.

Discreetly Picking Wedlock

Chapter 3 regarded courtship from the perspective of social institutions that promoted or obstructed female characters' courtship aspirations, while the present chapter has approached courtship as a field of ritual interactions that could be taught and learned. I have highlighted the multifaceted critical category of discretion in order to foreground the practical teaching function that animated early modern women's courtship plots. However, it must be stressed that an important difference distinguishes the courtesy models that these novellas promulgate from the paradigms disseminated by contemporary courtesy manuals such as Castiglione's *The Book of the Courtier* and Gracián's *The Oracle*. Whereas the latter aim primarily to tutor men in the art and craft of courtesy, women's courtship fictions feature narrative situations and conduct strategies especially applicable to young maidens facing the prospect of marriage.

As elucidated above, the *Desengaños amorosos*, by showing men to exercise a degenerate form of discretion divorced from moderation and morality, schools prospective brides in the risks inherent in courtship. Only Zayas's intradiagetic character, Lisis, triumphs over men's duplicity, an achievement Zayas squarely links to Lisis's uncommon discretion. Carvajal's *Navidades* tutors readers in the art and craft of courtesy by asserting an unequivocal causal linkage between discretion and success in courtship, a link that enables all of *Navidades de Madrid*'s heroines to realize their matrimonial goals. Leonor de Meneses unhinges courtship from principles of discretion in the *Desdeñado más firme*. By representing simulacra of dysfunctional courtship, Meneses too avows the positive value of discreet action. Discretion is conspicuous not only for its ineffectiveness within the fictional economy of Meneses's novella, but also for its overall suppression. Intrinsically defective, the courtship mechanisms operative in the *Desdeñado* fail to conduct young women and men forward into matrimony.

Finally, in addition to approaching courtship as a social formation worthy of imitation (chapter 3) and as a field of empowering ritual interactions that requires training (chapter 4), chapter 5 situates courtship tropes within the political domain. Considered within the dynastic context of the H`apsburg Court, courtship leading to wedlock mattered not only to prospective couples and their families; it also constituted a pressing matter of state upon which the destiny of the Spanish empire depended. Zayas, Meneses and Carvajal picked powerful political figures to whom to dedicate their novels, men and women who favored particular matrimonial solutions to Spain's ongoing succession crisis. Chapter 5 identifies and reconstructs the royal courtship scenarios that Zayas, Meneses and Carvajal figuratively espoused in their courtship narratives.

Notes

1. As David Castillo notes, Baltasar Gracián distinguished between the *sujeto,* or brute subject, and the *persona,* or public subject constructed through writing ("Gracían and the Art of Public Representation," in *Rhetoric and Politics: Baltasar Gracían and the New World Order*, ed. Nicholas Spadaccini and Jenaro

Talens, Hispanic Issues 14 [Minneapolis: University of Minnesota Press, 1997], 203-204).

2. The example of Queen Isabel of Spain that will be cited below represents a conspicuous exception to this rule.

3. For example, Evangelina Rodríguez, following Edward Riley, characterizes the short stories popular in seventeenth-century Spain by their sentimentality, eroticism and violence (*Novelas amorosas, de diversos ingenios del siglo XVII* [Novels of romance by various wits of the seventeenth century] [Madrid: Castalia, 1987], 27).

4. This dialogue on the attainments of the scholar is staged between the rector of the University of Salamanca and nine professors. Probably written in the 1550s, it was not published until this century. See Peter Burke, *The Fortunes of the Courtier: The European Reception of Castiglione's* Cortegiano (University Park, Pa.: The Pennsylvania State University Press, 1995), 84-85.

5. Similarly, Francisco Rodrigues Lôbo's 1619 courtship novel, *Côrte na aldeia e noites de inverno* [Village court and winter nights] has been found to draw its dialogic conception and numerous themes from Castiglione's *Courtier* (Burke, *Fortunes*, 94-95).

6. Boscán's adaptation of Castiglione's work accommodates the civic values of the Italian text to the political reality of the Hapsburg monarchy. For a comparison of the original with its adaptation, see Margherita Morreale, *Castiglione y Boscán: El ideal cortesano en el renacimiento español* [Castiglione and Boscán: The ideal courtier in the Spanish renaissance] (Madrid: Anejos del Boletín de la Real Academia, 1959), Vol I, 109-112. All subsequent Spanish citations of the *Cortesano* refer to Boscán's adaptation.

7. "en definitiva, el argumento esencial de la nobleza solía ser la posesión inmemorial, la exención de pechos, el desempeño de cargos o la pertenecia a cofradias de nobles; el vivir noblemente y, en definitiva, el haber sido siempre reputado él y sus ascendientes como nobles" [in short, the essential definition of nobility was usually based on their possession of lands in perpetuity, their exemption from paying tributes, the way in which they performed their official duties, or their membership in fraternal organizations of nobles; living nobly, and most importantly, always having been recognized as noble of character and not just of lineage] (Antonio Domínguez Ortiz, *La sociedad Española en el siglo XVII* [Spanish society in the seventeenth century] [Madrid: Consejo Superior de Investigaciones Científicas, 1965], Vol. I, 179).

8. In 1635, Ana Caro dedicated her *Relación de las fiestas y octava de la Iglesia de San Miguel* [Tales of religious festivities at the Church of St. Michael] to Doña Leonor de Luna Enríquez, Countess of Salvatierra. Within that work, she dedicated the first of its three versified sections to another woman, Agustina Espínola, wife of the naturalized Genoese banking magnate, Carlos Strata (Lola Luna, *Leyendo como una mujer: La imagen de la mujer* [Reading like a woman: The image of the woman], 143-145). In 1655, Leonor de Meneses writing under the pseudonym "Laura Mauricia," dedicated her novel entitled *El*

desdeñado más firme to Doña Luisa María de Meneses, Countess of Portalegre and Marchioness of Govea.

9. *Tesoro,* hereafter.

10. The phenomenon by which an embedded narrative exerts perlocutionary force upon its frame has been called "intercalated narrative": "When telling and acting are not simultaneous, but follow each other in alternation, narration is of the fourth type, namely 'intercalated.' Classic examples of this type are epistolary novels, such as Laclos' *Les liaisons dangereuses* [Dangerous liaisons] (1782) in which the writing of letters often serves both to narrate an event of the recent past and to trigger an event of the near future" (Shlomith Rimmon-Kenan, *Narrative Fiction: Contemporary Poetics* [London: Methuen, 1983], 90).

11. *Declaración magistral de los Emblemas de Alciato con todas las Historias, Antigüidades, Moralidad y Doctrina tocante a las buenas costumbres* [Magisterial declaration of the "Emblems of Alciato" with all the history, antiquity, morality and doctrine that relate to proper manners and respectability] (Nájera, 1615). The edition cited is that of Valencia (1655), 107.

12. Stith Thompson's *Motif-Index of Folk Literature*, 6 vols. (Bloomington, Ind.: Indiana University Press, 1966), devotes an entire classification unit (H) to "Testing." The testing of suitors occupies sub-heading H310 (Vol. 3). Seduction by disguise appears under sub-heading K1310 (Vol. 4).

13. The disruptive behaviors by which Jacinto and Beatriz achieve symbolic leverage represent a state of alienation from interaction ritual. Jacinto is here engaged in "external preoccupation," that is, the deliberate disruption of a a social interaction by means of redirecting attention to an unconnected concern." Beatriz's counter-offensive, that of becoming ill in reaction to Jacinto's snub, has been called "self-consciousness," or summoning an improper degree of attention to one's own welfare. See Erving Goffman, *Interaction Ritual: Essays on Face-to-Face Behavior* (Garden City, N.Y.: Anchor/Doubleday, 1967), 117-120.

14. Prometheus was credited with bringing the knowledge of fire to mortals. Proteus changed form to avoid answering Odysseus's questions in *The Odyssey* IV. See Lillian Feder, *The Meridian Handbook of Classical Literature* (New York: Meridian, 1986).

15. The genesis of the modern novel, however, was to take a different tack. It is an irony of literary history that the exclusionary courtship novel would be repaid in kind as, one by one, readers would definitively close the covers on a genre that, on Christmas in 1663, had left them out. The only known reissue of the *Navidades* was undertaken in 1728 by Alonso de Padilla, who added two additional novellas by different authors and called the ensuing collection the *Noches entretenidas* [Nights of amusement].

5: Courtship as Political Allegory

> —Vuesa merced me excuse con ese señor, que yo no soy bueno para palacio, porque tengo vergüenza y no sé lisonjear[1]
>
> (—Your grace must excuse my behavior with that gentleman, as I am not fit for palace life, being both bashful and inept at flattery.)
> —Cervantes, "El licenciado vidriera" [Licentiate of glass] (II 56)

Chapters 3 and 4 demonstrate that Zayas Carvajal and Meneses "do" different things with courtship motifs, yet each testifies that the marriage vow, implicit or explicit, present or absent, constitutes the formative utterance of their respective narrative adventures. Having inquired into courtship and marriage tropes *in* early women's fiction, let us conclude by turning to fiction itself *as* courtship, as an exchange between a patron and a writer, a release of symbolic capital into the power nexus constituted by Philip IV's royal Court. The object of this final chapter will be to determine the mutual benefit that publication of the *Desengaños,* the *Desdeñado* and the *Navidades de Madrid* might be thought to accrue to their respective authors and dedicatees. The premise underlying this approach is that traces of client-patron power relations can be decoded in the novels and their paratexts. The key to deciphering the novels and recovering these traces has been lost to modern readers, simply because it was an ephemeral rather than a durable key, stamped in the flimsy tin of current events rather than tempered on the putative forge of universal truth. By bringing the situational specificity of each story to bear upon its interpretation, a range of signification opens to view that casts additional light upon women's convergence on the courtship novel genre.

Dedicated novels are bivocal, at once addressing both the consumer-at-large (implied reader) and the historically specified patron (explicit reader). Zayas, Meneses and Carvajal dedicated their courtship novels to influential explicit readers. María de Zayas dedicated the *Desengaños* [Disenchantments] to d. Jaime Fernández de Silva, primogenitor of the Ducal House of Híjar. Leonor de Meneses dedicated the *Desdeñado más firme* [Scorned yet steadfast] to a powerful relative, Luisa María de Meneses, Countess of Portalegre. Mariana de Carvajal dedicated the *Navidades de Madrid* [Christmastide in Madrid] to Eusebio von Pötting, an Austrian count with personal ties to the Holy Roman Emperor, Leopold I of Austria.

Courtship novels dedicated to powerful patrons served a variety of ambitions and purposes, evidence for which arises at textual, paratextual and metatextual levels of discourse. Metatextually, the novelist and her patron occupied unique sites in a complex political nexus based on dynastic marriage alliances. Each writer and her dedicatee favored different courtship resolutions to the Spanish succession crisis that rocked Philip IV's Court between 1647 and 1663. By correlating historical data with textual evidence, many situationally specific elements of courtship plots spring into relief. Paratextually, the dedication projects an idealized representation of the balance of power between client and dedicatee, revealing and simultaneously cloaking under heavy folds of conventionalized rhetoric the political motivation for courting the dedicatee's favor. Textually, patron-writer ambitions are inscribed allusively in imagery, plotting mechanisms and narrative structures.

I begin this inquiry into women's courtship plots as political gestures with an overview of literary patronage in early modern Europe, taking Elizabethan England as a paradigm.[2] After setting forth a number of incentives that literary patronage offered to authors and a corresponding number of benefits that patronage entailed for the dedicatee, I will then pose the following set of questions for each novelist/patron pair: "What benefit might a given author (Zayas, Meneses, Carvajal) expect from a given patron or patroness (De Silva, Meneses, Von Pötting) (or vice versa) at the time of publication?" "By what rhetorical means does each author court her patron/patroness's favor and how does her fiction benefit her patron/patroness in return?"

Literary Dedications and the Politics of Patronage in Golden Age Spain

Dedicating a novel to an illustrious personage could be an act of solidarity, appeal, flattery and/or persuasion. Sponsoring the authorship of fiction could likewise serve many functions. To choose a dedicatee demands a double reading: first such a choice requires inferring that a given work will please a selected patron, and second, the selection of an actual or prospective patron requires discerning that he or she occupies a position from which to return the favor in a manner useful to the author/client. Regardless of whether the author selected her patron before or after writing the novel (or whether the author even composed the dedication at all), someone—author, testator or entrepreneurial bookseller—matched a certain novel with a certain powerful recipient. This "match" between a work of fiction and a potential protector holds great promise for revealing what Cedric Brown and Arthur Marriotti call the "particular local circumstances which shaped the understanding and interpretation of particular works" (1).

How a novel would satisfy its explicit reader, and how the explicit reader could satisfy an author are questions that point to the novel as a courtship gesture rather than as a disinterested, atemporal work of "art." As such, these questions help to return imaginative literature to the historical circumstances that informed its creation. As M. D. Jardine notes of literry patronage in Renaissance England, "The products of patronage are often occasional and historically specific; of all texts, they are the most likely to bear the trace of the material circumstances of their production, and are therefore resistant to the aesthetics of intertextuality" (304). While it might be thought that attention to material circumstance of a novel's production limits interpretative freedom, it is also true that any critical approach necessarily precludes another. For example, Paul Julian Smith rightly observes with respect to Gracián's *Criticón* [The master critic] that "the privileging of voice and literal meaning . . . is bought at the cost of the repression of writing and figuration; and critics' praise of . . . unity and coherence . . . is at the expense of a model of structure which would account for substitution and play" (108). Certainly, locating meaning at a specific historical juncture inhibits the critic's personal brand of playfulness; however, this need not impoverish or reify the reading process. Rather, politicized interpretation can reveal textual subtleties that contemporary readers enjoyed, but from which latecomers are excluded due to unfamiliarity with referential frames that prevailed at the time of publication. Original writers and readers understood the text's "multiple cueing," its "systematic concatenation of signals in more or less the same direction . . . coded into a text by a writer" (Vasvari, 1, 2) Modern readers who aspire to an equivalent linguistic competence must concertedly acquire the extralinguistic field of reference taken for granted by contemporary readers, through historical research and reconstruction. Therefore, prior to analyzing the client-patron power relations represented in each novel, it will be convenient to specify the historical parameters that shaped this dynamic.

Patronage engaged writers and their protectors in an exchange which benefited both parties. Materially speaking, client/authors aimed to gain prestige and influence at Court while patrons also wished to promote themselves and to extend their sphere of influence. Let us first outline five benefits that a patron could bestow upon the author/client. Obviously, patrons often granted authors who dedicated their work to them "money from their own pockets" (Griffin 2). Additionally, citing the patron's name in a dedication lent weight and legitimacy to the author's claims. Melinda Zook speculates that this was British author Aphra Behn's motive for finally turning to patrons after publishing her first nine plays without dedications:"she may well have felt the need for publicly-acclaimed alliances with powerful men and women" (79). Third, familiarity with the patron could lead to being introduced to other influential members of the patron's circle. Fourth, the "protection" that a patron extended could shield the author from slander, libel or censure. And finally, the patron's name functioned as a form of credit or "symbolic capital" that elevated the author's prestige and increased the value of future writings (Griffin 18-26).

Less obvious are the benefits that the author/client bestowed upon his or her patron. Dedications chiefly benefited their dedicatees by honoring them. Just as the duty and occupation of the courtier was to glorify his king, dedications aimed to exalt the dedicatee, whether he or she occupied the apex of the power pyramid at Court, or a lower rung.[3] To understand the value of this honoring function in a social hierarchy that placed a premium on honor, it is useful to contemplate the curious specter of a monarch deprived of courtiers, as envisaged by novelist Gabriel García Márquez in *El otoño del patriarca* [The autumn of the patriarch]. Márquez depicts the apocalyptic landscape of a Court erased of courtiers. Fear of sedition has eliminated even the most servile display of loyalty. Courtyards and salons where once intriguing sycophants clustered now languish abandoned and despoiled by herds of feral cows. By contrast, seventeenth-century European monarchs still relied upon the aristocracy to help them dramatize their power, while courtiers in turn relied upon other courtiers of inferior rank for the same purpose. Although early modern rulers distrusted their courtiers (a historical reality at which Calderón de la Barca's uxurcide drama, *El médico de su honra,* [The physician of his honor], hints by portraying His Majesty prowling the streets to espy the common gossip) kings still depended upon huge retinues of subjects to enact spectacles of sovereignty and submission. For Alan Sinfield, "the monarch is always a monarch with courtiers. The royal figure is frozen into a sheer representation of power, but this power can be exercised only through the courtiers, whose devotion to the person of the monarch only lightly masks a competition for the possession of a part of his or her authority" (263-264). Philip IV's capital, Madrid, according to Jonathan Brown and John Elliot, provided "the vast supporting cast necessary to ensure that every public appearance of the king became a major spectacle" (38). Among that loyal supporting cast one finds novelists, whose labors enhance their patron's prestige and cachet.

In addition to honor, writers pledged their patrons loyalty. Golden Age authors commonly asserted loyalty in their dedications through the conventionalized language of vassalage. For example, Carvajal's dedication closes with the formula "B. L. P. de V. Exc." meaning "besando los pies de Vuestra Excelencia" [kissing Your Excellency's feet] (4). Adulation represents another loyalty trope; dedications normally expend a great deal of ink accumulating the patron's credentials and praising his or her achievements. The frontispiece of Zayas's *Desengaños amorosos,* for example, identifies its dedicatee as follows:

Al Excelentissimo Señor Don Jaime Fernández de Yxar, Silva, Pinos, Fenollet, y Cabrera, Duque y Señor de Yxar, Cõde de Belchite, Marques de Alenquer, Cõde de Valfagona, Viscõde de Canet y Illa, Señor de las Baronias de la Portella, Peramola, Grions, Alcaliz, Estacho, y Gentilhombre de la Camara de su Magestad & etc. (111)

(To the most excellent gentleman d. Jaime Fernández de Yxar, Silva, Pinos, Fenollet y Cabrera, Duke and Lord of Yxar, Count of Belchite, Marquis of Alenquer, Count of Valfagona, Viscount of Canet and Illa, Lord of the baronies of Portella, Peramola, Grions, Alcaliz, and Estacho, and Gentleman in Waiting to His Majesty and etc.)

This heaping of the patron's decorations and titles produces a secondary benefit that Dustin Griffin calls "magnificence," a necessary attribute of power that enhances the patron's prestige. Fame was another corollary perquisite that accrued to the dedicatee. Wherever the volume to which the dedication pertained circulated, the patron's renown would spread. Furthermore, once a work had been dedicated to a patron, it became his or her "intellectual property." Just as an art collector of the period by amassing the works of great artists of the day augmented his or her status, the literary patron "possessed" each work that inscribed his or her name in its dedication (Griffin, 30-42).

Finally, author/clients could support their patron's political causes in present and future writing. For this reason, Griffin insists that the matching of clients and patrons is necessarily a politically motivated gesture: "It is very difficult for us to separate their 'political' activities from their work as 'patrons' of literature, just as they too would have found it difficult to separate 'politics' from 'literature'" (43). This is not to say in the process of courting their patrons' favor that novelists blindly endorsed their protectors' views; to the contrary, the writer might well assume an admonitory posture aimed at reorienting the patron's outlook. In assessing the impact of the patronage context on the meaning of a dedicated text, it is important not to assume a simplistic "top-down" flow of power. The chain of command from royal authority to the production of fictional texts passed through patrons, writers and implied readers. Patrons themselves adhered to competing factions; the writers who served them held differing views than their sponsors, and prospective consumers also influenced the final shape of the text. It is impossible, amid this dance of conflicting vectors to expect cultural production to "obey" or mirror imperial policy. Rather than representing "cultural control," a servile survival strategy for starving poets, or a brute exercise of royal prerogative, the patronage system consisted of an elaborate exchange network, a traffic in images, influence and wealth. This is as true of the latter Hapsburg Court as it was for the Court of Elizabeth I of England, of which Alan Sinfield writes:

> We should, therefore, perceive the Elizabethan state not as a static totality whose power structure is revealed in the ideology of monarchy, but

as diverse and changing, the site of profound contradictions. Then contest will not be a matter of individual, abstract and totalized subversion ... but of the continual exploitation of diverse opportunities for specific classes, fractions and categories to confirm or extend economic, political or ideological power. And literary texts will be perceived as involved in such contest, striving through their handling of fictions and images (including royal images) for power in and through the cultural apparatus. (265)

If ideology is defined as a strategy of legitimating inequality and exploitation "by representing the social order which perpetuates these things as immutable and unalterable—as decreed by God—or simply natural" (Dollimore, Sinfield 211, 212), patrons sought ideologically compatible writers who would ratify their rights and privileges. Likewise, writers selected their dedicatees with the expectation that their text would please that personage by satisfying his or her ideological and aesthetic requirements. The danger, however, lay in the fact that the patronized writer often occupied a different rung of the social ladder than the patron, and likely disagreed with his viewpoint. Client-writers mastered the art of encoding their own personal caveats, interests and perspectives into the patron's script without too blatantly appearing to do so. In this manner they continued to promote their own interests while retaining the necessary loyalty of their protectors.

"Context does not determine meaning," affirms Dustin Griffin, "but it alerts us to a wider range of possibilities, and proposes a world of diverse interests and controversies in which original writers and readers operated" (3). To specify the balance of client-patron interests inscribed in dedicated novels with any precision, to discern in this manner the "trace of the material circumstances of their production" (Jardine 304), those circumstances must first be known. Ignorant of the stakes for which patrons and writers were vying, it is easy to overlook textual traces of a Court, a dynasty and an empire only vaguely familiar to the modern reader. In the following section, I outline in the broadest of strokes, one facet of Hapsburg political life that preoccupied the nobility of Court with particular urgency in the latter years of Philip IV's rein: the dynastic crisis of 1646-1661. A courtship intrigue in its own right, the diplomatic struggle to marry off King Philip IV's two daughters so as to secure Spain's destiny finds its rejoinder in Zayas, Meneses and Carvajal's respective courtship narratives.

The Hapsburg Succession Crisis: 1646-1661

Martín de Cellorigo's *Memorial* [Memorial], cited in chapter two, promoted a vigorous pro-marriage policy to replenish Castile's war- and epidemic-ravaged population. However, wedlock attained even more sharply politicized connotations in an empire that cemented international allegiances through matrimonial union. Foreign policy in such a society aimed to perpetuate the Crown's power through dynastic succession, matrimonial alliance and military aggression. For the autocratic monarchs of seventeenth-century European ruling families, aristocracy and peasantry existed, not as beneficiaries of government (as subsequent Enlightenment rhetoric would profess), but solely for the sake of securing these dynastic ends. As historian John Lynch pointedly observes with respect to Philip IV, "He had no conception of a national monarchy transcending dynastic interests" (171).

Royal women comprised an unavoidable feature of the dynastic landscape. Spain's queens and princesses (in contrast, for example, to England's famous Virgin Queen, whose corporeality was uneasily gendered male) were awkwardly necessary female bodies, without which the monarchy could not very well get along. By virtue of both their biological indispensability in producing heirs, and their capacity to wed foreign princes, thereby thickening the thin waters of political allegiance with blood loyalty, infantas, queens and their vast retinues installed themselves deep within the halls of power of the House of Hapsburg (Magdalena Sánchez 1-10 and *passim*). In this light, royal women's role, not only as heir-incubators, but as arbiters of a nation's destiny, cannot be overstated.

A telling event early in Philip IV's reign illustrates the decisive role that courtship plots played in Hapsburg Court politics. In 1621, just as young Philip IV was succeeding his father to the Spanish throne, the Prince of Wales (Charles I) appeared unannounced in Madrid to extend a marriage proposal to Philip's sister, María Infanta [Princess María]. Although the gesture took Spain by surprise and horrified an Infanta for whom wedding a heretic amounted to hurling her soul into infernal perdition, the advantages of a British-Spanish allegience were obvious: safety on the high seas and a powerful ally against Spain's fractious neighbor to the north. Even the prince's Anglicanism was justified by means of papal dispensation to clear the way for the match. The Count-Duke of Olivares characterized the anticipated union of the England and Spanish royal families as nothing less than the "greatest matter ever to present itself to this Monarchy."[4] Indeed, the disintegration of those marriage negotiations was followed, in the year 1625, by an Anglo-Dutch naval attack on the Spanish seaport of Cádiz (Elliott 240, 241).

Dynastic politics assumed particular urgency from 1646-1700, the period during which Zayas, Meneses and Carvajal converged upon the courtship novel genre. A protracted succession crisis dominated the latter half of Philip IV's reign and beyond. In 1644, Queen Isabel of Bourbon died, and two years later, Crown Prince Baltasar Carlos also died, leaving Spain with no male heir and no means of producing one. Until a viable male successor was born, Philip's dynastic hopes would rest in the lap of his daughter, the Infanta María Teresa, legally enti-

150   *Chapter Five*

tled to inherit the throne in her own name, or to confer the right to rule upon her consort. Confronted with these prospects, public opinion condensed around various possible politically motivated marriage alliances. Thus, in 1647, the year that Zayas published her *Desengaños amorosos,* politics at the Hapsburg Court consisted largely of advocating one royal courtship scenario over another.

Before looking ahead to the political circumstances that Meneses and her patron encountered in 1655, several complicating factors facing Zayas warrant further remark. For 1647 was also the year that Philip was obliged to declare bankruptcy to relieve his treasury's debt, thereby calling into doubt his ability to dower the Infanta. The political climate was further troubled by the king's recent dismissal of his unpopular *valido* [royal favorite], d. Gaspar de Guzmán, the Count-Duke of Olivares in January of 1643. As the count-duke's influence waned, the ensuing power vacuum had given rise to various coup attempts, conspiracies and assassination plots. For example, Spain lost a vast landholding in 1640 when the Duke of Braganza crowned himself King João IV of a newly liberated Portugal. The following year, João's brother-in-law, the Duke of Medina Sidonia attempted (without success) to duplicate the Portuguese coup by naming himself sovereign of Andalusía (Lynch 160). Amidst this tumult, courtiers were divided with regard to the future of the Spanish Crown. Aside from secessionary and regicidal impulses, some factions sided in favor of succession by Philip's bastard son Juan José ("el Serenísimo" [The Most Serene]) of Austria; others favored the Infanta, María Teresa. Further disagreement arose as to whom María Teresa should wed: future Holy Roman Emperor Leopold I of Austria, or the future Louis XIV of France. These are some of the "material circumstances" in which Zayas and her patron, Jaime Fernández de Silva were likely to have been embroiled and whose traces in the *Desengaños* remain to be explored.

By the time Leonor de Meneses published the *Desdeñado más firme* in 1655, Philip IV had remarried. His second wife, fifteen-year-old Mariana de Austria was originally intended to wed Philip's son, Baltasar Carlos, but was hastily betrothed to Philip when the young prince died. The consanguineous proximity of this uncle-niece pair doubtless contributed to their reproductive woes, for, although the couple produced an astounding number of progeny, few survived their first year. The shining exception was the birth in 1651 of a second Infanta, Margarita of Austria, the rosy-cheeked blonde princess immortalized in Velázquez's *Las meninas* [The maids of honor]. Meanwhile, João IV had died, leaving Portugal in the hands of his widow, Leonora de Guzmán. Now more than ever, the diplomatic stability and internal order of the Iberian peninsula depended upon the courtship of princesses and queens, their politically motivated marriage alliances, and the mysterious working of their reproductive organs.

The Hapsburg dynastic crisis had assumed a new form by the time Carvajal's *Navidades de Madrid* came into print in 1663. France finally agreed to terminate its draining war with Spain, in exchange for which Louis XIV claimed María Teresa as his bride. The Peace of the Pyrenees Treaty solemnizing Maria Teresa's role as the "instrument of Franco-Spanish reconciliation" was signed in 1659 (Elliot 541). This turn of affairs necessitated the betrothal of the younger Infanta, nine-year-old Margarita, to her uncle, Leopold I of Austria, who had long cherished hopes of wedding María Teresa. The projected Spanish-Austrian marriage was meant to reassert the mutual loyalty of the two halves of the Hapsburg dynasty. Furthermore, on November 11, 1661, Queen Mariana gave birth a male child, Charles II *el hechizado* [the bewitched]. Unfortunately, Charles, too sickly to rule, developmentally delayed and, as events would prove, sterile, hardly represented a solution to Philip IV's predicament.[5]

Because politics and courtship converged during the seventeenth century in the question of royal marriages, it is reasonable to speculate that courtship plots provided a platform for critiquing the most gripping political issue of the period: the crisis of dynastic succession facing the latter Hapsburgs. Three conditions prepared early modern readers to expect so called "escapist" literary genres to participate in political discourse: the Baroque penchant for allegory in general, the necessity of speaking indirectly demanded of the perfect courtier, and autoreferential promptings of the texts themselves.

Accustomed to viewing *Autos sacramentales* (elaborate outdoor spectacles allegorizing the Mystery of Christ), readers of the period were deeply imbued with an allegorical sensibility. Historian R. Trevor Davies illustrates this allegorical mindset and the ease with which conventional symbols could encrypt political messages in his account of Philip IV's estrangement from his illegitimate son, Juan José of Austria. According to Trevor Davies, Juan lost his father's favor after calling on him at the palace: "to show him an enamel representing Saturn looking complacently at the amours of Jupiter and Juno (who were supposed to be brother and sister), hinting thus at a plan for marrying his half-sister, the Infanta Margarita, as a way of strengthening his claim on the throne" (110). Philip, "shocked and depressed by his son's apparently measureless ambition, refused ever to see him again, even on his deathbed" (110-111). For Philip IV, mythological figures habitually represented something other than themselves. Similarly, in France during the same period another overspent symbolic system, the pastoral romance, would succumb to allegorical reinscription. In the midst of the French civil war of 1648-1652, Madame de Scudéry would publish the first volume of her famous 14,000-page, ten-volume novel, *Artamène ou Le Grand Cyrus,* [The grand Cyrus] discovered shortly thereafter to mirror novelistically the political events of the Fronde (DeJean 44).

Another aspect of Baroque culture conducive to allegorized political commentary was the courtier's ideal of *sprezzatura,* translated by Boscán into Castilian as *descuido*. *Sprezzatura* demanded the outward appearance of indifference while charming, impressing and ultimately, winning the loyalties of onlookers or interlocutors. How could a writer engage in political reflection or invective while affecting disinterest in such matters? In the realm of letters, the bivalent courtship plot provided an allegorical screen for writing about power machinations at Court without appearing to do so.

Finally, by novelizing the act of interpretation itself, courtship fictions actually teach their readers to read between the lines. In Zayas and Carvajal's cases, the novels' intradiegetic (frame) narrative interprets events narrated at the diegetic (story) level. In Meneses's unframed narrative, characters nonetheless recite or send verses, which other characters then interpret. As fictional audiences rehash and evaluate the novels and poems that they have just heard, they model an interpretative process for the reader to emulate. For example, Zayas's characters gloss not only the *desengaños* [tales of disillusionment], but also the poetry recited betimes. In the following excerpt from the *Desengaños'* frame tale, Estefanía criticizes Isabel for depicting a cruel lady in her poem, thereby vindicating men's complaints about women. Estefanía automatically generalizes from the case of Isabel's cruel lady to the case of all women, and fears that this analogous interpretation will fuel the misogynistic discourse that the women are trying to curtail: "—Cierto hermosa doña Isabel, dijo, acabada la música, doña Estefanía—, que probaremos muy bien los engaños de los hombres cuando vos estáis notificando en vuestros versos rendimientos de un galán y desdenes de una dama" ["It is true, lovely doña Isabel," said Estefanía once the music had ceased, "that we will prove beyond question the deceits of men, and yet in your verses you are making a case for the submissiveness of a suitor faced with the scorn of a damsel"] (Yllera 408). However, Isabel rebukes Estefanía for this overly-literal approach to her verse. Whereas poetry may represent experience, she admonishes, it also symbolizes fantasy or desire: "—No todos los versos tienen héroes—respondió Isabel—, y advertid, señora doña Estefanía, que yo he cantado lo que ha de ser, que no lo que es. Y tengo por sin duda que no todos los poetas. sienten lo que escriben; antes imagino que escriben lo que no sienten" ["Not all poetry has heroes," responded Isabel, "and observe, Lady Estefanía, that I have sung of what must come to be, and not what is. And I consider it beyond question that not all poets feel what they write; rather, I imagine that they write things they do not feel at all"] (408). Not only Estefanía, but the reader as well learns how to read the *Desengaños* properly: not as brute testimony about what is (history), but, as an allegorical fantasy about what could be (poetry).

Ross Chambers coined the apt phrase a "story and situation" to theorize the historicity of fictional texts. By positing a loosely allegorical relationship between Court politics (actual or projected) and courtship fictions, I aim in the explications that follow to underscore previously unobserved points of textual contact between story and situation, between narratives and the conditions of their narrativation. I assume that each dedicatee, as a powerful Court figure, preferred a particular outcome to Spain's succession crisis, and that each author, and/or publisher either endorsed or opposed the explicit reader's preference. These situational convergences or divergences of interest produced a series of political fantasies, allegories that symbolically addressed specific political outcomes. The explications that follow correlate key passages and narrative features of each text with available data regarding the political position of its dedicatee. Clearly, pending additional documentation and scholarship, these analyses must remain less conclusive than conjectural. My aim with each explication below is not to convince the reader of its truth, but rather to call attention to a historical likelihood, an inquiry that welcomes future challenge, refinement and documentary support.

"Engolfada en mis desventuras" [Adrift amid my misfortunes]: Courting Jaime Fernández de Silva

Nicolás Antonio catalogued the earliest known edition of María de Zayas's *Desengaños amorosos,* that of Zaragoza, 1647, entitled *Parte segunda del sarao y entretenimiento honesto* [Second part of the soiree and decorous diversion] (Yllera 70). The volume was dedicated to Jaime Fernández de Silva, eldest son of Rodrigo Sarmiento de Silva, Duke Consort of Híjar. If the *Desengaños* was a courtship gesture directed to the young Duke of Híjar, what benefit might Zayas and her protector have gained from entering into this client-patron relationship in the year 1647? By what rhetorical means does Zayas court Jaime Fernández's favor in the *Desengaños* and how do the *Desengaños* benefit the future duke in return?

It comes as little surprise that Zayas's *Desengaños* should invoke the protection of a descendent of one of Zaragoza's most illustrious lineages of writers and literary patrons. Jaime Fernández's grandfather, Diego, Count of Salinas, was a renowned poet; his father, d. Rodrigo de Silva, Duke Consort of Híjar, distinguished himself as a generous patron and doyen of literary culture. Numerous luminaries of the day paid homage to Jaime Fernández's father. In 1635 the royal chronicler, Joseph Pellicer de Tovar, dedicated to d. Rodrigo a treatise entitled *Idea de la Comedia en Castilla: Preceptos del Teatro de España.* [The idea of the comedy in Castille: Precepts of the Spanish theater].[6] Luis Vélez de Guevara dedicated his satiric *El diablo cojuelo* [The limping devil] of 1641 to de Silva, whom he dubs "patria general de los ingenios donde todos hallan seguro asilo" [common fatherland of clever souls, where all find certain sanctuary], and to whom he ascribes the initiative for rescuing the *Diablo* manuscript from the oblivion of the author's files.[7] The duke participated in the "Insigne Academia de Madrid" [Distinguished Academy of Madrid], a select literary academy presided over by Francisco de Mendoza that met in Madrid from 1623 through 1637, and he collaborated with Sebastian Francisco de Medrano in an unsuccessful effort to establish an even more exclusive academy,"La peregrina" [the wayfarer]. Jaime's father also judged and sponsored numerous *certámenes* [poetry contests] and literary festivals (141-147).

However, it was fellow Zaragozan, Baltasar Gracián, who delivered the most daring tribute to d. Rodrigo de Silva in *El discreto* [The discreet gentleman] (1641), an instruction book on good governance dedicated to young Crown Prince Baltasar Carlos. Gracián closed *realce* [highlight] XIX of *El discreto,* "Hombre juicioso y no-tante" [The judicious and observant man], by asserting that de Silva epitomized the essential quality of discretion, and that Gracián had modeled his portrait of the ideal prince on the duke himself:

> De esta suerte discurría con el autor el comprensivo, el grande entendedor de todo, el excelentísimo señor, duque de Híjar, sucesor en lo entendido y discreto del renombre de Salinas y Alenquer, no sólo en el título, sino en la eminente realidad, *que es eco este discurso de tal magistral oráculo.* (117, my emphasis)[8]

> (And thus, the author would speak with this sympathetic man whose great mind understands all things, this most excellent gentleman, the Duke of Híjar, successor of Salinas and Alenquer in knowledge and discretion, not in name alone but in eminent reality, and *of such a masterful oracle this treatise is merely a poor echo.*)

Less discreetly put, the influential Jesuit in the passage above endorses the Duke of Híjar as Baltasar Carlos's worthiest guide and tutor in matters of statecraft, effectively nominating him for *valimiento* [the position of royal favorite and confidant] to the future King of Spain.

Several circumstances suggest that Zayas and Jaime Fernández's father traveled in the same cultural circles. Zayas and d. Rodrigo both shared Madrid-Zaragoza connections. Zayas first published both of her novel collections in Zaragoza, home to Rodrigo's third wife, Doña Isabel Margarita, Fourth Duchess of Híjar, through whom Rodrigo rose to his title.[9] In Madrid, Zayas is thought to have participated in Mendoza and Medrano's literary academies (Yllera 13 n14) where she likely coincided with the duke. An intertextual link has also been detected. Historian Ramón Ezquerra Abadía posits formal and thematic similarities between a lyrical interlude found in Zayas's 1637 novella "El desengañado amado y premio de la virtud" [The disillusioned lover and virtue's reward] and an undated poem of Rodrigo de Silva anthologized in volume 6 of *El parnaso español* [The Spanish Parnassus] (135, 136). Zayas's verse appears on the left and the duke's on the right below:

Fugitivo pajarillo que por el aire te vas, inconstante a mis finezas, ingrato a mi voluntad (136n1)	Gilguerillo fujitibo que bien supiste buscar a pesar de mi cuidado la preciosa libertad (135)
(Fleeing little bird that soars away through the air, fickle when faced with my favors, never repaying my fondness in kind)	(Little bird that so adroitly did flee in spite of my attentions in search of precious liberty)

If indeed the use of so commonplace a baroque conceit as that of a bird escaped from its cage can be burdened with intertextual portent, a question of literary indebtedness arises: who imitated whom? I contend that d. Rodrigo's verse relied upon and refashioned Zayas's, and that the similarity between the two represents a tribute to Zayas's poetic prestige. Híjar's high regard for Zayas would arguably magnify the latter's incentive for dedicating her future work, the *Desengaños amorosos,* to the Duke of Híjar's primogenitor, d. Jaime Fernández.

In order to comprise a tribute, Híjar's verse must be shown to have been composed later than Zayas's. A subsequent stanza of Híjar's poem sheds further light on its date of composition relative to Zayas's 1637 poem. In the following stanza, the poet remains imprisoned while the bird flies free to enjoy the company of the Sun and Moon:

Goza [el pájaro] del Sol y la Luna
mientras que la obscuridad
de la noche me acomapña
en tan larga soledad (136)

(Have your romp with the Sun and Moon
while I languish in such long-lived loneliness,
with only the darkness of night
for company)

A standard poetic convention during this period of kings and favorites was to depict the monarch as a sun and his *valido* or favorite as a lesser orb that revolves around and reflects the monarch's brilliance. In Cervantes's *Exemplary Novel,* "La gitanilla" [The little gypsy girl], for example, Ronald Cueto identifies a similar planetary conceit in one of its eight intercalated poems: "Junto a la casa del Sol / va Júpiter; que no hay cosa / difícil a la privanza / fundada en prudentes obras" [Wherever the house of the Sun goes, so goes Jupiter; for nothing is difficult for favor founded in wise works] (Sieber I, 68. In

Cueto 65). Read allegorically, the Sun in the Duke of Híjar's stanza, cited above, may be seen to allude to Philip IV, the Planet King, and the "Moon" to his *valido*. From 1621 to 1643, Philip favored as his *valido* the Count-Duke of Olivares, whom he subsequently replaced with Luis de Haro. Híjar's poetic narrator complains that a prolonged solitude, "tan larga soledad," imprisons him in darkness, removed from the twin light sources mentioned above. But which "moon," Olivares or de Haro, does the poem invoke? By answering this question, the text can be dated before 1643, during the Olivares years, or after, during de Haro's *privanza* [tenure as favorite or confidant of the king].

Rodrigo de Silva fell into disgrace and was exiled from Court during de Haro's ministry. According to Ezquerra Abadía, Híjar "aspiraba ardientemente a ser valido de Felipe IV" [ardently aspired to become Philip the Fourth's favorite] (120). When De Haro rose to power, the duke and a clutch of similarly disgruntled nobles confabulated to discredit the king's new minister. Their machinations exposed, Híjar alone suffered punishment. De Haro exiled him from Court to Villarubia de los Ojos in La Mancha, where he remained isolated and humiliated from March 1644 until 1646 (128). The "moon" from which the poet complains that he is estranged may well be Luis de Haro, which would date Híjar's verse seven to nine years after the publication of Zayas's "Fugitivo pajarillo" [Fleeing little bird]. During the "larga soledad" [long-lived loneliness] of his exile to La Mancha, Rodrigo de Silva, held Zayas's writing in sufficiently high esteem to appropriate her poetic image of the inconstant warbler in order to allegorize his desire to return to Court.

Even without taking into account this somewhat circumstantial evidence of the duke's high regard for Zayas's writing, it is not difficult to surmise that Zayas stood to derive protection and possible support by dedicating her novel to the son of a well-known literary patron of her day. In fact, it made more sense to make d. Jaime the dedicatee than his father, a trend that Enrique Suárez de Mendoza would emulate in 1665, when he devoted the second edition of his *Eustorgio y Clorilene* [Eustorgio and Clorilene] (158) to d. Jaime. Not only was Rodrigo still out of royal favor in 1647, he was also reputed to be embroiled in an elaborate scheme to assert his hereditary rights (acquired through marriage to doña Isabel) to the Aragonese throne. If he succeeded, Jaime Fernández stood in line to become the next King of Aragon. Although secret, the duke's alleged plot may have been known to Zayas. At the very least, she would have known that Rodrigo's prestige had declined as a result of the de Haro affair, while Jaime's honor was still intact. Surely it made more sense to dedicate the *Desengaños* to the impressionable younger Híjar than to his maverick and controversial father.

Events soon proved the sagacity of Zayas's selection of dedicatee. In August of 1648, d. Rodrigo and two coconspirators were arrested and charged with attempting to overthrow the king. The plot that Rodrigo would be convicted of masterminding called for assassinating Philip IV, neutralizing Infanta María Teresa's claim to the throne by kidnapping her and marrying her off in Portugal or France, cleaving the united kingdoms of Castile and Aragon with military assistance from France, crowning Híjar himself sovereign of Aragon, and, in the absence of a legitimate heir to Castile, pressing Híjar's claim (as Philip IV's cousin) to the Castilian throne as well (Ezquerra Abadía 9-21). Híjar's coconspirators confessed and were duly executed. The duke, who, even under torture, denied his role in the coup-attempt, remained imprisoned for the rest of his life.

Turning from the benefits that Zayas might have been expected to derive from her client-patron relationship with d. Jaime, to the benefits that the dedicatee stood to gain, 1647 marked a propitious year to impart a boon to d. Jaime Fernández de Silva, future duke of Híjar. Most conspicuously, before the reader turns the first page of the *Desengaños,* Zayas's dedication, cited earlier, glorifies and publicizes the younger de Silva's many titles and landholdings. Offered at a time when d. Jaime's father was still recovering from the scandal of 1644-1646, this heaping of magnificence offered the young Duke a welcome dividend. In addition to adulation, Zayas grants de Silva the honor of association with her prestigious name. Zayas had earned renown as a novelist with the publication of the *Novelas amorosas* [Love stories] in 1637, which had undergone at least six reprintings in the decade following its initial release (Yllera 69).

The year 1647 also marked a decisive year for marriages in the Híjar family, creating new opportunities to serve the younger duke. That year, Jaime Fernández's sister, Teresa Sarmiento de la Cerda wed the Marquis of Valero, d. Juan de Zúñiga y Sotomayor y Mendoza, future Duke of Béjar (131, 132), and the elder duke delegated a trusted family agent to begin negotiating Jaime Fernández's match.[10] The coincidence of surnames between Zayas and Teresa's intended (María de Zayas y Sotomayor and Juan de Zúñiga y Sotomayor y Mendoza) raises conjecture that the author of the *Desengaños* may have been related to d. Juan, and that the marquis's union with Teresa also ushered Zayas into the vast familial network of the house of Híjar just as her novel was being finalized for publication. Zayas's dedication could have served as a preliminary calling card to remind Jaime Fernández that his sister's marriage had just related him to a powerful literary figure and potential political ally.

It is also likely that Zayas knew that Teresa's wedding paved the way for contemplating Jaime's marriage prospects. By dedicating her courtship novel to d. Jaime Fernández at a time when his marriage was being negotiated and plots were afoot that would poise him to inherit the throne of a newly independent Aragon, Zayas arrogated to herself the positioned of counselor or *privado* to one of Spain's (or at least one of Aragon's) most potent political figures. Although it may well have been unseemly or difficult for Zayas (as a woman, perhaps as a newcomer to the family) to counsel Jaime Fernández directly, the subterfuge of fiction permitted her to impart political advice to her dedicatee without restraint. Thus I propose a bivocal interpretation of the *Desengaños*. To its implied readers, Zayas's cautionary tales delivered an anti-matrimonial invective, while to its dedicatee, the young duke preparing to realize his father's exalted political ambitions, Zayas's narrative served, paradoxically, as a marriage guide and *Regimiento de príncipes*, or Guide to princes.

Joan Scott makes it easier to read the *Desengaños* as a veiled political guidebook by calling to mind that "gender is a primary way of signifying relationships of power" (1067). Whereas for the implied reader, Zayas's *desengaños* paint a bleak picture of the battle of the sexes, for Zayas's explicit reader, d. Jaime Fernández, men's victimization of women in the *Desengaños* figures allegorically for brute political aggression that obeys no laws and respects no boundaries. As such, the tales offer a series of instructive vignettes on how not to abuse the power that Zayas's young dedicatee would soon wield should his father's political designs bear fruit. This cautionary impulse is evident in *desengaño* four, "Tarde llega el desengaño" [A lesson learned too late], in which the principal character learns two lessons about political survival and diplomatic marriage invaluable to a future ruler. It is significant that the character who learns these lessons is named Jaime of Aragón, for in the event that Jaime Fernández de Silva were to inherit the Aragonese throne, he too would bear that title.

First d. Jaime of "Tarde" learns the folly of conceding too much power to a woman, and second, he discovers the foolishness of the opposite extreme, that of conceding to her too little. Lucrecia, the first woman with whom d. Jaime becomes involved, holds excessive power as symbolized by her leading Jaime, passive and blindfolded, into her chambers. Jaime jeopardizes this arrangement by disobeying Lucrecia's demand for anonymity and revealing her face, prompting her to issue orders for his assassination. Forced to flee for his life, Jaime soon replaces Lucrecia with her double, Elena, a perfect "retrato" [likeness] (247), the sole difference being that now the power relations are reversed because Elena is poor and dependent on Jaime.

Whereas blindfoldedness had symbolized Jaime's earlier powerlessness, now muteness, or the lack of an opportunity to verbally defend herself, evidences Elena's lack of autonomy with respect to Jaime. In effect, an African slavewoman jealous of Jaime's favoritism toward Elena persuades d. Jaime that Elena had cuckolded him by consorting with her cousin. Jaime readily believes this self-serving lie, and without stopping to hear Elena's version of the story, at once burns the supposedly offending cousin alive. Instead of killing Elena as well, he consigns her to subsistance at the margins of his Court, forcing her to beg for scraps under the table, and to drink water out of her cousin's skull. Then Jaime elevates the tale-bearing slavewoman to the heights of prestige that Elena had formerly enjoyed:

> *La otra* que por la puerta salió era una negra, tan tinta, que el azabache era blanco en su comparación, y sobre esto, tan fiera, que juzgó don Martín que si no era el demonio que debía ser retrato suyo, porque las narices eran tan romas, que imitaban los perros bracos que ahora están tan validos. . . . Traía la fiera . . . una saya entera con manga en punta, de un raso de oro encarnado tan resplendeciente y rica que una reina no la podía tener mejor. (237, my emphasis)

> (*The other woman* who came through the door was a negress, so inky-skinned that obsidian would appear white by comparison, and moreover, so wild that d. Martin judged her to be, if not the devil himself, then quite a faithful likeness of him, for she was so snub-nosed that her face looked just that of one of those pug dogs so popular now. The beast wore a gown made of a reddish-gold satin with dolman sleeves which was so rich and resplendant that not even a queen's raiments could have been finer.)

The elevated slave-woman, who completely infiltrates the precincts of Court represents the "Other," in this terrifying emblem, in stark contrast to the legitimate wife, literally cast down by her ill-counseled husband. D. Jaime precipitates this monstrous violation of the "natural" hierarchy by heedlessly acting on the unsubstantiated testimony of an underling. If Jaime Fernández wishes to conserve his power and resist similar manipulation and usurpation, Zayas's parable directs him to tread a middle path between relationships of excessive servility or extreme autocracy. Likewise the narrative counsels Jaime with respect to his own impending marriage. Both marrying "up," symbolized by Jaime's match with the tyrannical Lucrecia, and marrying "down," represented by his union with impoverished Elena, produce imbalances of power. Instead, the narrative closes on a note of matrimonial parity as the witness character, d. Martin, "escarmentado en el suceso" [forewarned by the incident] (254), returns home to wed his cousin, that is, his exact equivalent in pedigree.

In addition to instructing Jaime Fernández in the art of governance and directing his gaze toward a suitable spouse, Zayas's narratives may be seen to lend allegorical support to the Híjars' political goal of founding a new Aragonese dynasty. As noted earlier, in 1647, with no male heir to the Spanish throne and no queen to produce one, Castilian political stability rested with the marriage prospects of Philip IV's daughter, María Teresa. The likelihood that the Infanta marry a foreign prince who would strengthen and unify the Spanish Crown "boded ill" for the Híjars' separatist aspirations. As chapter 3 demonstrates, Zayas's novellas, particularly "Mal presagio casar lejos" [Only disaster awaits a bride far from home] and "La perse-

160   *Chapter Five*

guida triunfante" [The triumph of the fugitive damsel] portray exogamy in a negative light. In fact, any royal marriage, endogamic or exogamic, represented a threat to the Híjars' reputed plans by raising the specter of competing claims to the throne. This may explain why Zayas limns even domestic marriages such as those of Pedro and Rosaleta (Italians living in Palermo) of "El verdugo de su esposa" [His wife's executioner], or Jaime and Elena (Spaniards who spent summers in the Canary Islands) of "Tarde llega el desengaño" as disastrous.

On the other hand, sending the Infanta María Teresa into religious reclusion would forestall the possibility of a male heir to the Spanish throne and perpetuate the unstable conditions favorable to the Duke of Híjar's separatist designs. Again, Zayas offers allegorical support for her patron's interests. Inés of "La inocente castigada" [Her innocence punished], Beatriz of "La perseguida triunfante" [The triumph of the fugitive damsel], Isabel of "La esclava de su amante" [Her lover's slave-girl] and Lisis of the *Desengaños*'s frame tale all step off the *camino real* [11] [royal road] of matrimony yet appear none the worse for taking the road less traveled (see chapter 3) to the convent. Even a strategy of postponing marriage for a later date (Lisarda's choice in Zayas's frame tale) receives higher marks from Zayas than immediate wedlock.

Any whisper favoring the disinheritance of Spain's sole legitimate heir to the throne, María Teresa, harbored sedition. While Rodrigo de Silva's reputed pretensions to the Aragonese and perhaps Castilian thrones derived from legitimate genealogical and legal claims, his alleged efforts to usurp those of María Teresa, and to murder her father, Philip IV, in order to assert those prerogatives were clearly unlawful. Did Zayas go so far as to support her patron's alleged disloyalty to the crown? The *Desengaños*' first novella, "La esclava de su amante" lends itself to seditious interpretation by obliquely discrediting the king, thereby justifying his overthrow.

Onomastic allegory may be detected in the names of "La esclava"'s principal characters, Isabel and Manuel. A false "savior," Manuel dishonors and abandons Isabel, just as her namesake, Spain's recently deceased Queen Isabel of Bourbon had been dishonored by her philandering husband, King Philip IV (whose nocturnal escapades were widely blamed for his failure to produce a viable male heir, thereby precipitating the present succession crisis). However, Manuel receives due punishment when murdered by an indignant ally of Isabel. By comparing Philip IV to a false savior, the fictional discourse rationalizes his removal (assassination) and replacement by a worthier monarch. The text further challenges the king's authority by situating the action against the backdrop of the Catalonian revolt of 1640, an insurrection motivated by mounting disillusionment with Hapsburg leadership.

"La esclava" closes with a *romance* [ballad] on the *topos* of jealousy which fans the flames of Zayas's anti-monarchical subtext. Mingled amidst its clichés ("nacen celos del amor","es tan malo darlos que tenerlos" [of love jealousy is born; it is just as bad to provoke jealousy as it is to be jealous]) the poem's fourth stanza warns that those whose unfaithfulness provokes jealousy prove themselves to be unworthy of esteem:

> Quien pide celos no estima
> las partes que le dio el Cielo,
> y ensalzando las ajenas,
> abate el merecimiento.
>
> Está a peligro que elija
> su mismo dueño por dueño
> lo que por reñir su agravio
> sube a la esfera del fuego. (168)

(He who provokes jealousy does not respect
the shares of love that Heaven granted him,
and in exalting those which belong to another,
he degrades his own merit.

He is in danger who chooses his own master,
supplanting the master provided for him by Heaven,
for the latter, proclaiming herself wronged,
will enlist heaven's wrath on her behalf.)

Philip's notorious infidelity, stanza four insinuates, represents a failure to fulfill his sacred duty as king, and jeopardizes his Divine right to rule ("abate el merecimiento" [he degrades his own merit]). Stanza five at first appears utterly commonplace. He who pledges his love to another always runs the risk of inciting his mistress's jealousy, which she will proclaim to the very heavens. However the juxtaposition of the last verse of stanza four with the first verse of stanza five—"abate el merecimiento / Está a peligro" [he degrades his own merit / He is in danger] sounds an ominous note. Like Isabel's unfaithful lover, Manuel, unfaithful King Philip IV has placed himself in danger. Yet Isabel (de Bourbon)'s dishonor will be avenged, according to this allegory, by appealing to "la esfera del fuego", the "sphere of the Sun King", young Louis XIV of France, from whom Rodrigo de Híjar hoped to obtain military aid for his coup.

Finally, it should not be forgotten that the story of an indomitable female character named "Lisis" frames all ten *desengaños*. Only Lisis succeeds in containing the matrimonial disenchantments exposed during her *sarao* and transforming them into a happy ending ("No es trágico fin, sino el más felice que se pudo dar" [This ending is not tragic, but rather the happiest possible]) (510) (see chapter 3). While it is tempting to subject Lisis's name to onomastic scrutiny, such an inquiry is unlikely to establish a univocal role for the *Desengaños*' central character. Like the image of the sun, which iconographically could represent Louis XIV the Sun King, or Philip IV, the Planet King, *lis,* the lily, carried associations to both Spanish and French royalty. On one hand, the *fleur de lys* symbolized French sovereignty; French troops wore the *fleur de lys* emblazoned on their shields. On the other hand, a lily also adorned the Spanish crown. Historian Martin Hume relates that as queen Isabel of Bourbon lay on her deathbed on October 5, 1644, she requested that the crown be brought to her chamber because its lily was reputed to contain a fragment from the true Cross (392), a powerful symbol of both personal and national redemption. The inscription of a triumphant *flor de lys* in the heart of the *Desengaños amorosos* emblematizes the deliberately ambiguous operation of Zayas's double-edged discourse. To the implied (loyalist) reader, the lily points to the conspicuously vacant seat of the Spanish Queen, to the expectation either that Philip IV would soon remarry and regenerate his lineage, or that the Infanta María Teresa's marriage would achieve a similar effect. However to Jaime Fernández, Zayas's explicit reader and destinatary, the lily's bellicose petals point beyond the Pyrenees to France, whence Jaime's father awaited his deliverance in the form of military aid for the Aragonese cause.[12]

In conclusion, for Zayas and her dedicatee in the year 1647, mutual benefit lay in the elder duke's alleged pretensions, whether they took the form of dispossessing the Infanta and placing Jaime on the throne of an autonomous Aragon, or merely resulted in recuperating royal favor. Either sequence of events would presumably elevate Zayas as an Híjar supporter to the inside track—in Madrid, or at a newly constituted Zaragozan Court—where the author could now tutor her protégé freely, without recourse to the subterfuge of fiction.

"No temo la censura" [I do not fear censure]: Courting the Countess of Gouveia

Leonor de Meneses dedicated her courtship novel, *El desdeñado más firme* [Scorned yet steadfast] of 1655 to a relative, Luisa María de Meneses, Countess of Portalegre and Marchioness of Gouveia. In piecing together an account of the mutual rewards that the two relatives might have garnered by entering into a patron-client relationship in 1655, five helpful generalizations emerge. First, Leonor and Luisa Maria were longtime companions; second, Leonor de Meneses's intellectual accomplishments enhanced her family's established record of cultural achievement; third, by the year 1655, when the

Desdeñado came into print, d. Luisa had come to occupy a higher rung of the recently restored Portuguese Court hierarchy than her novelistically-inclined relation d. Leonor; fourth, the *Desdeñado* appears to have circumvented both Spanish and Portuguese vetting systems, and finally, client and patron shared royalist (pro-Portuguese, anti-Spanish) sympathies. After adducing paratextual, biographical and historical support for these claims, I will specify in greater depth the pair's common political vision. Finally, I will locate traces of this vision within *El desdeñado más firme*.

Leonor's life up to the year 1655 may be chronologically outlined as follows. Born around the year 1625, at sixteen the author of the *Desdeñado* became a lady-in-waiting to Queen Luisa of Portugal where her relative d. Luisa served in the same capacity. D. Leonor married d. Fernando Mascarenhas, Count of Serem, around the age of eighteen (1643). Fernando owed his elevation to the title of count to having fought in Bahia in favor of João IV's rebellion against Spanish rule.[13] Within the next six years, the young countess gave birth to a son who died shortly after she was widowed in 1649. Six years later, in 1655, the thirty-year-old widowed countess, possibly residing in Paris, dedicated the *Desdeñado* to her relative and former serving companion, Luisa Maria. D. Leonor died in her late thirties in the year 1664, apparently due to complications arising from the birth of her fourth child by her second husband, whom she wed in 1661. (Whitenack, Campbell 2-4).

Whether Luisa and Leonor met for the first time in Lisbon in the service of Queen Luisa, or whether they knew one another since childhood remains to be established. At any rate, a document dated January 1, 1641, entitled "Nomina das Pessoas q tem ordenado e moradias da Caza da Raynha Nossa" [Directory of titles and salaries of those persons belonging to the House of Our Queen], listing members of Queen Luisa's royal household, includes the names "Dona Luiza Maria de Menezes" and "Dona Lyanor de Menezes" among those of fourteen ladies-in-waiting (*Damas*) whose salaries were set at 10,000 reales each.[14] It must be recalled that the royal household was in its infancy at this time, following the nearly bloodless revolt of 1640 known as the Restoration that elevated King João IV, formerly known as the VIII Duke of Bragança, and his wife, Andalusian heiress Luisa Francisca de Guzmán, to the throne of Portugal.[15]

Leonor de Meneses's intellectual standing within a family renowned for its erudition has also been established. Whitenack and Campbell indicate that she mastered philosophy, music, mathematics, Castilian, French and Latin (5). And while Luisa Maria de Meneses's consanguineous relationship to Leonor de Meneses remains unknown, the illustrious Gouveia clan into which Luisa married in 1649 also boasted cultural attainments. The Gouveias had been enshrined in French letters since the famous Portuguese humanist André de Gouveia, hailed by Montaigne as "the greatest principal of France" had founded the College of Guyenne in Bordeaux in 1534) (Marques *History* 194). Luisa's husband, João de Silva, seventh Count of Portalegre and second Marquis of Gouveia (Whitenack, Campbell 68) bestowed two new titles on his bride: marchioness and countess. Thus, while in 1641, Luisa Maria and Leonor had enjoyed social parity as ladies-in-waiting to the queen, their subsequent marriages elevated Luisa to a higher social rank, a disparity that Leonor emphasizes in the dedication by comparing the countess-marchioness to a sun and to a sanctuary:

> Las faltas de la pluma, excelentíssima señora, enmienda el acierto de la Dedicatoria, y aunque el discurso no admire por grande, respectos de grande adquiere con la *protección* de V. Exc., a quien suplico sea su patrocinio. Que aunque el valor se busca para mayores empeños, advierto que siendo la última parte de la tarde la menor del día, el sol (sin desechar assumpto tan pequeño) no le desprecia, antes se inclina a él.
>
> Los ojos de V. Exc. tienen la misma calidad. Yo soy el águila más presumida; no podían parar en otra parte de mi presunción los buelos. De las manos de V. Exc. se vale esta fábula, primera de las que el enfado de un dilatado ocio me ocasiona escriuir. No *temo* la *censura,* que si el templo del Aurora fue *sagrado* de los riesgos, no *peligrarán* mis discursos, teniendo en mi fauor essos dos templos. Dios guarde V. Exc. infinitos siglos. Paris. 30 de Mayo de 1655
>
> Esclava de V. Exc. más afectuosa, que su planta besa. (68-70, my emphasis)

(The pen's failures, most excellent lady, are compensated for by the success of one's Dedication, and although this volume as a whole is undeserving of regard, it acquires aspects of grandeur with the *protection* of Your Excellency, of whom I implore its patronage. Even though great value is sought in greater endeavors, bear in mind, as I do, that even as the waning afternoon is the briefest of all the parts of the day, the sun (not underestimating such a minor event) does not disregard it, but rather is inclined towards it.

Your Excellency's eyes possess these same solar qualities. I am the most presumptuous eagle; my flights of fancy could lead me nowhere but to you. Held in Your Excellency's hands, some value accrues to this little tale, the first of many that the exasperation of prolonged idleness provoked me to write. I do not *fear censure,* for if the temple of Aurora was a *sanctuary* for daring souls, my words, so favored by the twin temples of your eyes, *will not be in any danger* at all. May God eternally protect Your Excellency. Paris, May 30, 1655.

Your Excellency's most affectionate slave, who humbly kisses the soles of your feet.)

Like twin suns that "incline" (set) toward the humblest part of the day—the afternoon—the Countess of Portalegre's eyes incline favorably toward the humble pages of the *Desdeñado*. Furthermore, her sun-eyes are architectural spaces, "templos de Aurora" [temples of Aurora], in which Leonor seeks asylum and protection for her novel. By "inclining" toward the text and sheltering it, Maria Luisa fulfills the role of patroness.[16] The dedication intensifies the asylum conceit by pairing safety (*protección . . . no temo . . . sagrado . . . no peligrarán* [protection . . . I do not fear . . . sanctuary . . . will not be in danger]) with the patroness's favor.

The implied "danger" from which d. Leonor seeks shelter arises from two sources: her own impertinence and the rancor of her detractors. Paradoxically, the author's impertinence in soliciting her relative's protection causes the very peril from which she seeks relief. Dedicating the novel to *V. Exc.* [Your Excellency] is presented as a brazen (*presumida*) gesture. With feathered pen in hand, d. Leonor compares herself to a presumptuous eagle who could as easily offend as charm the countess-marchioness by aspiring to soar to the heights of her approval.

Whitenack and Campbell observe that the phrase "No temo la censura" [I do not fear censure] in d. Leonor's dedication insinuates that without her relative's imprimatur, d. Leonor feared reproach or even censorship: "It is also possible that Meneses felt the need of protection from Castilian censors" (11). D. Leonor's use of a pseudonym, the choice of Paris as the place of publication instead of Madrid or Lisbon, and a noticeable lack of standard front matter (prologue, approbations, publisher's colophon) reinforce the impression that d. Leonor expected her text to provoke reprisal. Anonymity, particularly during a period when anonymity was outlawed in Spain, publication outside of the precincts of Spanish censorship and without the customary signs of having passed through official channels all suggest that Meneses was maneuvering evasively around Spanish and Portuguese authority to bring the *Desdeñado* into print in 1655. Faced with these omissions, Whitenack and Campbell are forced to question whether "Leonor de Meneses's *El Desdeñado* was ever licensed for publication" (9). Until the discovery of other editions proves otherwise,[17] Meneses's seventy-nine-page novel might well be characterized as an "underground" publication.

As I demonstrate below, although d. Leonor aimed *El desdeñado más firme* at a Spanish readership, the novel promoted a political vision hostile to Spanish dynastic aspirations and friendlier to French and Portuguese interests. By dedicating her anti-Spanish courtship novel to Luisa Maria, d. Leonor honored her more powerful relative and enhanced her magnificence, fame and status. At the same time, since the Gouveia family was well-known in French letters (see above), the dedication to Luisa Maria may have helped d. Leonor to attract a Parisian publisher for a volume certain to have been banned in Spain and likely to have provoked reprisal from the Portuguese Inquisitorial apparatus, which remained under Spanish sway. In this manner, an anti-Spanish novel nonetheless written in Castilian by a Portuguese noblewoman came to be published under dubious official supervision in Paris in 1655.

In order to draw closer to an understanding of Luisa and Leonor's political ambitions in 1655 it is useful to specify the dynastic courtship plot that was unfolding in Lisbon at this time. Circumstantially speaking, it is very likely that d. Leonor and her relative, d. Maria Luisa supported the struggle to safeguard Portuguese sovereignty against Spanish military aggression. First, d. Leonor owed both her position in the queen's retinue and her title, Countess of Serem, to the overthrow of Spanish rule. Secondly, in her dedication to d. Luisa, Leonor seeks refuge in a more powerful relative who had also served the queen when the Restoration was still in its infancy, which suggests that d. Luisa shared d. Leonor's royalist leanings.

Furthermore, d. Leonor appear to have supported the succession claims of King João IV and Queen Luisa's youngest son, Pedro, over those of their second son, Alfonso. With three sons and a daughter, the Portuguese sovereigns looked beyond Madrid for dynastic allies. Beset by Spanish military aggression, pro-Portuguese strategists did not consider matrimonial allegiance with Spain a possibility for strengthening their position. As Harold Livermore states, "It had long been clear that the Braganças would only wring recognition from Spain with the collapse of the latter or after a long interval" (182). Already in 1646, negotiations had been initiated to wed Crown Prince Teodósio to Louis XIII's niece, La Grande Demoiselle. However, Teodósio suddenly died in 1653, necessitating the investiture of his younger brother, Alfonso, with rights to the throne. Partially paralyzed by a childhood illness and considered mentally deficient, Alfonso was twelve years old in 1655, his younger brother, Pedro, was seven, and his sister, Catherine, future Queen of England, was seventeen (Livermore 173).

Subsequent events would prove that Queen Luisa favored Pedro's ascension rights over those of Alfonso.[18] Armed with the certainty of hindsight, Hipólito Raposo reconstructs the Queen Mother's ruminations as the fledgling country mourned Teodósio's death and celebrated Alfonso's investiture:

Ao coração da Mãe e ao espíritu da Rainha seria angustioso o confronto do filho morto com o filho vivo e inválido; de D. Teodósio, flórida esperança nas letras e nas armas, com D. Alfonso VI, pungente realidade, a ofrecer o constante espectáculo do seu irremediável alejão. (242)

(A mother's heart and a queen's spirit would find it painful to compare her deceased son to her surviving invalid son and to compare d. Teodosio, a florid hope in arms and letters, with the dismal reality of d. Alfonso VI, who could only offer the ongoing spectacle of his incurable affliction.[19])

Evidence that d. Leonor probably remained loyal to Queen Luisa (and therefore also supported Pedro's succession rights over Alfonso's) emerges from the author's second marriage of 1661, which would unite her with a powerful ally of the queen, d. Jerónimo de Ataide, sixth Count of Atouigia, who owed the queen his 1659 appointment as Governor of Arms of Alentejo (Whitenack, Campbell 3n7).[20] If the Count of Atouigia supported Queen Luisa, it is likely that he chose a wife who would share and promote his convictions, as well.[21]

As the preceding outline of Portugal's dynastic prospects indicates, political courtship plots abounded in Lisbon in 1655. Moreover, King João IV, afflicted with gout, increasingly relied on Queen Luisa to carry out matters of state (he would expire the following year) (Livermore *New* 185). If Queen Luisa were effectively running Portugal in 1655, a courtship novel written by one former member of her entourage and dedicated to another would be likely to comment on current matters of import at the Portuguese Court. Therefore it is surprising that the *Desdeñado* offers so many indications that it aimed to reach a Spanish audience, and that its courtship intrigues take place in Madrid rather than in Portugal. Written in Spanish[22] under a Spanish pseudonym (Laura Mauricia), with the spellings of such Portuguese names as Meneses (Menezes), Luisa (Luiza) and Govea (Gouveia) hispanized, the *Desdeñado* narrates the courtship prospects of two maidens rather than two gentlemen, a configuration, as we shall see, more conducive to allegorizing Hapsburg rather than Bragança dynastic dynamics, since the former depended on the marriages of two princesses, and the latter on the rivalry of two princes.

The two Spanish princesses upon whom the Hapsburg succession depended in 1655 were María Teresa Infanta, the seventeen-year-old daughter of Queen Isabel de Bourbon and Philip IV, and her half-sister, Margarita Infanta, four-year-old daughter of Philip and his second wife, Mariana of Austria. For nine years, the monarchy had lacked an heir-apparent (the short-lived Philip Prosper would be born two years later, in 1657). In 1655, Philip IV hoped to wed the elder Infanta to his brother-in-law, Leopold I of Austria, but Louis XIV of France sought María Teresa's hand as well. Since an Ibero-Austrian alliance would strengthen the Hapsburg dynasty while an Ibero-French alliance would leave Spain vulnerable to the possibility of takeover by the foreign Bourbon dynasty, Portuguese loyalists seeking the debilitation of their belligerent neighbor to the east were likely to favor Louis's suit over Leopold's.

Turning to the text of the *Desdeñado* it is now possible to discern how the *Desdeñado* might be construed as an "underground" critique of Hapsburg dynastic politics draped in the guise of a courtship novel. Certainly Queen Luisa de Guzmán's former lady in waiting could be expected to paint an unflattering picture of Spain, one which would necessitate its author's anonymity as well as the publication of her text outside the peninsula, where her anti-Spanish views would be more readily indulged.[23] I propose in the following pages to demonstrate that *El desdeñado más firme* allegorically defames King Philip IV, mocks his ineffectual dynastic machinations and proposes alternative courtship scenarios more favorable to the Portuguese cause. Furthermore, Leonor de Meneses fancifully scripts the younger Infanta, Margarita, as a traitor who valiantly flings Hapsburg dynastic aspirations out the window, a scenario both reminiscent of the Braganza coup of 1640 and conducive to current Portuguese political designs. Finally, I will uncover a cameo inscription of d. Leonor's patroness, the Countess of Portalegre herself, allegorically cast as the loyal servant of the indomitable Portuguese Queen Luisa Maria.

As chapters 3 and 4 indicated, the *Desdeñado* charts the confused courtships of five suitors competing for the favor of two cousins who live together in Madrid. Both cousins are named Lisis, once again inviting onomastic speculation regarding the allegorical significance of this name. Just as Zayas's central character Lisis suggested links to royal women either north or south of the Pyrenees, Meneses's double Lises also draw analogies to Bourbon or Hapsburg princesses. However, the *Desdeñado* dispels all ambiguity by situating both Lises within the household of a father-uncle figure named Felipe, thereby nearly duplicating the familial configuration of the half-sister Infantas, María Teresa and Margarita living under the authority of their father, King Philip IV.[24]

Glancing at the names of other principal characters in the *Desdeñado* for additional onomastic clues, the name César stands out. Whitenack and Campbell remark on the rarity of this name in Spanish letters of the day. Noting that the name César appears in none of Lope de Vega's plays, they speculate that the name may have suggested ironic comparison with the Roman Emperor (Caesar Augustus), or it may have alluded to a relative of the same name (71, 72n124). Indeed, a Cezar de Menezes does enter Portuguese histories of the 1660s.[25] However, César was not only a name but a title synonymous with that of Holy Roman Emperor (*Su Magestad Cesárea*). In Meneses's novel, César is juxtaposed against the names Felipe and Luis. This constellation, César, Luis and Felipe, is unavoidably evocative of dynastic events of the 1650s, in which the Holy Roman Emperor Leopold I competed with Louis XIV of France for the hand of Philip IV's daughter, the Spanish Infanta, María Teresa.

In addition to César and Luis, three other suitors descend upon the Lises of Meneses's novel: Carlos Félix, Jacinto and an unnamed marquis, the former making but a brief appearance at the start of the narrative, only to bow gallantly out of the picture at Lisis's request at the close of Discourse I (112). Jacinto too departs the before novel's end, horizontally, a brace of bullets lodged firmly in his flesh precluding his return. Finally, Felipe consents that the mysterious marquis wed Lisis of Toledo, while he promises d. Luis the hand of his daughter, Lisis of Madrid.

One of the most bizarre features of Meneses's courtship novel is that it achieves its desired outcome without conflict or effort in the very first paragraphs of the second discourse.[26] Felipe willingly grants César his daughter's hand in marriage as he requests. This appearance of an event that would normally herald narrative closure—the scene in which a desired courtship is agreed upon by the maiden's father—turns out to be chimeral however, for César, mistaking one Lisis living at d. Felipe's address for the other, had asked for the wrong maiden's hand. Preposterous as it sounds, César knew so little about the woman in the carriage who had smitten his heart, that he managed to ask for the wrong Lisis's hand in matrimony, and Felipe cared so little for his daughter's preferences that he didn't check with her first (if consulted, the "right" Lisis, Felipe's niece from Toledo, would have declined anyway, since she despised all suitors). The *Desdeñado* unravels from this false resolution through an infinite regression of arrested courtship initiatives. After a mortified César ducks out of his mistaken pledge, d. Felipe selects a marquis to wed his daughter. However, the other Lisis, Felipe's niece from Toledo, vanquishes the Marquis's heart. Meanwhile, Lisis of Toledo's brother Luis comes to visit and begins wooing Felipe's daughter, who meanwhile remains faithful to d. Jacinto. Luis and the Marquis receive permission from Felipe to swap Lises, Luis eliminates his rival Jacinto by murdering him, and amidst all of these peripeties of fortune aimed at fixing the two Lises' marriages, no vow is ever exchanged. As I queried in chapter 3:

> the reader is left with a disturbed impression at novel's end. What does it mean that the ostensible patriarch (Felipe) and the perfect courtier (César) fail to control the outcome of events? Why do the maidens remain unwed and what is the significance of this indeterminacy? By resisting the temptations of comicity and closure, *El desdeñado* renders more significant and enduring the misfirings of its peculiar plot.

The narrator excuses the novel's lack of closure by promising a sequel: "De los demás sucessos suyos, los de Lisis, y otras personas, daré cuenta en la segunda parte" [I will give an account of their outcomes, those of Lisis and other characters, in the second part] (150). Six years would pass before the "dilatado ocio" [prolonged idleness] (Dedication 69) of Meneses's widowhood would cede once again to the responsibilities of matrimony, ample time to fulfill her promise and publish a sequel. Yet no notice of such a novel is recorded. Inconclusiveness, on the other hand, is entirely consistent with a plot that reiteratively "trips over its own hoop skirts" (Lisis of Madrid's hapless caper in Discourse II), pits non-rivals in deadly combat against one another in the dark (César and Luis's error in Discourse III), and loses itself in labyrinthine passageways (César's misfortune in Discourse IV).

I contend that the infelicitous, botched, miscalculated and unruly courtships that *El Desdeñado más firme* plots, collectively denigrate the character d. Felipe, and through him, the King of Spain, Philip IV. The more d. Felipe proves himself incapable of reining (reigning) in the courtship chaos that surrounds his daughter and niece, the more ineffectual and hollow he appears. The discourse clearly marks Felipe as a villain. He is calculating: "Y en esto de casamientos, no se ha de seguir otro norte más que la comodidad" [And in this marriage business, no other compass but that of convenience need be followed] (124), greedy: "el interés es estímulo para la resolución" [our collective gain is the catalyst of resolution] (125), vain, "En mi casa . . . entráis a manchar los resplandores de su siempre bizarra reputación" [You all dare enter my house, sullying the splendors of its ever-sterling reputation] (118) and offensive: "Con ella (his daughter, upon engaging her without her consent to the marquis) no hizo su padre la ordinaria ceremonia de practicársela; a la otra Lisis lo dixo, y se vino a entender della" [Lisis' father did not even take the customary step of informing her of her engagement; he did, however, tell the other Lisis about it, and it was from her cousin that his daughter finally heard the news] (125, 126) in exercising his patriarchal prerogatives.

This portrait of an unscrupulous, preening, autocratic authority figure who nonetheless utterly fails to subordinate courtship events to suit his will, easily translates into a scathing satire of Philip IV attempting to negotiate the two Infantas' marriages to Spain's advantage in the year 1655. In fact, like Felipe, Philip IV did try to marry his elder daughter to (His Majestic Caesar) Leopold I, but ongoing machinations on the part of Louis XIV of France forced him to retract this arrangement. When the narrator of Discourse II comments, "En este laberinto estava César" [this was the labyrinth César found himself in] (115), she could well be describing Leopold's plight from 1655 until 1663, suspended between Infantas and entrapped by courtship circumstances that increasingly demonstrated Luis XIV's ascendancy over both Houses of Hapsburg. Finally, in 1663 King Philip would cede the "other Lisis," Margarita's hand to the emperor, although the royal wedding itself would be delayed for five additional years (see below). Meanwhile Meneses's most vigorous suitor figure, d. Luis, pugnacious to be sure, but admirable in his Machiavellian determination, stabs and shoots his way toward the marriage he seeks with his cousin, Lisis of Madrid just as Louis XIV moved inexorably through military and economic domination toward union with his mother's niece, the Spanish Infanta María Teresa.

My reading of the *Desdeñado* as a politically motivated *román a cléf* must remain loosely rather than strictly allegorical until further historical research can be conducted. For example, I have not yet identified historical equivalents for Carlos Félix or Jacinto. The fifth suitor, the mysterious marquis favored by d. Felipe, prompts many conjectures. The marquis character could refer to the hispanophile Marquis of Vila-Real, known as Portugal's wealthiest nobleman (Marques *History* 283). Another high-profile Portuguese marquis of the period was João IV's ambassador to France in 1642, d. Vasco Luis da Gama, Marquis of Niza (Livermore 177). In Spain the marquis might allude to the eldest son of Philip IV's favorite, Luis de Haro, the Marquis of Eliche. The Marquis of Eliche first attained notoriety in 1656 for spending 16,000 ducats staging a 100-plate banquet for 1,000 guests to entertain the Spanish monarchs. A few days later, Philip IV ("predictably") raised the marquis to the title of grandee (Hume 450, 451).[27] Eliche, awaiting elevation to grandeeship in 1655 corresponds closely to the *Desdeñado's* marquis who attracted Felipe "con aventajado estado, título de marqués y pretensiones de grandeza" [with his enviable status, his title of marquis and his aspirations to grandeur] (125).

Two additional features of Meneses's allegorical satire remain to be explicated: the defenestration scene, and the assistance that Lisis of Toledo receives from her maid to carry out this defiant act. Defenestration held special political significance for Restoration Portugal because it was by this method that the Portuguese literally "overthrew" Spain. On December 1, 1640, revolutionary Portuguese forces arrested the Spanish Governess of Portugal, the Duchess of Mantua, but they shot and defenestrated her secretary, Miguel de Vasconcelos (Livermore 172). One of the most memorable episodes that the *Desdeñado* narrates is that of César's inadvertent nocturnal intrusion into his beloved Lisis of Toledo's chambers. As described in chapter 3, Lisis coolly demands César's sword, stabs him with it, and then dumps his inert body out the window with the help of her maid. While wildly improbable, the scene nonetheless coincides with Lisis of Toledo's *dama esquiva* [aloof damsel] role, indeed consecrating her character with a final and irrefutable act of rebelliousness.

The defenestration scene humiliates César and foregrounds Lisis of Toledo's strength of character. As a projection or fantasy of political desire, it represents the dream of a Spanish Infanta with the savvy of an Andalusian heiress. If only the Infantas were less compliant and more *esquiva* [aloof], they too could help Portugal. If only they sparked with the seditious zeal that brought Luisa de Guzmán to the Portuguese throne! Queen Luisa's initiative had been decisive to the insurrection against Spain. Without her energy, historian Harold Livermore doubts whether King João, the former Duke of Braganza, would have hazarded his fortunes on the David-meets-Goliath adventure of 1640. In his words, the Duke of Bragança "might never have risked his vast possessions in a long and arduous struggle for the throne had it not been for the resolution of his Spanish wife" (173). What a glorious day for Portugal if Margarita should arise like a latter-day Luisa de Guzmán to oppose her Hapsburg suitor, César, at dagger-point, vanquish him, ally herself with the Braganças and throw all Austrian hopes for dynastic renewal out the window.

Although fantastic, the preceding interpretation of the defenestration episode helps explain a puzzling detail: the role of Lisis's maid. In a stop-action-like moment, with César's body crumpled before them, Lisis quarrels with an unnamed *moça* about how best to dispose of this damning evidence of dishonor. To forestall scandal, Lisis asks the serving-girl to help her haul the body out of the window, but instead, the maid scolds her mistress for stooping to murder: "Replicóle la criada, diziendo que era crueldad que desluzía mucho su nobleza, acabar de matar aquel caballero tan impiamente" [The maid dared retort, saying that Lisis' having just killed that gentleman so ruthlessly was an act of cruelty that greatly diminished her nobility] (147, 148). Unmoved by this unsolicited sermon, Lisis secures the maid's assistance to eject César's body from the room. Of this juncture, Whitenack and Campbell judiciously remark,

> It is not clear why the narrator would give us a report on the opinion of this servant (a completely new character to the reader) on the problem of what to do with César's body. However it could be a device to introduce the next sentences, which will further explain Lisis's actions (148n431).

Should one agree to posit a wistfully analogous relationship between the indomitable Lisis of Toledo and the indomitable Queen Luisa, it becomes possible to glimpse a playful moment of myth-making in Meneses's text. Granting that the figure of Lisis of Toledo defenestrating César represents a Queen Luisa-like gesture of insubordination against the House of Hapsburg, then Lisis's pert maid analogously becomes a maid of the Queen. The maid is portrayed positively as a quick-witted yet loyal character concerned with the queen's reputation. Yet why should an allegorical maid to the queen of Portugal—let alone an outspoken one—enter the narrative at all?

The chain of displacement that allows Lisis's maid to represent a maid of Queen Luisa can once again be summarized as follows: Heroic and rebellious Lisis of Toledo represents a fanciful dream of the Spanish Infanta Margarita betraying Spain just as Luisa Francisca de Guzmán betrayed Spain in 1640 when she turned her back on Andalusia and embraced the Portuguese cause. A servant of Lisis of Toledo may therefore be seen to represent an idealized servant of Queen Luisa. Extending this allusive chain back to the opening lines of the *Desdeñado,* it will be recalled that a servant of Queen Luisa had appeared earlier after all—in the *Desdeñado*'s dedication. Meneses's dedicatee, Luisa Maria, the Countess of Portalegre, had held the post of Queen Luisa's lady-in-waiting at the dawn of the Restoration (as did d. Leonor). If linking the unnamed maid of the defenestration episode to the *Desdeñado*'s dedicatee appears farfetched, it probably escaped most readers as well. As d. Leonor's explicit reader, the countess belonged to a select inner circle uniquely equipped to trace the text's allegorical chain of associations through the *dama esquiva* [aloof damsel] character of Lisis de Toledo through the Spanish Infanta (likewise courted by a certain Caesar) to the heroic Queen of Portugal, and to trace Lisis's unnamed *moza* [serving-girl] to a loyal maidservant of the revolutionary Queen, one of queen Luisa's original ladies-in-waiting. A parenthetical curtsy to the Countess of Portalegre, the maid's fable fulfills the same function as the dedication, depicting Leonor's patroness in a valiant, protective role, speaking out to safeguard her queen's interests.

If the *roman à clef* reading that I propose is admitted, it is not difficult to see why Meneses should chose to publish this work in Paris. Not only does *El desdeñado más firme* insinuate an unflattering portrait of the Spanish monarch in the greedy yet ineffectual figure of d. Felipe, but it also favor s Louis XIV's claim to the Infanta's hand, a claim the French monarch would collect in the Peace of the Pyrenees treaty four years later. Since by 1655 Spain still hadn't formally recognized the sovereignty of renegade Portugal, d. Leonor de Meneses also did well to ingratiate herself to Spanish readers by writing under the more Spanish-sounding pseudonym, Laura Mauricia. Finally, by dedicating the novel to her relative, Luisa Maria de Meneses, Countess of Portalegre and Marchioness of Gouveia, d. Leonor promoted their mutual political interests and may have increased her marketability in Paris by association with the prestigious Gouveia family name.

"Para grandeza de ambas coronas" [For the greatness of both crowns]: Courting Eusebio von Pötting

Mariana de Carvajal's 1663 courtship novel, the *Navidades de Madrid y noches entretenidas* ["Christmastide in Madrid and nights of amusement"] is dedicated to Count Eusebio von Pötting, the Viennese ambassador charged with negotiating Infanta Margarita's marriage to Holy Roman Emperor, Leopold I of Austria.[28] After highlighting von Pötting's political ascent in the service of Leopold I, I will subject Carvajal and her dedicatee to the same set of questions that were asked of Zayas and her patron, d. Jaime Fernández de Silva, and of d. Leonor de Meneses and her patroness, Maria Luisa de Meneses. How did Carvajal and von Pötting each stand to gain by entering into a client-patron relationship in 1663? By what rhetorical means does Carvajal favor von Pötting and how does association with von Pötting benefit Carvajal in return?

Born on August 10, 1627 in the Styria region of Austria to Count Friedrich von Pötting and Countess Elisabeth Kunigunda Sternberg, Francisco Eusebio von Pötting enjoyed close ties with Leopold I since youth (von Pötting was thirteen years older than the prince).[29] The future ambassador began working for the Austrian Crown before he reached twenty years of age, and by the age of twenty-two, he had been named vice-chancellor of Bohemia and chief chamberlain to young Leopold (xxxix). Von Pötting married twice, first in 1650 to María Margareta Löbel, daughter of the Baron of Grünberg, through whom he succeeded in naturalizing himself and his family to her native Bohemia. María Margareta Löbel died eight years later, in 1658. After receiving the title of Imperial Count in 1655, von Pötting was called to serve on Leopold's Privy Council in 1660. The count wed Princess Marie Sophie Dietrichstein on April 16, 1662. He also acquired several new titles through the second marriage (duly enumerated in the *Navidades's* dedication): Baron de Oberfalkenstein, Señor de Groskircheim, Rumburg, Milchzin, y Burgravio hereditario de Lienz [Baron of Oberflakenstein, Lord of Groskircheim, Rumburg, Milchzin, and Burgrave, Heir of Lienz] (3).

Von Pötting's second marriage further augmented his status and sphere of influence. Among his bride's family connections could be counted her brother, chief chamberlain to the Spanish Queen Mariana (Leopold's sister), and to Mariana's uncle, Count Lamberg, former ambassador to Madrid, as well as the powerful Cardona family of Spain. Nieto Nuño attributes von Pötting's appointment to Madrid not only to these new connections, but, in large measure, to his wife's strategic importance as a future companion to Austrian-born Queen Mariana:

> Este segundo matrimonio resultó decisivo para el nombramiento de Pötting como embajador en Madrid, donde, por ser la Reina austríaca y hermana del Emperador, se quería una embajadora de la mejor sangre que pudiera acompañar convenientemente a la Soberana y compartir con ella largas pláticas en su propia lengua materna. (xl)[30]

(This second marriage turned out to be the decisive factor in the naming of Pötting to the post of ambassador in Madrid where, because the Queen was both Austrian and the Emperor's sister, it was imperative that the ambassador's wife be of the best possible breeding so that she could provide Her Highness with suitable companionship and could chat at length with her in her native tongue.)

Five months after their marriage, the von Pöttings set out for the Spanish Court. The emperor had charged his special envoy with two matters: first, to press forward the stalled negotiations for Leopold's marriage to Margarita Infanta, and, second, to seek financial support from the Spanish Crown for the Austrian campaign against the Turks.

This was not an easy task. María Teresa's dowry to Louis XIV had never been paid and everyone knew that there was no money for Margarita either. Dissension, intrigue, indecision and numbing protocol, had bogged down negotiations between the monarchies for years. Emperor Leopold placed his latest hope in the von Pöttings.

The von Pöttings arrived in Madrid on January 3, 1663, replacing interim ambassador (and Queen Mariana's confessor) Father Everardo Nitthard, who was preceded in his ambassadorial post by Count Lamberg (xl). Although the ambassador succeeded in formalizing the desired engagement between the Infanta Margarita and Emperor Leopold I within a year of his arrival at Court, the royal marriage would not take place for another five years. Spain's notorious bureaucracy plagued the count. As the British ambassador complained in a letter dated 1689, "lo de España me da pena, porque ni hacen nada, ni conocen lo que se hace" [what goes on in Spain aggrieves me, for the Spanish manage both to do nothing and to not realize what they do]. Emperor Leopold himself became so exasperated with the slow pace of negotiations that he expressed the opinion in a letter dated September 10, 1667 that the Spanish walked with "feet of lead" (xx, xxi). Duke Medina de las Torres, to whom the marriage arrangements had been delegated, procrastinated on the grounds that he was overburdened with other affairs. In fact, Philip's health was failing, and any momentum propelling the marriage ahead soon dissipated amid power-struggles catalyzed by the king's impending death. Another setback for von Pötting was his failure to convince Philip to abandon the war with Portugal for the sake of diverting resources to Austria. During von Pötting's eleven years in Madrid, two special envoys were dispatched to assist him. He returned to Vienna in 1674, where he occupied the military post of chief marshall until his death in 1678 (xliv-lii).[31]

The *Navidades de Madrid*'s dedication to Count von Pötting does not bear Carvajal's name, only "Quien más le desea servir" [the person who most wants to serve you] (4). Carvajal's publisher, Gregorio Rodríguez, not Carvajal herself, probably both composed the dedication and selected von Pötting as its recipient. Von Pötting too attributed the dedication to a male writer, for on January 13, 1664, five months after the *Navidades* was published, his diary would record, "A uno que me dedicó un libro llamado *Navidades de Madrid* he dado 10 doblones" [To *him* who dedicated a book called Christmastide in Madrid to me, I have given ten doubloons] (Nieto Nuño, ed. 10, my emphasis). A professional reader, if you will, Gregorio Rodríguez discerned a compatibility of vision between Carvajal's fiction and the Austrian ambassador in Madrid. In the act of dedicating the *Navidades* to von Pötting, Rodríguez both courted the count's favor and protection, and lent support to his proxy courtship of Margarita Infanta.

Four factors made von Pötting an attractive dedicatee. First, he enjoyed a reputation as a generous patron of the arts. According to historian Nieto Nuño, "su pasión por los libros fue conocida al poco de llegar [a Madrid], y así acudieron a él autores y libreros con volúmenes dedicados" [his passion for books became known shortly after his arrival in Madrid, and therefore authors and booksellers bearing volumes dedicated to him came calling] (li). Second, the *Navidades* being Carvajal's inaugural publishing venture, Rodríguez needed to enhance the marketability of the work by linking Carvajal's "pequeña oferta" [little offering] (4) to a more prominent figure "que hiciese plausible este libro" [who would make the book praiseworthy] (4), as he states in the dedication. Von Pötting, who arrived in Madrid with all the pomp befitting an envoy of the Holy Roman Emperor, as recorded by a contemporary gazetteer, must have appeared an ideal dedicatee:

> Vino el Conde de Petin, Embaxador, en nombre de su Principe Leopoldo de Austria, Emperador de Alemania, á pedir en casamiento a la Serenissima señora Doña Margarita de Austria, Infanta de las Españas, hija segunda de nuestro Catolico Monarca Felipe Quarto, que Dios guarde, y hizo su entrada con la obsentación y grandeza competente a su Estado: saco librea de felpa guarnecida con terciopelo açul, y quaxadas las mangas con un bastoncillo al canto de las faxas. (xliii)

> (So came the Count of Petin, Ambassador, on behalf of his Prince, Leopold of Austria, Emperor of Germany, to ask for the hand in marriage of Her Most Serene Highness, doña Margarita of Austria, Princess of the Spanish Kingdoms, second daughter of our Catholic Monarch Philip IV, may God keep him, and with the pomp and grandeur befitting his office he made his entrance in Madrid: he wore his military regalia, a loose-fitting felt tunic embellished with blue velvet whose sleeves were lavishly adorned with braiding that hung all the way to the sashes that wound about his waist.)

What onlookers did not know was that von Pötting himself would go into debt to fund this lavish display.[32]

Third, timing favored selecting the count as dedicatee. I conjecture that at some point during the eleven-month period between September 1662, when the *Navidades* received approval for publication,[33] and August 13, 1663, the date that the volume was actually bound,[34] Gregorio Rodríguez selected von Pötting to be the *Navidades*'s *post-factum* dedicatee. Von Pötting's eye-catching arrival in January of 1663 fell within this window, and his prestige at the Spanish Court continued rising rapidly thereafter. For example, on March 9, 1663, von Pötting received his first royal audience, and just one month later, on April 5, Philip IV verbally agreed to the Infanta's engagement to Leopold I. Shortly afterwards, Leopold I inducted von

Pötting into the Order of the Golden Fleece (*Toison de Oro*) the most prestigious aristocratic distinction in Europe. It appears likely, then, especially since the ambassador was still living in Austria in September 1662 when the volume was first approved, that Rodríguez's eyes fell on the Viennese ambassador during this initial period of visibility and success.[35]

However, the choice of von Pötting as dedicatee represents much more than the selection of a current darling of Court to promote an unknown author's work. The *Navidades*, as I will demonstrate below, lends strong support to von Pötting's goal of Hapsburg reunification through Margarita's marriage to Leopold I. Rather than theorize any direct link between Carvajal and her patron, I instead propose that the same occasion inspired their respective literary and diplomatic efforts: Charles II's birth in November of 1661. The birth of a male heir to the Spanish throne fifteen long years after the death of Baltasar Carlos in 1646, granted Spain a final hope for peaceful dynastic continuity. With a Crown Prince waiting in the wings, Philip IV could finally contract matrimony for Margarita Infanta, relieved of the threat that her consort might usurp the Hapsburg Crown. By wedding Margarita to her mother's brother, the aging monarch could add the unification of the divided House of Hapsburg to his legacy, a prospect that he had long cherished (albeit with María Teresa in mind rather than Margarita). According to the interpretation that I elaborate below, Mariana de Carvajal's *Navidades de Madrid y noches entretenidas* aligns itself with those political forces favoring the Infanta's union with Leopold, in opposition to those factions that supported the monarchical ambitions of the Infanta's illegitimate half-brother, Juan José of Austria. This orientation aligns the *Navidades* with von Pötting's mission, a concurrence of political interests upon which Rodríguez capitalized in his choice of dedicatee.

Although Carvajal's novellas resist strict allegorical interpretation, allusions to the contemporary political situation pervade the narrative, beginning with the surname of the principal character, Lucrecia de Haro. (As noted above, Luis de Haro had succeeded the Count-Duke of Olivares as Philip IV's favorite after 1643). These allusions, coupled with Carvajal's scrupulous attention to legalistic and courtly protocols (see chapters 3 and 4), subvert the fairy-tale ambiance evoked by such motifs as imprisoned damsels, jousts and wicked stepmothers, and return her courtship plots to the referential field of the Hapsburg Court. Through a technique of scattering, moreover, the narrative fractures and disperses various cues, indirect favorable references to Leopold and Margarita's union, throughout the novellas and their frame tale. I shall delineate six of these resituated elements below: first, the exaltation of matrimony, especially exogamy; second, vilification of illegitimate siblings who would threaten the orderly exercise of succession rights; third, privileging of the art of courtly diplomacy; fourth, condemnation of delayed marriages; fifth, the pairing of diplomatic marriage with international peace; and, sixth, a close correlation between the death of the maiden character's father and realization of her courtship aspirations. Although individually none of these inferences would have carried sufficient weight to affront opponents of Margarita and Leopold's match, cumulatively, their scrambled presence confers an oblique endorsement upon von Pöting's courtship mission, encouraging him in his diplomatic efforts.[36]

By exalting matrimony, Carvajal's courtship plots favor the Infanta's marriage to Holy Roman Emperor Leopold I. Just as María de Zayas's *Desengaños* had indirectly lobbied against wedding the elder Infanta María Teresa by casting all marriage in a bleak light, the *Navidades* supports the younger Infanta betrothal to her Austrian uncle by championing nuptiality in general and exogamy in particular. Not only do all eight of Carvajal's narratives end happily in matrimony, the frame tale too closes on a festive note with triple engagements. The *Navidades* emphasizes the mutual benefits that marriage affords to the bride, the groom and their families. For example, indigent yet aristocratic Beatriz of "La industria vence desdenes" ("Effort vanquishes scorn") gains wealth by marrying Jacinto, while Jacinto burnishes his lineage by wedding noble Beatriz. Doristea of "La dicha de Doristea" ("Doristea's good fortune") retrieves her lost honor by wedding d. Carlos, while d. Carlos gains entry into one of Seville's most exclusive families (see chapter 4).

The last novella of Carvajal's collection, "Amar sin saber a quién"("Her mystery lover"), extols the practice of exogamy among royalty in terms easily translatable to Margarita and Leopold's situation. Several parallels may be traced between Margarita and Carvajal's Scottish princess, Lisena. Like the Spanish Infanta, whose engagement to Emperor Leopold was deferred until after the birth of Charles II in 1661, Lisena remains unwed until her father's second wife produces a male heir (see chapter 3)."Amar's" happy ending, Lisena and Enrique of Navarre's engagement and the bride's departure for her husband's realm, read more like an instruction booklet on royal diplomacy than an escapist romance. For example, the passage below specifies the duties of the ambassadors who negotiate the couple's wedding on foreign soil:

> Con esto se efectuaron los conciertos, con los requisitos acostumbrados. Despachó el embajador por la posta, enviando a decir por su carta estaba señalada la ciudad de Estella en el dicho Reino de Navarra, para las entregas, diciendo el día efectivo que había de llegar a ella.
>
> Desposóse el Rey con su hija en virtud de los poderes. (213)

> (And with that the agreed-upon actions were taken, in accordance with the customary guidelines. The ambassador sent the news by post, and in his letter he let it be known that the city of Estella in the aforemen-

tioned Kingdom of Navarre had been chosen as the site of the ceremony, and he also specified the date by which all parties were to arrive in Estella.

The King gave his daughter's hand in marriage, complying with the conditions established by the ambassadors of both kingdoms.)

"Amar" also treats issues of dynastic security and continuity as integral to the courtship plot. After his engagement to Lisena, Enrique spends four days behind closed doors hammering out safeguards to the dynastic interests of both parties: "Cuatro días estuvo de secreto, confiriendo algunas cosas importantes a la conservación de los reinos" (He was in seclusion for four days, resolving some things that were of great importance for the integrity of both kingdoms) (214). These concerns addressed, the foreign groom returns to his homeland to prepare a spectacular welcome for his new bride and, significantly, to reward those who had supported his lengthy courtship: "Y dándole al Almirante un decreto real, le dijo: —Por eso os hago merced de seis lugares en mi reino, con título de Duque de Sangüesa" [And giving a royal decree to the Admiral, the groom said to him: "In recognition of your service, with the title of Duke of Sangüesa I ceed to you control of six villages in my kingdom"] (214).[37] This novelistic flourish raises speculation that Carvajal or her relatives hoped to receive similar remuneration from Austria in recognition of their loyalty to Leopold. "Amar" closes by assuring the reader that Princess Lisena's marriage to a foreign prince yields both happiness for the new queen, and dynastic stability: "Reinó Lisena largos años, colmando el cielo su dicha con ilustres descendientes" [Lisena reigned for many years, and Heaven showered her with good fortune, blessing her with illustrious descendents] (214). It is interesting in the context of the loosely allegorical reading that I propose that only Lisena's and not Enrique's happiness preoccupies the narrator in novella's closing line, for it is the Infanta's fate, rather than that of Leopold I, that would have concerned Carvajal's Spanish readership.

The *Navidades* also favors Leopold's courtship aspirations by reproaching illegitimate inheritance claims. Opposing Margarita and Leopold's union, a faction at Court favored the royal pretensions of Philip IV's illegitimate son, d. Juan José of Austria. The uncharacteristically harsh portrait that Carvajal paints of Esperanza's illegitimate half-brother, Leonardo, in "Quién obra siempre acierta" ["Kindness always pays"] (see chapter 3) exposes Juan José's alarming potential to destabilize Margarita's succession claims. However, as noted earlier in this chapter, Philip himself also opposed Juan José's pretensions. Therefore, an allegorical rebuke of Juan José needed by some means to protect his philandering father from defamation. Once again, a scrambling device attenuates criticism of the king in Carvajal's narrative.

Whereas a "straight" allegory might thinly veil Philip IV and Juan José in the guise of a king and his evil bastard son plotting to undermine the inheritance claims of a legitimate daughter, "Quién bien" protects the monarch's image by refracting and recombining these elements. "Quién bien" contrasts Leonardo, whose dubious rank is evident from the start ("Tengo por mi desdicha un hermano bastardo hijo de mi padre" [It is my great misfortune to have the bastard son of my father for a brother], 113), with Esperanza's father and her suitor, d. Luis, both respected *veinticuatros*, or city councilors. Because the two are equals, Luis cannot prosecute Esperanza's father for his attempt on Esperanza's life. Instead, the case is heard by the king, who defends Esperanza's right to wed Luis. By casting the king as a fair judge who restores order, the narrative delicately finds the means to castigate the bastard son, without attacking his (profligate) royal father. The text reinforces its support of Margarita's succession claims by naming "Quién bien's" rightful heiress Esperanza, meaning Hope.

The *Navidades's* careful attention to interactive courtesy rituals represents a third allegorical curtsy to Leopold and Margarita's projected allegiance. As chapter 4 explicated, the *Navidades de Madrid* may be read as a novelized courtesy guide that anatomizes both observable and concealed facets of discreet behavior. Rodríguez's choice of von Pötting as the *Navidades'* dedicatee can clarify the purpose and timing of publishing such a guide in 1663, when diplomacy was not the only option for settling the Infanta Margarita's future. Against the sort of coercive or violent solutions to Spain's succession crisis that Juan José would be forced to deploy, the *Navidades* lends unequivocal support to peaceful diplomatic courtship strategies. By rewarding characters who master complex interactive codes, and penalizing those who violate the same codes (see chapter 4), the *Navidades* reinforces its support for Leopold's legitimate suit over Juan José's audacious pretensions. The strict reward and punishment schema of Carvajal's text not only motivates potential suitors such as Leopold I to try for Margarita Infanta's hand, but also teaches them (or their delegates) how to navigate the treacherous shoals of Madrid Court etiquette.

In chapter 4, "El amante venturoso" [The lucky lover] illustrated the extent to which questions of *politesse* control plot outcome in the *Navidades*. "El amante," it will be recalled, expounds the predicament of a willing, well-matched young couple, Carlos and Teodora, enmeshed in rigid courtship codes. Their situation closely matches Leopold I's stalemated courtship of Margarita, which von Pötting would be summoned to resolve. The first two verses of this love poem to Teodora compare Carlos's helplessness to the plight of a sailor lost at sea: "Engolfado navegaba / el mar incierto de amor" [Cast adrift, I navigated the uncertain sea of love] (85). If Carlos pushes his suit for Teodora's hand too hard, he shows impatience and disrespect. If he acts indifferently, he insults his lady. Likewise, if Teodora breaks her show of diffidence, she cheapens herself. If she remains aloof, she discourages Carlos.

Fortunately, Carlos's poem provides the solution to this impasse; the pole-star of hope for the deadlocked couple lies to the North:

> era la tormenta brava,
> salió el Norte y descubierto,
> me guió con tal acierto
> que, siguiendo su hermosura,
> viento en popa mi ventura
> llegó mi esperanza al puerto. (84)

> (the squall was fierce,
> but the North Star appeared, and once visible
> it guided me so infallibly
> that, following its beauty,
> my good fortune the wind at my back,
> my hope found its way home.)

Should "north" allude to Spain's geopolitical north-star, the Viennese Hapsburgs, then Carlos's poem implies that patience, determination and diplomatic savvy will bring about a happy courtship resolution for Margarita Infanta and Leopold I. In fact, consistent with the narrative "scrambling" technique observed throughout the *Navidades,* a character named Margarita plays the role of diplomatic go-between in "El amante." By carrying missives back and forth between the lovers, Margarita helps their stalled courtship to regain momentum.[38] No one more urgently needed the encouragement and instruction that these vignettes offered than the individual charged with defying the "extremos paralizantes" [paralyzing extremes] (xlv) of the Spanish Court on Emperor Leopold's behalf, the *Navidades*' dedicatee, Count Eusebio von Pötting.

In its condemnation of delayed marriages, the *Navidades* offers a fourth sort of encouragement for Margarita and Leopold's speedy engagement. Both "Celos vengan desprecios" ("Jealousy avenges disdain") and "La dicha de Doristea" [Doristea's good fortune] dramatize the risks of protracted courtship. Narcisa's refusal to favor either of the two suitors who seek her hand in "Celos" leads to an escalating cycle of rivalry that nearly culminates in tragedy for the maiden (see chapter 4). "La dicha de Doristea" blames Doristea's father for failing, for selfish reasons, to settle his daughter's marriage before he died: "Amábala tanto, que se puede decir que fue causa de su desgracia—cosa que sucede muchas veces, pues el mucho amor de los padres quita la suerte a los hijos, por no apartarlos de sí" [He loved her so much that one could say that he was the cause of her misfortune—something that happens quite often, for the exaggerated love of parents is injurious to their children's futures, the former not wishing their progeny separated from them] (46). As a result of her father's procrastination, Doristea would fall prey to an unscrupulous gambler who would nearly take her life. These vignettes imply that the duty of Spain's aging monarch, once a male heir had been born in 1661 was to overcome his paternal attachment and wed Margarita with all dispatch.

A fifth means by which the *Navidades* champions the Holy Roman Emperor's courtship of the Spanish Infanta is by coupling the prospect of diplomatic marriage to international peace. Uniting the divided halves of the Hapsburg empire would fortify both members of the allegiance against their common enemies, most notably, the Ottoman Turks. Among Carvajal's eight narratives, "Del esclavo de su esclavo" [His slave's slave] stands out generically as the collection's sole byzantine romance, a format that credibly blends both prongs of von Pötting's mission: marriage negotiations and peace with the Turks (depicted as Algerians in Carvajal's text). It will be recalled that "Del esclavo" narrates Count Rudolfo of Barcelona's efforts to retain external and internal control over Catalonia. Unable to sire an heir, Rudolfo jealously guards his sister Blanca from marriage lest her consort usurp his rule. At the same time, seafaring Algerian pirates threaten the Catalonian coast. In defiance of her autocratic brother, Blanca takes Rudolfo's prime minister, Felix to be her lover, by whom she bears a daughter named Matilde. Raised in secret, Matilde is taken captive and carried off to Algiers. After many twists of plot, Matilde's parents gain control of Barcelona, Matilde is repatriated, she marries one of her rescuers and they inherit the realm.

Significantly, Matilde's rescue, return and wedding are explicitly linked to Barcelona's political revival in Carvajal's text: "Tuvo Matilde dos hijos varones que Reinaron después con gloriosa memoria" [Matilde gave birth to two sons who eventually reigned in accordance with her glorious memory] (105). In Madrid, if young Margarita Infanta wed Leopold I, she could become Matilde's analogue agent of national regeneration. Like Matilde, the Infanta would have to embark on a dangerous trip (to Vienna rather than Algiers), but the fruits of this adventure, according to the novella, would be peace, prosperity and widespread religious conversion for Spain (Matilde's Algerian allies convert to Christianity). Furthermore, "Del esclavo"'s diplomatic fantasy satisfies von Pötting's second goal, that of peace with the Turks. In Carvajal's version, the "Rey moro" [Moorish king] pays tribute to his former captive, Matilde, "con . . . perpetuas paces, empeñando su real palabra de no quebrantarlas" [with uninterrupted peace, pledging on his royal honor never to disturb it] (104).

Although technically Carvajal's plot weds Matilde in her native land of Catalonia while Margarita Infanta would be married on foreign soil to a foreign king, this incongruity is only apparent. Since

Margarita's mother, Mariana, was Viennese, one could argue that the pale Infanta lived in "exile" at the southern Hapsburg Court awaiting the opportunity to return to her uncle and future husband's home in Vienna. This was Matilde's situation: even before her dramatic capture and removal to Algiers, she already lived in exile, for Blanca bore her in secret on Monjuich and sent her to be raised on the periphery of the Court. Blanca and Félix "vivían melancólicos" [lived in perpetual gloom] (92) until events permitted them to be reunited with their daughter.

A sixth and final discursive feature that promoted Leopold's efforts to wed his niece—literally over Philip IV's dead body—is the dead-father motif. It wasn't that Philip IV opposed the Ibero-Austrian match; however, no matter of state as important as a royal marriage alliance could move ahead while Philip IV teetered on the brink of death. Carvajal's *Navidades* is strewn with the corpses of marriageable maidens' fathers. In "Del esclavo," the event that restores Blanca and Matilde to power is the Count Rudolfo's death: "Y desembarcados, supo que el Conde era muerto, y que Blanca había dado la mano de esposa a don Félix, su señor" [And, once they had disembarked, it was discovered that the Count was dead and that Blanca had conceded her hand in marriage to her lord, d. Félix] (100). Leonor of the frame tale and Beatriz of "La industria vence desdenes" are courted under the auspices of their widowed mothers, Juana and Guiomar, respectively. Doristea of "La dicha de Doristea," is wed with the consent of her guardian aunt, Estefanía. Teodora's wedding in "El amante venturoso" would wait until Teodora's father, Octavio Esforcia, had succumbed to illness, and Floripa, of "La Venus de Ferrara" [The Venus from Ferrara], would not marry her cousin Astolfo, the Duke of Ferrara, until her father had surrendered to a glorious military death: "dio la batalla a tanta costa que murió en ella" [he surrendered himself so fully to battle that it took his life from him] (30).

Not only do these dead-father plots expose an unsuspected advantage attendant upon the father's demise, they also express faith in the surviving widows' capacity to execute a favorable match. Both Lucrecia de Haro, and Juana de Ayala appear in the *Navidades*'s frame tale as widows who arrange favorable aristocratic marriages for their offspring. Their positive role constitutes a vote of confidence in Queen Mariana, who, following Philip IV's death, would soon assume the title of regent until Charles I reached his majority.[39] However, Queen Mariana's situation even more closely resembled that of a third widow of Carvajal's collection, Guiomar de Meneses, who in "La industria vence desdenes" lacks a dowry to wed her noble daughter, Beatriz de Almayda. Analogously, Mariana, queen of a monarchy forced to suspend bank payments in 1647 and again in 1652, and to renege on delivery of Infanta María Teresa's dowry to Louis XIV of France, lacked a dowry for Margarita Infanta. Guiomar de Meneses's strategy of entrusting her affairs to her confessor, d. Pedro, recalls

Queen Mariana's controversial reliance on the leadership of her Austrian confessor, Abbot Nitthard. Surely the dowry settlement gallantly offered for Beatriz de Almayda's hand in "La industria" would have appealed to Spanish advocates of an Ibero-Austrian alliance: "No he menester riqueza; bástame su calidad y virtud" [I've no need for riches; her character and virtue are enough for me] (176).[40]

In "La Venus de Ferrara," Astolfo, Duke of Ferrara marries Floripa "con moderada pompa" [in subdued splendor] in recognition of Teobaldo's recent death (31). However, when Margarita Infanta "returned" to Vienna to marry her uncle Leopold one year after the death of her father, Philip IV in 1666, her lavish wedding lasted for six weeks. Emperor Leopold commissioned the architect Burnacini to erect a new 1,500 seat Comedy House for the occasion. The following year, the extravagant five-and-a-half hour equestrian opera *Il pomo d'oro* honored Austria's new empress. Scored by Italian court poet Francesco Sbarra and composed by Marc Antonio Cesti, *Il pomo* rescripts the classical apple of discord myth with Margarita beating immortal contenders Venus, Athena and Juno for the title of most beautiful among the goddesses.

Yet, just as Carvajal's courtship plot, "La Venus de Ferrara," does not close with Floripa and Astolfo's wedding, but continues to recount the courtship adventures of their daughter, Venus, the Hapsburg dynastic courtship plot would not end with Emperor Leopold's long-awaited union with Empress Margarita. As historian John Spielman observes, "Leopold was the last male in a dwindling dynasty" (55). Allegorically, the final scene of Sbarra and Cesti's opera projects this anxiety in a larger-than-life wish-fulfillment tableau:

> The concluding scene was set against a monumental allegory representing the Court of Austrian Glory, with statues of Leopold and Margareta set in the center of the stage, surrounded by pictures of their illustrious ancestors: . . . behind the Imperial couple were ranged images of a large and prosperous progeny, received with joy by allegorical figures representing not only the hereditary lands and states, but also friendly foreign powers, chief among them the Spanish Habsburg dominions. (Spielman 55)

In 1663, neither Carvajal, her publisher, Gregorio Rodríguez nor their dedicatee, Austrian Ambassador Eusebio von Pötting, could have anticipated that Infanta Margarita would ultimately win the apple they envisaged for her: that of becoming Holy Roman Empress. But they could mobilize their respective and combined diplomatic, rhetorical and entrepreneurial talents to promote this goal. The *Navidades de Madrid,* as I have attempted to explicate in the preceding pages, advocates Hapsburg political regeneration through Margarita's marriage to Emperor Leopold I of Austria, exhorts its readers and its influential patron, Count Eusebio von Pötting, to favor their cause, and provides instruction for attaining this courtship outcome.

Notes

1. Ronald Cueto notes that Cervantes recurrently thematizes the problem of patronage at Court, including the Licenciado Vidriera's apology, cited above ("Patronage, Politics, Religion and Cervantes' *Novelas ejemplares*," in *After Cervantes: A Celebration of 75 Years of Iberian Studies at Leeds*, ed. John Macklin, Leeds Iberian Papers Series [Leeds, England: University of Leeds, 1993], 44).

2. The field of seventeenth-century Spanish literary patronage remains to be described systematically. For the purposes of this investigation, I have found it both convenient and enlightening to extrapolate from research on early modern England carried out by Cedric Brown and Arthur Mariotti, eds. (*Texts and Cultural Change in Early Modern England* [New York: St. Martin's Press, 1997]), M. D. Jardine ("New Historicism for Old: New Conservatism for Old? The Politics of Patronage in the Renaissance," in *Patronage, Politics and Literary Traditions in England, 1548-1658*, ed. Cedric C. Brown [Detroit: Wayne State University Press, 1993], 291-309), Dustin Griffin (*Literary Patronage in England: 1650-1800* [Cambridge: Cambridge University Press, 1996], and Melinda Zook ("Contextualizing Aphra Behn: Plays, Politics and Party, 1679-1689," in *Women Writers and the Early Modern British Political System*, ed. Hilda L. Smith [Cambridge: Cambridge University Press, 1998], 75-93).

3. Alternately, William Egginton describes power relations at the Spanish Court as depicted in Gracián's 1647 *Oráculo Manual* [The oracle] not as a pyramid, but as "a series of concentric circles representing ever increasing 'reputation' or social eminence as one moves toward the center, and a corresponding increase in the power to wield one's will over those inhabiting the outer rings" ("Gracían and the Emergence of the Modern Subject," in *Rhetoric and Politics: Baltasar Gracían and the New World Order*, ed. Nicholas Spadaccini and Jenaro Talens, Hispanic Issues, Vol. 14 [Minneapolis: University of Minnesota Press, 1997], 154).

4. Fray Francisco de Jesús, *Narratives of the Spanish Marriage Treaty*, ed. S. R. Gardiner (N.p.: Camden Society, Vol. 101, 1869), 67-71, quoted in John H. Elliott, *The Count-Duke of Olivares* [New Haven, Conn.: Yale University Press, 1986], 209n26).

5. John Crow minces no words in his dismissal of Charles II's reign, contending: "When Charles II came to the throne in 1676, everything was lost" (*The Root and the Flower* [Berkeley and Los Angeles: University of California Press, 1985], 226). For a concise summary of Hapsburg dynastic woes from 1644-1666, see John Spielman, *Leopold I of Austria* (New Brunswick, N.J.: Rutgers University Press, 1977), 45.

6. See Ramón Ezquerra Abadía, *La conspiración del Duque de Híjar (1648)* [The conspiracy of the Duke of Híjar] [Madrid, 1934], 140-141). Unless otherwise noted, all historical references in this section refer to Ezquerra Abadía.

7. "V.E. . . . ha solicitado mi desconfianza para rescatar del olvido de una naveta, en que estaba entre otros borradores míos, este volumen que llaman *El diablo cojuelo*" [Your Excellency, for reasons I cannot fathom, has seen fit to save this volume they call "The limping devil" from the oblivion to which I had consigned it in a desk drawer, where it was hidden from sight along with other lackluster rough drafts of mine] (Luis Vélez de Guevara, *El Diablo Cojuelo*, ed. Enrique Rodruíguez [Madrid: Cátedra, 1984], 65). For his part, the Duke provided Luis Vélez de Guevara's daughter with the dowry necessary to enter religous orders (Ezquerra Abadia, *La conspiración*, 136).

8. Ezquerra Abadía cites fragments of this passage (*La conspiración* 136).

9. The duke preferred to make the Court his home. His palace occupied the site of the future Palace of Buenavista (Ezquera Abadía *La conspiración* 134).

10. After Jaime's sister Teresa was wed in 1647, "para casar al primogénito, don Jaime encargó otra negociación a don Luis Fernández de Córdoba, marqués de Priego y Duque de Feria" [in order to marry off the eldest son, d. Jaime undertook another negotiation with d. Luis Fernández de Córdoba, Marquis of Priego and Duke of Feria] (Ezquerra Abadía *La conspiración* 132).

11. "Del Maestro Fray Luis de León a Doña María Varela Osorio" [From her Master, Friar Luis de León, to Lady María Varela Osorio], prologue to Luis de León's *La perfecta casada* (1583) [The perfect wife] (Barcelona: Grandes Autores, 1990), 5.

12. Ironically, Zayas's emblematic lily foretold an unanticipated third scenario, that of France's *fleur de lys* taking root on Spanish soil. France's rapid usurpation of Spain's imperial eminence began with the 1659 Peace of the Pyrenees treaty by which María Teresa was betrothed to Louis XIV, and was ratified in 1700, with the founding of the Bourbon dynasty in Spain.

13. D. Fernando's father, Viceroy of Brasil from 1639-1641, also supported the Portuguese cause.

14. A virtual roll-call of Portuguese nobility, including members of the Mendoça, Meneses, de Castro, Noronha and Guzmán families, the fourteen *Damas* occupied the second tier of the queen's retinue, drawing less compensation for their services than maids of honor (*Damas de Honor*), who earned 12,000 reales, and more than chambermaids (*Donnas da Cámara*), who earned 6,000. National Library of Portugal, Codice 4173 (Hipólito Raposo, *Dona Lvisa De Gvsmão, Dvquesa e Rainha (1613-1666)* [Lisbon: Empresa Nacional de Publicidade, 1947], 401).

15. The duke was the closest living collateral relation to the former Avis dynasty. See H. V. Livermore, *A New History of Portugal* (Cambridge: Cambridge University Press, 1966), 171.

16. The immediate antecedent to "templos" [temples] is, as Judith Whitenack and Gwyn Campbell point out, not the dedicatee's eyes but her hands (Introduction to *El desdeñado más firme* [Scorned yet steadfast], by Leonor de Meneses [Potomac, Md.: Scripta Humanistica, 1994] 70n117). However, I prefer to view the phrase "De las manos de V. Exc." [in the hands of Your Excellency] as parenthetical to a loosely unified sun conceit constituted by the associative series: tarde / día / sol / inclina / ojos / templo de Aurora / dos templos [afternoon / day / sun / inclines / eyes / temple of Aurora / two temples].

17. The Biblioteca Nacional [National Library] (Spain) edition (R 25004) is the only known extant copy of the *Desdeñado* (Whitenack and Campbell, introduction to *Desdeñado* , 8).

18. After João's death in 1656, Alfonso VI did succeed him, but Pedro managed to oust his brother in 1667. In what Livermore terms a "matrimonial coup d'etat," Alfonso's wife of one year, Marie Françoise of Nemours, Princess of Savoy, appealed to have her marriage annulled owing to her husband's impotence, thereby initiating a revolt that would install Pedro on the throne, whom she would promptly wed instead (Livermore *Portugal* 67; A. H. de Oliveira, *History of Portugal: From Lusitania to Empire* [New York: Columbia University Press, 1972], 332).

19. Translated from the Portugeuse by Charles Perrone.

20. On the other hand, the Count of Atouguia belonged to Alfonso VI's "triumverate" of privy counselors (Edmund B. D'Auvergne, *The Bride of Two Kings* [London: Hutchinson, 1910], 76).

21. In a final twist of Lisbon's courtship plots, Mazarin dispatched the Chevalier de Jant to Lisbon in 1655 to raise the possibility of wedding João's elder daughter, Catherine de Bragança to Louis XIV in return for Portuguese military assistance against Spain (Livermore *Portugal* 181-84). This prospect subsequently foundered when France and Spain made peace in 1659 and Louis XIV wed the Spanish Infanta, María Teresa. For her part, Catherine would wed Charles II to become Queen of England.

22. It is not surprising to find a Portuguese noblewoman raised during the Spanish protectorship writing courtship novels in Spanish. According to A. H. de Oliveira Marques, "A majority of literary works printed in Portugal during the same period [1580-1640] were in Castilian" (*Lusitania to Empire* 323).

23. The fact that both the Archbishop of Braga and the Portuguese Inquisitor-General belonged to the hispanophile faction (Livermore *Portugal* 176-177) may have inhibited publication of anti-Spanish literature within Portugal.

24. The coats of arms of two branches of the Meneses family bore lily designs. That of d. Alfonso de Menezes (d. 1656), Chaimerlain to Alfonso VI, is vertically bisected. The right half of the field is red decorated with five gold lilies (*Os Restauradores de 1640 e a sua descendência* [The restorationists of 1640 and their descendants] [Lisbon: Publipor, 1990], 15-17). That of D. Antonio Luis de Menezes, Marquis of Marialva is quartered. The lower left and upper right quadrants display a blue background with three gold lilies arranged on each quarter (*Os Restauradores* 43-45).

25. The historical d. Cezar was a rival of Alfonso VI's *privado,* d. Luis de Vasconcelos, Count of Castelmelhor. Accused in 1666 of conspiring to unseat Alfonso VI, he was exiled to Algarve, although the accusation was never proven (D'Auvergne *Bride* 90-91).

26. The *Desdeñado* is divided into four chapters called *Discursos*, or Discourses.

27. Eliche aspired to succeed his father to the position of Keeper of the Retiro Palace, however, Philip granted the post to the Duke of Medina de las Torres instead. Eliche was later accused of conspiring to blow up the palace (Martin

Hume, *The Court of Philip IV of Spain in Decadence* [New York: Brentanos, 1927], 489).

28. "Para grandeza" are the closing words of the *Navidades'* dedication. (M.ariana de Carvajal y Saavdra, *Navidades de Madrid y noches entretenidas en ocho novelas* [Christmastide in Madrid and nights of amusement in eight novellas] (1663), ed. Catherine Soriano [Madrid: Clásicos Madrileños, 1993], 4). All citations from the *Navidades* refer to the Soriano edition.

29. A letter written in 1663 by the widowed Empress Eleonora alludes to the long-standing friendship between the two youths (M. Nieto Nuño, ed., *Diario del Conde de Pötting, Embajador del Sacro Imperio en Madrid (1664-1674)* [The diary of Count Pötting, embassador of the Holy Roman Emperor in Madrid] [Madrid: Biblioteca Diplomatica Española, 1990] xxxix). All historical citations and diary entries in this section unless otherwise noted refer to Nieto Nuño.

30. Indeed, von Pötting's diary confirms Sophie's importance at Court. In January 1664, the (pregnant) countess is recorded to have visited Queen Mariana four times and to have sent her gifts once, while in the same period, von Pötting only visited the queen once, the king twice, and sent gifts to the king once. Sophie's schedule during the year 1664 included attending at the palace, paying visits, receiving visitors, sitting for portraits and attending Mass (Nieto Nuño *Diario* 7-77).

31. Nieto Nuño vigorously denies that von Pötting failed in his mission. The fact that both envoys (Baron von Lisola and the Marqués de Grana) were recalled from their posts in Madrid during von Pötting's term of service suggests rather that the emperor continued to hold faith with von Pötting, but required (as did Charles II of England) more than one representative to navigate the diplomatic shoals of the Spanish Court (*Diario* xlviii).

32. "Las demandas de dinero para cubrir con decoro su respresentación las encontrará el lector [del diario de von Pötting] repetidas veces. Y como no fueron la mayor parte de las veces satisfechas, se vio el embajador en la necesidad de empeñar al 20% de interés sus alhajas. Como el Conde de Castellar en Viena, que no pudo dejar la Corte Cesárea cuando fue requerido por tener elevadísimas deudas que satisfacer, igualmente hubo de retrasar Pötting su partida de Madrid por inconfesadas razones semejantes" [In the diary of von Pötting the reader will find his numerous requests for money to cover the expenses incurred for his presentation at Court. And as these requests were not generally granted, the ambassador found it necessary to pawn his finery, at twenty percent interest. Like the Count of Castellar in Vienna, who could not leave the Court of the Holy Roman Emperor when it was required of him because he had an extraordinary amount of debt to pay off, in the same way Pötting had to delay his departure from Madrid, due to similar embarrassing circumstances] (Nieto Nuño *Diario* lii).

33. The Licencia del Ordinario [permit granted in civil court] signed by Notary Pedro Palacio reads, "El Licenciado D. García de Velasco, Vicario desta Villa de Madrid y su partido: por el presente y por lo que a Nos toca, damos licencia para que se imprima un libro intitulado: Novelas, de Doña Mariana de Caravajal y Saavedra. . . . Dada en Madrid, a veinte y cinco de Setiembre de mil seiscientos y sesenta y dos años" [The Licenciate d. García de Velasco, deputy of this town

of Madrid and its administrative districts: on this day and by the powers vested in us, we grant permission for the printing of a book entitled "Novellas," by d. Mariana de Carvajal y Saavedra . . . Given in Madrid, on the 25th of September, 1672] (Carvajal *Navidades* 7).

34. According to the "Suma de la Tassa" ["Summary of Official Rates and Charges"], on August 13, 1663, the price of the *Navidades* was set at *siete reales y un cuartillo* [less than three pesetas per copy (*Diccionario de la lengua española, Real Academia Española. 20a ed.* [Madrid: Espasa-Calpe, 1984])], calculated on the basis of number of folio sheets needed for printing (10).

35. On December 18, 1663 (four months after the *Navidades* had been printed), the marriage settlement (*capitulaciones*) was officially proclaimed at the palace, accompanied by a lavish fireworks display: "y el dia de los conciertos hizo festivas demonstraciones de su regocijo, con repetidas inuenciones de fuego, y fuentes de diversos licores, á su usança" [And the day their wedding was solemnized there were festive demonstrations of delight with fireworks and fountains from which various liqueurs flowed, as was their custom] (Nieto Nuño *Diario* xliii-xliv).

36. Carvajal also combines techniques of fragmentation and redistribution in the salacious "Fábula de Eurídice y Orfeo" [The tale of Eurydice and Orpheus] with which she closes the Christmastide festivities. Instead of describing vanquished Eurídice from head to foot as classical precedent demanded, Leonor declaims her charms from the outside inward, elaborating the rich fabrics and adornments of Eurídice's attire, then presenting her nipple as though it were a decorative flower: "un botón de mosqueta / que adornaba curiosa una roseta / blanca, que parecía / que el pico del botón la desprendía" [the bud of a climbing rose, which made a quaint decoration for a white rose-blossom, and it seemed that the tip of the rosebud protruded quite noticibly from the rosette from which it had sprung] (Carvajal *Navidades* 220). Similarly, in the "Fábula de Dafne y Apolo" [The tale of Daphne and Apollo], Carvajal permits Lucrecia to anatomize Dafne "amores por abajo" [lovely qualities from the bottom up], that is, feet first (Carvajal *Navidades* 179). Elsewhere, I have named the procedure whereby intercalated verse mirrors narrative operations *desdoblamiento*, redoubling (Shifra Armon, "Rhymes and Reasons: Verse Interpolation in Golden Age Fiction," Caliope [2001]: forthcoming).

37. This gesture of largesse recalls a similar juncture in "Del esclavo de su esclavo," in which Carvajal's plot bestows rich rewards on Audalia and Xarifa, who collaborated to unite Matilde with her future husband in Catalonia: "gozando Audalia el oficio de Mayordomo Mayor y Xarifa el de Camarera" [Audalia was elevated to the post of chief steward, and Xarifa to that of chambermaid] (Carvajal *Navidades* 105).

38. Painstakingly scrupulous courtships also occupy "La industria vence desdenes" [Effort vanquishes scorn] and "Amar sin saber a quién" [Her mystery lover], whose suitors, Jacinto and Enrico respectively must court insistantly, yet without causing offense.

39. Mariana of Austria shared power with a Junta of five ministers as stipulated by Philip IV's will. The *Junta de Gobierno*, as it was called, was composed of the president of the Council of Castille, the vice-chancellor of Aragon, the

archbishop of Toledo, the inquisitor general, a councillor of state and a grandee to be named. "Thus," in John Lynch's words, "although the queen mother was in a sense the chief executive, she did not have sovereign power, for she had to act with the advice of the Junta, which was instructed to assemble daily" (*The Hispanic World in Crisis and Change: 1598-1700* [Oxford: Blackwell, 1992], 236).

40. In the same novella the sibling cooperation between Pedro and his twin sister Jacinta to rejuvenate their dying lineage reminds the reader that Emperor Leopold and his sister, Mariana, Queen of Spain, could also join forces in order to revitalize the gasping Hapsburg dynasty.

Afterword: Picking Wedlock

Literary historians have long treated courtship narratives written by women writers either in isolation from one another or simply as sharing the common trait of female authorship. They made comparisons, to be sure—González de Amezúa favored Zayas's melodramatic intrigues but found Carvajal pedestrian; Ludwig Pfandl admired Carvajal's uncluttered style but deemed Zayas indecorous. Frank Warnke and Katharina Wilson anthologize Zayas and Carvajal's prose (together with Ana Caro's poetry) in a chapter of *Women Writers of the Seventeenth Century* dealing with Spain, yet, until now, no one has questioned the remarkable coincidence that, of the three known female novelists publishing Spanish fiction in the seventeenth century, all three picked narratives of courtship and wedlock.

Studying and teaching these narratives over the past decade, I have found at least three areas of commonality that justify treating women's courtship novels as a distinct generic category. Lucas de Gracián Dantisco's courtesy guide, the *Galateo español* [Spanish Galateo] (1534), first convinced me that fictions about courtship were ideally adapted to teaching noblemen and noblewomen the art of self-presentation required to succeed at Court. In order to instruct his (mostly male) readers in the art of recounting extended narrative, Gracián Dantisco interpolated into his manual an entire novel, "La novela del gran Soldán" ["The novel of the Great Sultan"]. I reasoned that if a conduct manual could mobilize the energies of fiction to teach its readers successful interactive strategies, courtship fictions removed from that explicitly didactic framework could do the same. But who taught aristocratic women the winning skills that they needed at Court? I conjectured that women's courtship narratives filled this gap.

The second area that women's courtship novels share is their instructive implse. This is most easily seen in Mariana de Carvajal's 1663 *Navidades de Madrid,* in which the maiden figure always "gets her man" after demonstrating a repertoire of successful courtship strategies. Zayas's 1647 *Desengaños amorosos* takes the opposite tack, depicting the unsatisfactory outcomes attendant upon abandoning codes of courteous interaction, and contrasting them with the stellar exception of a character named Lisis, who outmaneuvers her opponents with masterful ease. The two Lises of Leonor de Meneses' 1655 *Desdeñado más firme* (Scorned yet steadfast) flounder about in a fictional world devoid of courtesy and, as such, serve as objects of Meneses's derision.

A third element that women's courtship plots share is their commitment to representing women's experiences in courtship. Zayas, Meneses and Carvajal consistently identify aspects of female subjectivity that the dominant discourse neglected or suppressed. For instance, Zayas and Carvajal highlight the pleasures and rewards of prolonged courtship rather than its frustrations, Carvajal acknowledges that widowed mothers could arbitrate courtship outcomes, and Meneses creates two practically indistinguishable female characters who demonstrate great individuation in their responses to the same courtship initiatives. These enduring examples of *imperfectas no casadas* [imperfect unmarried women] remind the modern reader that female subjectivity emerged in contestation with other discourses rather than through the imposition of a univocal story of female subjugation.

Appendix

Twenty-One Women's Courtship Narratives: Synopses of Nineteen Novellas and Two Cornices—Published by Women in Spanish between 1647 and 1663

Parte segunda del Sarao y entretenimiento honesto
[Desengaños amorosos]
[Second part of the soiree and decorous diversion (Disenchantments of love)] (1647)
By María de Zayas y Sotomayor (Chapter titles by Pablo Campins, 1734).

Cornice

The *Desengaños amorosos* fulfills a noblewoman named Lisis's promise to avenge her suitor Juan's disloyalty. In the narrative that frames the first part of the *Sarao*, subtitled the *Novelas amorosas y ejemplares* [Exemplary and amorous novellas], published in 1637, Lisis loses Juan to her cousin, Lisarda. When another suitor, Diego steps in to claim Lisis's hand in marriage, the noblewoman becomes ill, languishing on the brink of death for over a year. Juan's and Lisarda's visits only intensify her fever. Lisis finally recovers her health when her aunt sends a beautiful slavewoman named Zelima to serve as her companion. Lisis agrees to wed Diego on the condition that she be allowed to host an engagement party at which her female guests recount "true" tales of men's perfidy. After listening to ten of these *desengaños* [tales of disillusionment], Lisis announces that the horror-stories have convinced her that it would be foolish to marry any man, and that she instead plans to enter a convent. Although prior to the engagement party, such an assertion might have elicited disapproval, the collective testimony of the *desengaños* now prompts a sympathetic response. Lisis's mother, Laura, and Zelima (whose *desengaño* revealed that she is really a disillusioned noblewoman named Isabel) even join Lisis in religious reclusion, with Isabel taking vows. Diego becomes so distraught by Lisis's decision that he abandons himself to dangerous military service, dying shortly thereafter in Catalonia. Shaken by the ten horror stories that she has just heard, Lisarda breaks off her relations with Juan, and several months later, weds a wealthy foreigner. Although Lisarda never suspects that Lisis has deliberately manipulated her into spurning Juan, Juan does catch on to Lisis's strategy. When news of Lisarda's marriage reaches him, Juan realizes that he himself must bear the blame for having lost both Lisarda and Lisis. The inconstant suitor falls ill and dies in a paroxysm of remorse, effecting the *Desengaños* "happy ending": Lisis gives Juan a taste of his own disillusioning medicine, while she herself retains her mother's loyalty and sidesteps an unwanted match.

1. "La esclava de su amante" [Her lover's slave girl]
(narrated by Isabel Fajardo, formerly the *morisco* slave, Zelima)

Lisis's slavewoman Zelima surprises everyone at Lisis's storytelling *sarao* by confessing that her real name is Isabel Fajardo of Murcia. Her *desengaño* recounts the story of her disgrace. Isabel had moved to Zaragoza with her father when he was called to fight in Catalonia. The family rented rooms from a noblewoman whose son, Manuel, seduced Isabel with false promises of matrimony, a scandal which became widely known throughout Zaragoza. Her reputation ruined, Isabel secretly followed Manuel to Sicily, hoping to persuade him to honor his obligation to marry her. The shock of her disappearance killed Isabel's father, and sent her mother packing for Murcia. In order to travel with greater ease, Isabel disguised herself as a slavewoman named Zelima. Once ashore in Sicily, Isabel arranged a meeting with Manual on a coastal island; however Moorish corsairs intercepted them and brought them to Algiers. There Manuel and "Zelima" entered the service of a noblewoman named Zaida who fell in love with Manuel and arranged for all of them to return to Zaragoza, where she promised to convert to Christianity and wed Manuel. Back on Spanish soil, Zelima revealed her prior claim on Manuel, who nonetheless insisted that he would still marry Zaida. Upon hearing Manuel's renouncement, Isabel's loyal servant shot Manuel to death, which moved Zaida to stab herself in the heart. Isabel then sold herself back into slavery to symbolize the enslavement of her soul. Lisis's uncle purchased her for one hundred ducats whereupon he began harassing her for favors. Zelima confided in Lisis's aunt, who removed her from the her husband's reach by giving her as a gift to her ailing niece, Lisis. Now that she has explained how she came to be called Zelima, Isabel asks Lisis's permission to marry the only Spouse that will not deceive her: God.

2. "La más infame venganza" [Vengeance most foul]
(narrated by Lisis's cousin, Lisarda)

Beautiful Octavia allows Carlos, the son of a wealthy Milanese senator, to seduce her. However, in a matter of years, Carlos tires of Octavia, whose gambling father and brother had squandered her inheritance. Carlos deceives Octavia into relocating temporarily to a convent, where he abandons her to wed the wealthier, albeit less lovely Camila, the daughter of one of his father's friends. Stranded at the convent, Octavia summons her brother, Juan, to avenge her dishonor. Juan conceives a diabolical plan to repay Carlos in kind by dishonoring Camila. Unable to seduce Camila with words, Juan finally rapes her. Carlos blames Camila for her "unfaithfulness" and she flees to a convent to escape his ire. After a year of separation, Carlos's father, convinced of her innocence, persuades Camila to returns home. Unfortunately, Carlos refuses to eat or sleep with her for a full year. Finally, Carlos poisons Camila, who dies with her belly and limbs gruesomely distended. Juan and Carlos's crimes are never discovered. Octavia realizes how much better off she is behind convent walls, and takes the vows of a Bride of Christ.

3. "El verdugo de su esposa" [His wife's executioner]
(narrated by Nise)

In Palermo, Sicily, Roseleta valiantly resists the seductive efforts of her husband Pedro's friend, Juan, to whom Pedro had overzealously confided the charms of his new bride. However after receiving Juan's sixth love letter, Roseleta enlists Pedro's aid to repel further advances. Husband and wife agree that Roseleta will feign an assignation with Juan and that Pedro will ambush him en route. However, Juan stops on the way to the tryst to worship the Virgin Mary, who intercedes in the form of a talking cadaver to protect him from the danger that awaits. Juan repents and enters Orders, but Roseleta's problems continue. Another woman, Angeliana, resents that Roseleta had interrupted her idyll with Juan, who had promised to marry her. To avenge this affront, she seduces Pedro and sets his heart against Roseleta, a simple task since Pedro already suffers from widespread rumors that Roseleta and Juan actually had cuckolded him. Pedro has his wife "accidentally" bled to death, returning to Angeliana's house for consolation.

4. "Tarde llega el desengaño" [Disillusioned too late]
(narrated by Filis)

Returning home to wed his cousin after serving the Spanish Crown in Flanders, d. Martín of Toledo is shipwrecked and tossed ashore on Grand Canary Island. There he seeks refuge with a nobleman named Jaime of Aragon, and witnesses the cruel captivity of Jaime's wife, Elena. As Jaime explains, he had originally fallen in love with a mysterious woman who only allowed Jaime to attend her blindfolded and in darkness. Although she paid him richly and favored him in every possible way, Jaime could not resist the temptation to see his exquisite partner, who finally identified herself as the princess of Erne, Madame Lucrecia. However, the day after the Princess had revealed her beauty to him, she ordered her men to kill Jaime, who was forced to flee for his life. One day, the disconsolate lover met a poor woman named Elena who seemed to him the very portrait of his beloved Lucrecia. The two were wed, and lived happily, until a black slavewoman, jealous of Elena's privileges and fortune, betrayed her. The slavewoman told Jaime that Elena had carried out an affair with her cousin. Enraged, Jaime burned Elena's cousin alive and forced Elena to use his skull as a vessel. He punished Elena by obliging her to beg for table scraps and to live in a small enclosure while he conceded to the devious slavewoman all of the privileges formerly enjoyed by his wife. On the night of d. Martín's visit, the slavewoman is stricken ill and confesses her lie, but it is too late, for Elena has just perished. Jaime goes mad from the shock, and Martín hastens home to wed his cousin, having learned never to place his faith in servants.

5. "La inocencia castigada" [Her innocence punished]
(narrated by Lisis's mother, Laura)

At the age of seventeen, Inés, a Sevillian noblewoman closely guarded by her brother and cruel sister-in-law, receives a marriage proposal from a wealthy aristocrat of the same region. In order to escape her confinement, Inés agrees to the match. Inés enjoys the freedom of movement that her marriage permits, but unfortunately, catches the eye of a gentleman named Diego, who begins an unremitting campaign to seduce her. Inés ingeniously repels all of his advances until he enlists the services of a Moorish sorcerer who confects a voodoo candle to entrance her. Whenever Diego lights the candle, Inés arises zombie-like from her bed and comes to Diego across the city in her nightgown. One night, a city patrol intercepts Inés, but she is exonerated once it is ascertained that magic has deprived her of free will. Diego, on the other hand, is carried off by the Inquisition. Unfortunately, Inés's brother, husband and sister-in-law believe that she invented the story of the spell to cover up her guilt. They buy a house in the city of Seville where they immure Inés in its chimney for six years. Festering in her own excrement, unable to move or lie down, Inés loses her sight in the pitch blackness of her prison. Finally a female neighbor hears her moans and musters both Church and civil authorities to effect her rescue. Inés's persecutors are tried and sentenced to death, and Inés inherits their collective fortunes. She recovers her former beauty, although not her eyesight, and takes her religious vows.

6. "Amar sólo por vencer" [Loving only to conquer]
(narrated by Matilde)

A well-bred maiden named Laurela lives with her family in Madrid. Espying her out for a ride in her carriage, a carpenter's son named Esteban falls madly in love with her. Posing as a servant-girl, Esteban inveigles his way into her household where he wins the family over with his musical abilities and charms. Soon "Estefanía" becomes Laurela's constant companion, even sleeping in the same room with her. However, when Laurela's engagement to a nobleman named Enrique is announced, Estefanía "confesses" to Laurela that he is really an enamored nobleman of Burgos. Impressed that her secret admirer had thus served her so selflessly for more than one year, Laurela surrenders to him without confirming his identity. Esteban convinces her to elope with him. The following day, he takes her jewels, and abandons her at the Church of Santa María, located near her aunt's house, and returns to his wife. Laurela's father and uncle determine that Laurela should remain in seclusion at the aunt's house, even though Enrique still wishes to marry her. Over a year later, the two orchestrate an "accident," causing a wall to cave in and kill Laurela. A servant tells Laurela's mother what really happened, and she and her surviving daughters take the veil.

7. "Mal presagio casar lejos" [Only disaster awaits a bride far from home]
(narrated by Luisa)

Luisa recounts the story of the tragic death of her great-aunt, d. Blanca. Blanca's two older sisters suffer by marrying afar: d. Mayor's Portuguese husband stabs her to death; d. Leonor's Italian husband strangles her with her own hair. Blanca's youngest sister, María, who had accompanied Mayor to Portugal breaks both legs jumping out of a window to escape her sister's fate. Blanca thinks she has learned from their mistake, and plans never to leave her brother's house, but after a Flemish prince devotes two years to courting her, she relents, weds him and moves to Flanders. There, her new father-in-law despises her and her new groom alternately ignores her and abuses her when she complains. Blanca's sister-in-law, Marieta comes to her aid, but soon Blanca walks into the dining room to find Marieta's cadaver sitting on a chair. When she discovers her husband has been consorting with his sixteen-year-old page, Arnesto, Blanca burns the offending bed, and threatens to do the same to the page. Instead, Blanca's husband and father-in-law murder her by bleeding her to death. María watches through a keyhole, and asks her beloved, Gabriel, to notify Blanca's brother, now a military governor of Flanders. He (the Duke of Alba) arrives and takes revenge on the Flemish people for his sisters' death. Four years later, when Blanca's body is transported to Spain, it is found to be incorrupt. María marries Gabriel, and when it is time for her daughter, María, to take a spouse, she weds her within her own close-knit Spanish social circles. Luisa, the narrator, is the product of this union.

8. "El traidor contra su sangre" [Traitor against his own kind]
(narrated by Francisca, Luisa's sister)

D. Pedro of Jaén has a daughter named Mencía and a son named Alonso. Wishing to concentrate his inheritance in Alonso, Pedro rejects all of Mencía's suitors and plans a religious vocation for her. However, Mencía's suitor, d. Enrique, remains undeterred. He and Mencía hope to soften Pedro's heart, but Clavela, Enrique's jealous ex-lover, denounces the pair to Alonso and Pedro. Alonso stabs his sister to death and places her cadaver in an exterior room where it appears to warn Enrique to flee while he still can. Alonso and his men then fall upon the stunned suitor and murder him. Alonso escapes to Italy where he falls in love with poor but noble Ana. He weds her without his father's knowledge, but repents when Pedro threatens to disinherit him. Alonso decapitates Ana, stuffing her body down a well and placing her head in a seaside cave. He flees by boat, but is apprehended and sentenced to death for his crime. Unperturbed, don Pedro announces to his card-playing cronies that he prefers a dead son to an ill-wed son. Ironically, when Pedro dies, Ana's and Alonso's child inherits Pedro's fortune.

9. "La perseguida triunfante" [The triumph of the fugitive damsel]
(narrated by Sister Estefanía)

King Ladislao of Hungary dispatches his younger brother, Federico, to escort his English bride across Europe. However, Federico falls in love with Beatriz and begins to pursue her. During one of Ladislao's extended absences, Beatriz resorts to trapping Federico in a cage in order to keep him at bay. Incensed, Federico retaliates by accusing Beatriz of trying to seduce him. Ladislao condemns Beatriz to be sent into the wilderness to be killed by beasts. The servants accompanying the innocent queen pluck out her eyes, steal her jewels and leave her for dead. A mysterious woman arrives, restores Beatriz's sight, provisions her with food and water, and disappears Late that day, Duke Octavio of Germany, out on a hunting excursion, finds Beatriz and takes her to his Court. Meanwhile, Ladislao ascertains Beatriz's innocence, and dispatches Federico to look for her. Federico enlists the aid of a sorcerer to help him do away with her once and for all, but Beatriz's mysterious intercessor rescues and comforts her over and over. Finally, a plague falls on Hungary which Beatriz cures with special herbs that the Virgin Mary gives her. The "miraculous doctor," Beatriz, finally confronts Federico, who is dying from the plague that the sorcerer is unable to treat. The disguised queen tells her brother-in-law that his only hope for recovery is publicly to confess his sins. Federico confesses and repents, Beatriz's clothing suddenly transforms into the royal raiments she wore when she was first carried away to die, and the evil sorcerer disappears in a cloud of smoke. Ladislao asks Beatriz to return to him, but she elects to become a nun. Ladislao also enters Orders, naming Federico to succeed him to the Hungarian throne. Federico weds Beatriz's younger sister, and Beatriz composes the story of her life as Estefanía herself (the narrator) read it on a trip to Italy with her parents.

10. "Estragos que causa el vicio" [The vicisstitudes of vice]
(narrated by Lisis)

D. Gaspar, a Spanish nobleman accompanying Philip III in Lisbon, enjoys the favors of a libertine lady. One night as he enters the gates of her house he finds a moaning cadaver, the sight of which helps convince him to stop visiting his lady. At Church, he espies two women, Florentina and Magdalena, whom he determines to pursue, but when he locates their house, he finds it strangely still. After a typical night of debauchery, Gaspar returns to the ladies' street and sees in the moonlight a woman's body stretched out on the ground. It is

Florentina, bathed in blood, who later recounts the events leading to her sorry state. Florentina had lived with her step-sister, Magdalena, under Magdalena's uncle's care. The uncle, not wishing to lose control over the girls' estates, delayed Magdalena's marriage to her suitor, Dionisis, for so long that Florentina too came to fall in love with Dionisis. After Magdalena and Dionisis were wed, Florentina confessed her love to Dionisis, who reciprocated her affection. Following the advice of a black maidservant, Florentina orchestrated a scene in which Dionisis entered Magdalena's chamber at night to find her in the company of a servant. Dionisis flew into a rage, murdering everyone in his path, and would have killed Florentina if the maidservant hadn't thrown herself between them. Upon hearing Florentina's tale, Gaspar defends her before the Portuguese authorities, and she takes the veil. Gaspar returns to Spain and marries in Toledo.

El desdeñado más firme [Scorned yet steadfast] (1554)
By Leonor de Meneses (Laura Mauricia)

Discurso primero [First discourse]

D. César, seeing four women in their carriage, asks them to unveil themselves. He falls in love with the as-yet-unknown Lisis of Toledo, the more beautiful of the two noble ladies in the coach, in his opinion. D. Jacinto tells César that their friend, Carlos Félix, had also recently declared himself devoted to the woman, that he himself is also pursuing her, and that her name is Lisis. Later, César finds Lisis (of Toledo) at the same spot, and she insists that she does not know Carlos Félix, and that at any rate she despises all men. This time, César trails her home, to the house of a friend of his father's, d. Felipe, a wealthy nobleman with a marriageable daughter (Lisis of Madrid). César sends Lisis a note, and while awaiting a reply listens to love poetry recited by his friends. D. Jacinto enters and shows him a bouquet of flowers from Lisis of Madrid, who has given him leave to ask her father for her hand. César, unaware that there are two Lises living in the same household, bitterly accuses his friend of betraying him, and Jacinto departs to ask Carlos Félix to desist in his pretensions. Carlos Félix gallantly relinquishes his claim, respecting Lisis of Madrid's choice.

Discurso segundo [Second discourse]

Jacinto asks for Lisis of Madrid's hand, but Felipe declines, considering César a better match for his daughter. Lisis (of Madrid) summons César to meet her at a window facing the garden at one o'clock in the morning. When César arrives, she stands to greet him, but trips over her hoop-skirt, causing several glass ornaments to crash to the ground. The noise awakens her father, who finds his daughter dressed in her finery. She attempts to persuade Felipe that she was looking for relief from the heat in her bedroom, and when César is caught hiding behind a bush, he lamely claims that he had entered the garden to dodge the police, who had mistaken him for a fugitive. Felipe retires and Lisis returns to talk to her cousin, Lisis of Toledo. The latter chides her for not having sent a maid to explain to César that he was betrothed to the wrong woman. Lisis of Madrid accuses Lisis of Toledo of allowing things to reach this pass by not disabusing César of his error much earlier, and resolves to send a maid tomorrow to let him know so that he can call off the engagement.

Discurso tercero [Third discourse]

The next day, César is relieved to hear from Lisis of Madrid's maid, d. Ana, that there are two women called Lisis, and that the one he adores is not pledged to Jacinto. He gives the maid a diamond rose for her help. César backs out of his engagement to the wrong woman, hinting to Felipe that he knows of another equally worthy gentleman —Jacinto—who is in love with Lisis of Madrid. Unmoved, Felipe engages his daughter again without her consent, and without even the courtesy of informing her directly of his decision, to a marquis with prospects for a grandeeship. When the marquis arrives, Lisis of Madrid remains faithful to Jacinto, and the marquis soon turns his gaze on her cousin, Lisis of Toledo. When Lisis of Toledo's brother, d. Luis Palomeque, arrives in Madrid, he takes a liking to Lisis of Madrid. In the dark outside Felipe's house Luis and César mistake one another for their respective rivals, and a duel ensues. César wounds his non-rival, Luis and flees. Lisis of Madrid secretly gives thanks that Luis was stabbed, but Jacinto, upon hearing of the duel assumes that she consented to be courted by another man. After Jacinto sends Lisis a complaint, she replies in kind, accusing him of bad faith.

Discurso cuarto [Fourth discourse]

Jacinto and Lisis make peace and Luis recovers, consoled to learn that his adversary had not been his rival. Luis and the marquis ask Felipe for a gentleman's swap: Lisis of Madrid will marry her cousin, d. Luis Palomeque, and Lisis of Toledo will now wed the marquis. One night, Jacinto is en route to speak to Lisis. Luis shoots him, claiming to the bereft Lisis of Madrid that his honor had demanded it. Before dying, Jacinto asks César to deliver to Lisis of Madrid certain personal items after he dies. On the night that César attempts to carry out his friend's final wishes, however, the hapless gentleman becomes accidentally trapped in Lisis of Toledo's room. Figuring that César has come to dishonor her, Lisis of Toledo takes his proferred dagger, stabs him with it, and calls a serving girl to help her throw the damning evidence of his body out the window. A passing friend of César finds him and carries home. Once recovered, César sends Lisis of Madrid the items that Jacinto had entrusted to him via his confessor, and leaves for Flanders after composing a final rhyme, leaving the details of what happened to the two Lises to a sequel.

Las Navidades de Madrid y noches entretenidas [Chrsitmastide in Madrid and nights of amusement] (1663)
By Mariana de Carvajal y Saavedra

Cornice

The advent of Christmas and the desire to comfort the recently widowed d. Lucrecia provide pretexts for convening a storytelling Christmas party attended exclusively by the eight residents of an urban Madrid household. A further underlying motive for the gathering, however, is courtship. Two widows, Lucrecia and Juana, wish to introduce their respective son, Antonio, and daughter, Leonor, to one another. Viscayan houseguest Vicente, who has come to Court with his friend, Enrique, to file grievance claims, pursues another guest, Gertrudis. Furthermore, in the course of successive banquets, giftgiving, music, dancing and flirtation, his countryman, Enrique, will pair up with another resident, Lupercia. Originally scheduled to last only five nights with one story to be recited per evening, the party is extended for three additional nights, allowing each guest an opportunity to recount a tale. Finally when additional guests arrive to celebrate the three abovementioned couples' engagements, narration gives way to the recitation of increasingly gay and bawdy poetry by alternating male and female guests. At the end of the evening Antonio announces that he has just received word that Vicente's and Enrique's court claims have been approved. This news spurs a final flurry of congratulations, giftgiving and delectation.

1. "La Venus de Ferrara" [The Venus from Ferrara]
(narrated by Gertrudis)

This bi-generational courtship narrative set in the Italian dukedom of Ferrara recounts how Floripa and her daughter, Venus, met, attracted and selected their spouses. Floripa is secluded in a castle and guarded by twenty men while her father, a general, fights in foreign wars. However, she secures the aid of her servant, Leucano, to attend her cousin, the Duke of Ferrara's birthday party. Although disguised as a peasant, Penosa, Floripa charms the Duke, Astolfo, and eventually wins his hand in marriage. The following year, with the birth of Venus, she and the Duke also deem it prudent to guard their daughter in a secluded wing. When Venus reaches the age of eighteen, the now-widowed Floripa realizes the need for her daughter's marriage and convenes a tournament for all of Venus's suitors to prove their worth to both mother and daughter. At the end, Venus is allowed to pick the husband of her choice from among them. During the tournament, Venus switches costumes with her maid, and one of the suitors, Alfredo, the Duke of Modena, also switches livery with his footman, Laureano. Venus is not fooled by appearances, however. In her ultimate selection of the "footman," she wins the duke, just as he deserves Venus's hand in marriage by favoring the apparent "maid."

2. "La dicha de Doristea" [Doristea's good fortune]
(narrated by Vicente)

A Sevillian nobleman is so attached to his daughter, Doristea, that he can make no arrangements for her marriage. When Doristea's father dies, the orphan is placed in her aunt's protection. Her aunt rebuffs the advances of a gambling ne'er-do-well named Claudio, who seeks to marry Doristea for her money. Outraged, Claudio vows to take revenge. He secretly courts Doristea, convincing her to elope with him. Once Doristea leaves her aunt's house with Claudio, he robs her and prepares to murder her. A passing nobleman, Carlos, rescues Doristea and shoots Claudio. Mortified, Doristea hides her identity from Carlos, who secretes her into his father's house, without informing his father of her presence. Little by little, Carlos begins to importune Doristea for favors, forcing her to flee to a convent, from which she writes him a letter revealing her high-birth and true identity. Carlos and Doristea are wed and Doristea is restored to her place of honor in aristocratic society.

3. "El amante venturoso" [The lucky lover]
(narrated by Lupercia)

Neighbors, childhood friends and social peers, Carlos and Teodora of Zaragoza are courting. However, the strict demands of decorum impede their efforts. After eight months of stalemate, Carlos's sister, Margarita, acts as intermediary to carry missives back and forth between the stranded lovers. Finally, Carlos and Teodora become engaged and a party is held. After much singing and dancing, an "Academy" is convened at which guests wittily versify glosses for a series of hieroglyphs on the topic of love.

4. "El esclavo de su esclavo" [His slave's slave]
(narrated by Enrique)

The Count of Barcelona, who has no heir, jealously prevents his sister, Blanca, from marrying, lest her offspring usurp his power. Blanca secretly consorts with one of the count's favorites, Félix Centellas, and gives birth to Matilde, who is surreptitiously raised by Félix's trusted secretary, Alberto, far from Court. However, Algerian corsairs capture Matilde and Alberto and carry them to Algiers. Matilde becomes a companion to a lady of the Court named Tarifa (Jarifa) and Alberto becomes a slave to Tarifa's suitor, the nobleman Audalia who, unbeknownst to him, sympathizes with the Christians. On a mission to the Catalonian coast, Audalia is captured by another favorite of the Count of Barcelona, Feliciano Torrellas. Although Feliciano treats Audalia with great courtesy, he notes his captive's unhappiness and asks the cause. Audalia confesses that he finds it unbearable to be separated from Tarifa, and promises that if Feliciano sets him free, he and Tarifa will become Feliciano's eternal slaves. Feliciano frees Audalia on the condition that he refrain from attacking Barcelona, and he returns home. Soon thereafter, Feliciano too is captured by corsairs and taken to Algiers, where Audalia recognizes him as being the enslaved Feliciano. Audalia and Feliciano, now disguised as Mustafá, conspire with Tarifa, Alberto and Matilde to carry out a daring escape. Upon returning to Barcelona, where the count had recently died, Audalia and Tarifa convert to Christianity, and the Sultan of Algeria, mollified by generous gifts, forgives his former captives, promising perpetual peace with Catalonia. Feliciano and Matilde marry, and their descendents succeed them to reign gloriously over Catalonia.

5. "Quién bien obra siempre acierta" [Kindness always pays]
(narrated by Lucrecia)

Returning to Córdoba from military service in Flanders, d. Alonso witnesses a terrible sight: a noblewoman pleading for her life while watching her own grave being dug. Alonso rescues the woman, who turns out to be his brother, Luis's fiancée, Esperanza. Esperanza's illegitimate half-brother, Leonardo, had made the attempt on her life with their father Álvaro's approval. Álvaro opposed Esperanza's choice of Luis as a spouse. In fact, he harbored the desire to disinherit Esperanza altogether and transfer her estate to Leonardo. The murder attempt was meant to eliminate Esperanza and frame Luis for the crime. Alonso brings the conspiracy to light, although there is no way to prosecute Álvaro locally since both he and Luis are city magistrates. The case is taken to the President of Castile, and a royal order is returned granting clemency to Álvaro. The king demands only that Álvaro separate from the concubine by whom he had fathered Leonardo, free her, and dower her to wed her social equal. The order further stipulates that Luis and Esperanza are to be wed.

6. "Celos vengan desprecios" [Jealousy avenges disdain]
(narrated by Antonio)

A Milanese lady, Narcisa, suffers the unwanted advances of two noblemen: Duke Arnaldo and Count Leonido. The more she disdains them, the more emboldened the two rivals become. A Spaniard named Duarte, poised to inherit the dukedom of Cardona, also admires Narcisa, but he limits himself to standing near her at church and disguising himself as a gardener in her country-house. Various occasion arise in which Duarte rescues Narcisa from her importuning suitors, but the gallant Spaniard remains anonymous, asking nothing in return. Finally, in the course of thwarting the duke's attempted ambush of Narcisa's carriage, Duarte sustains a wound that requires Narcisa's care. She recognizes him from church and offers him her hand in marriage.

7. "La industria vence desdenes" [Effort vanquishes scorn]
(narrated by Juana)

Noble parents from Ubeda lack the means necessary to dower their daughter or to establish her twin brother in a lucrative position. By sending both children into Orders, the parents secure the well-being of the twins, but also guarantee the extinction of their aristocratic lineage. After the parents die, Jacinta and her brother Pedro cooperate to restore their lineage. Pedro dowers his sister with his meager inheritance so that she can marry and raise a son. Meanwhile, Pedro cultivates his skill as a painter, earning lucrative sinecures in return for his services. Eventually, Pedro positions Jacinta's son, Jacinto, in his own household where the lad meets two women: rich but plebian Leonor and the poor but noble Beatriz. A protracted courtship reveals Leonor's flaws and Beatriz's superiority, however in order to overcome Beatriz's defenses, Jacinto must resort to an ingenious subterfuge. The two are wed, saving the family line not only from extinction, but also from contamination by intermarriage with non-nobility.

8. "Amar sin saber a quién" [Her mystery lover]
(narrated by Leonor)

The Queen of Scotland dies, leaving King Ludovico without an heir. His daughter Lisena is beset by eligible suitors, particularly Enrico, the King of Navarre, but disdains them all. When Ludovico remarries, the new queen is jealous of her subjects' love for Lisena. Sensing the friction that her presence causes, Lisena voluntarily retires to an island hunting retreat during the queen's pregnancy, which will result in an heir to secure the stability of the realm. Hearing of her departure, Enrico of Navarre pays the islandkeeper, Alberto, a generous pledge in exchange for the privilege of working on the island in his guise as a rich, simple man. Calling himself the "Rustic Lover," Enrico charms all who meet him with his droll speech, ball-playing skill and other courtly accomplishments. Soon, he catches Lisena's eye. When the Rustic Lover rescues Lisena from a fall into the river, Lisena appoints him her personal physician. In gratitude, he gives her his portrait, which she later verifies to be that of her original suitor, the King of Navarre. Hearing that the queen gave birth to a son, Lisena returns to her father's Court and selects Enrico to marry her. The engagement is held in Scotland, and, following lengthy negotiations to secure both parties' inheritance rights, the wedding itself is held in Navarre, where Lisena reigns for many years, followed by her descendents.

Bibliography

Alborg, Juan Luis. *Historia de la literature española: Época Barroca.* Vol. 2. Madrid: Gredos, 1967.

Alcalá, Ángel, ed. *Inquisición española y mentalidad inquisitorial.* Barcelona: Ariel, 1984.

Alchiati, Andrea. *Emblemas.* Eds. Manuel Montero and Mario Soria. Madrid: Editora Nacional, 1975.

Aleman, Mateo. *Aventuras y vida de Guzman de Alfarache.* Ed. Enrique Miralles García. Barcelona: PPU, 1988; Bruguera, 1982.

Anon. *El libro de Calila e Digna.* Eds. J. Keller and R. Linker. Clásicos hispánicos. Madrid: Consejo Superior de Investigaciones Científicas, 1967.

———. *Lazarillo de Tormes.* Ed. Francisco Rico. Barcelona: Planeta, 1983.

Antonio, Nicolás. *Biblioteca Hispana Nueva, o de los escritores que brillaron desde el año 1500 hasta el 1684.* Trans. Francisco Pérez Bayer. Madrid: Fundación Universitaria Española, 1999.

Arenal, Electa and Stacey Schlau. *Untold Sisters: Hispanic Nuns in Their Own Words.* Albuquerque: University of New Mexico Press, 1989.

Armon, Shifra. "The Paper Key: Money as Text in Cervantes's 'El celoso extremeño' and Camerino's 'El pícaro amante.'" *Cervantes: Bulletin of the Cervantes Society of America* 18 (1998): 96-114.

———. "Rhymes and Reasons: Verse Interpolation in Golden Age Fiction." *Caliope* (2001). Forthcoming.

Astete, Gaspar de. *Tercera parte de Padre Gaspar Astene de la Compañia de Iesvs, Del gouierro de la familia, y estado del Matrimonie: Donde se trata, de como se har de auer los casados con sus mugeres, y los padres con sus hijos, y los Señores con sur corados.* Valladolid: Alonso de Vega, 1598. Lexington, Ky.: University of Kentucky Libraries, Microfilm Center, 1965.

Barbeito Carneiro, Isabel. *Mujeres de Madrid Barroco: Voces testimoniales.* Madrid: Comunidad de Madrid, 1992.

Barca de Bolea, Ana Francisca. *Vigilia y octavario de San Juan Baptista.* Ed. María Angeles Campo Guiral. Huesca, Spain: Instituto de Estudios Altoaragoneses, 1994.

Bates, Catherine. *The Rhetoric of Courtship in Elizabethan Language and Literature.* Cambridge: Cambridge University Press, 1992.

Bennassar, Bartolomé. *La España del Siglo de Oro.* Trans. Pablo Bordonava. Barcelona: Crítica, 1983. Bloomington, Ind.: Indiana University, 1932.

Bourland, Caroline. "Aspectos de la vida del hogar en el siglo XVII según las novelas de doña Mariana de Carbajal." In *Homenaje ofrecido a Menéndez Pidal*, Vol. II, 331-368. Madrid: n.p., 1925.

———. *The Short Story in Spain in the Seventeenth Century.* New York: Lenox Hill, 1973.
Boyden, James. *The Courtier and the King: Ruy Gómez de Silva, Philip II, and the Court of Spain.* Berkeley: University of of California Press, 1995.
Brandenberger, Tobias. *Literatura de matrimonio (Península ibérica s. XIV-XVI).* Hispánica Helvética 8. Zaragoza: Pórtico; Lausanne: Sociedad Suiza de Estudios Hispánicos, 1996.
Brooks, Peter. *Reading for the Plot: Design and Intention in Narrative.* New York: Vintage-Random House, 1984.
Brown, Cedric and Arthur Mariotti, eds. *Texts and Cultural Change in Early Modern England.* New York: St. Martin's Press, 1997.
Brown Jonathan, and John H. Elliott. *A Palace For a King: The* Buen Retiro *and the Court of Philip IV.* New Haven: Yale University Press, 1980.
Burgos, Carmen de. *Al balcón.* Valencia: Sempere, n.d. [1913].
———. *El divorcio en España.* Madrid: Vuida de M. Romero, impresor, 1904.
Burke, Peter. *The Fortunes of the Courtier: The European Reception of Castiglione's* Cortegiano. University Park, Pa.: The Pennsylvania State University Press, 1995.
Butler, Judith P. *Excitable Speech: A Politics of the Performative.* New York: Routledge, 1997.
Cacho, María Teresa. "Misoginia y barroco: Baltasár Gracián." In *Literatura y vida cotidiana.* Actas de las Cuartas Jornadas de Investigación Interdisciplinaria, eds. María Ángeles Durán and José Antonio Rey, 173-186. Madrid: Universidad Autónoma de Madrid; Zaragoza: Universidad de Zaragoza, 1987.
Calderón de la Barca, Pedro. *El gran teatro del mundo.* Eds. John J. Allen and Domingo Ynduráin. Barcelona: Crítica, 1997.
———. *Love is No Laughing Matter/ No hay burlas con el amor.* Ed. and trans. D. Cruickshank and S. Page. Warminster, England: Aris and Phillips, 1986.
———. *El médico de su honra.* Ed. D. W. Cruickshank. Madrid: Cátedra, 1981.
———. *La vida es sueño.* Ed. Ciriaco Morón. Madrid: Cátedra, 1996.
Carvajal y Saavdra, Mariana de. *Navidades de Madrid y noches entretenidas en ocho novelas.* 1663. Ed. Catherine Soriano. Madrid: Clásicos Madrileños, 1993.
———. *Navidades de Madrid y noches entretenidas, en ocho novelas.* 192 fols. Madrid: n.p., 1663.
———. *Navidades de Madrid y noches entretenidas en ocho novelas.* Ed. Julio Jiménez. Ph.D. diss., Northwestern University, 1974.
———. *Novelas entretenidas.* Madrid, 1728.

Casey, James. *The History of the Family.* Oxford: Basil Balckwell, 1989.
Casey, James and Bernard Vincent. "Casa y familia en la Granada del Antiguo Régimen." In *La familia en la España mediterránea (Siglos XV-XIX)*, eds. James Casey et. al., 172-211. Barcelona: Crítica, 1987.
Castiglione, Baldassare. *El Cortesano.* Trans. Juan Boscán. Ed. Marcelino Menéndez Pelayo. Madrid: Consejo Superior de Investigaciones Científicas, 1942.
———. *Il libro del Cortegiano.* Torino: Einaudi, 1998.
Castillo, David. "Gracián and the Art of Public Representation." In *Retoric and Politics: Baltasar Gracián and the New World Order*, eds. Nicholas Spadaccini and Jenaro Talens, 191-208. Hispanic Issues 14. Minneapolis: University of Minnesota Press, 1997.
Castillo Solórzano, Alonso de. *Las harpías en Madrid.* Ed. Emiliano Cotarelo y Mori. Madrid: Librería de los bibliófilos, 1907.
Cervantes, Miguel de. *El Ingenioso Hidalgo Don Quijote de la Mancha.* Eds. Salvador Fajardo and James Parr. Asheville, N.C.: Pegasus, 1998.
———. *Novelas ejemplares.* Ed. Harry Sieber. Vols 1 and 2. Madrid: Cátedra, 1984.
Cesti, Antonio. *Pommo d'Oro.* 1667. Nationalbibliothek, Vienna. Seattle: University of Washington, 1976. Microfilm.
Chambers, Ross. *Story and Situation: Narrative Seduction and the Power of Fiction.* Theory and History of Literature 12. Minneapolis: University of Minnesota Press, 1984.
Charnon-Deutsch, Lou. "The Sexual Economy in the Narratives of María de Zayas." In *María de Zayas: The Dynamics of Discourse*, eds. Amy Williamsen and Judith Whitenack, 117-132. Cranbury, N.J.: Associated University Press, 1995.
Chartier, Roger, ed. *Passions of the Renaissance.* Trans. Arthur Goldhammer. Cambridge: Harvard University Press, Belknap Press, 1989.
Claramonte, Andrés de. *El valiente negro en Flandes.* In Nelson Lopéz, "Edición crítica para actores de *El valiente negro en Flandes* de Andrés de Claramonte." Ph.D. diss., University of Florida, 1998.
Clavero, Bartolomé. *Mayorazgo: propiedad feudal en Castilla (1369-1836).* Madrid: Siglo Veintiuno, 1974.
Clements, Robert J. and Joseph Gibaldi. *Anatomy of the Novella: The European Tale Collection from Boccaccio and Chaucer to Cervantes.* New York: New York University Press, 1977.
Coloma, Carlos. *Las guerras de los Estados Bajos, desde el año 1588 hasta el de 1599, recopiladas por C. Coloma.* N.p., n.d.

Córdoba, Martín de. *Jardín de nobles doncellas*. 1468. Reprint, with a foreword and notes by Félix García, Madrid: Ediciones Religión y Cultura, 1956.

Covarrubias Horozco, Sebastián de. *Emblemas morales* (1610). Ed. Carmen Bravo-Villasante. Madrid: Fundación Universitaria Española, 1978.

———. *Tesoro de la lengua castellana o española*. Madrid: Turner, 1979.

Crow, John. *Spain: The Root and the Flower*. Berkeley: University of California Press, 1985.

Cruickshank, D. W. "Literature and the Book Trade in Golden-Age Spain." *Modern Language Notes* 73.4 (1978): 799-824.

Cruz, Anne. "*La bella malmaridada:* Lessons for the Good Wife." In *Culture and Control in Counter-Reformation Spain*, eds. Anne Cruz and Mary Elizabeth Perry, 145-170. Hispanic Issues. Vol 7. Minneapolis: University of Minnesota Press, 1992.

———. "Studying Gender in the Spanish Golden Age." In *Cultural and Historical Grounding for Hispanic and Luso-Brazilian Feminist Literary Criticism*, ed. Hernán Vidal, 193-222. Literature and Human Rights Series 4. Minneapolis: Institute for the Study of Ideologies and Literature, 1989.

Cueto, Ronald. "Patronage, Politics, Religion and Cervantes' *Novelas ejemplares*." In *After Cervantes: A Celebration of 75 Years of Iberian Studies at Leeds*, ed. John Macklin, 43-90. Leeds Iberian Papers Series. Leeds, England: University of Leeds, 1993.

Dantisco, Lucas Gracián. *Galateo español*. Ed. Margherita Morreale. Clásicos Hispánicos 2: 17. Madrid: Consejo Superior de Investigaciones Científicas, 1968.

D'Auvergne, Edmund B. *The Bride of Two Kings*. London: Hutchinson, 1910.

Davis, Natalie Zemon. "'Women's History' in Transition: The European Case." In *Feminism and History*. Ed. Joan Wallach Scott, 79-104. Oxford: Oxford University Press, 1996.

Davis, Natalie Zemon and Arlette Farge. "Women as Historical Actors." In *Renaissance and Enlightenment Paradoxes*, eds. Natalie Zemon Davis and Arlette Farge, 1-7. In Vol. 3 of *A History of Women in the West*. Eds. Georges Duby and Michelle Perrot. Cambridge: Harvard University Press, Belknap Press, 1993.

Daza Pinciano, Bernardino. *Los emblemas de Alciato traducidos en rhimas españolas*. 1549. In *Alciato: Emblemas*, eds. Manuel Montero and Mario Soria. Madrid: Editora Nacional, 1975.

DeJean, Joan. *Tender Geographies: Women and the Origins of the Novel in France*. New York: Columbia University Press, 1991.

De la Cerda, Juan. *Libro intitvlado, Vida politica de todos los estados de mugeres en el qual se dan muy prouechosos y Christianos documentos y auisos, para criarse y conseruarse deuidamente las mugeres en sus citados.* Alcalá de Henares: Juan Gracián, 1599.
Delicado, Francisco. *Retrato de la lozana andaluza.* Manantial 37. Barcelona: Plaza and Janes, 1977.
Del Val, Joaquín. "La novela española del siglo XVII." In *Historia general de las literaturas hispánicas*, ed. M. Menéndez Pidal, 44-80. Vol. 3. Barcelona: Barna, 1953.
Diccionario de Autoridades. 1726. 3 vols. Ed. Facsim. Madrid: Real Academia Española, 1976.
Diccionario de la lengua española. Real Academia Española. 20a ed. Madrid: Espasa-Calpe, 1984.
DiPuccio, Denise M. *Communicating Myths of the Golden Age Comedia.* Lewisburg, Pa.: Bucknell University Press, 1998.
Dollimore, Jonathan and Alan Sinfield. "History and Ideology: The Case of *Henry V.*" In *Alternative Shakespeares*, ed. John Drakakis, 206-277. London: Methuen, 1985.
Domínguez Ortiz, Antonio. *La sociedad española en el siglo XVII.* 2 vols. Madrid: Consejo Superior de Investigaciones Científicas, 1965.
Dopico Black, Georgina. "Perfect Wives, Other Women: Signs of Adultery and Inquisition in Early Modern Spain." Ph.D. diss., Yale University, 1995.
Duby, Georges, ed. *A History of Private Life.* Cambridge: Harvard University Press, 1988.
Egginton, William. "Gracián and the Emergence of the Modern Subject." In *Rhetoric and Politics: Baltasar Gracián and the New World Order*, eds. Nicholas Spadaccini and Jenaro Talens, 151-169. Hispanic Issues. Vol. 14. Minneapolis: University of Minnesota Press, 1997.
Elias, Norbert. *Power and Civility.* Trans. Edmund Jephcott. New York: Pantheon, 1982.
Elliott, John H. *The Count-Duke of Olivares.* New Haven, Conn.: Yale University Press, 1986.
———. *Imperial Spain: 1469-1716.* 1963. Harmondsworth, England: Penguin, 1990.
El Saffar, Ruth. "The 'I' of the Beholder: Self and Other in Some Golden Age Texts." In *Cultural Authority in Golden Age Spain*, eds. Marina Brownlee and Hans Ulrich Gumbrecht, 178-208. Baltimore: Johns Hopkins University Press, 1995.
Enciclopedia del idioma: Diccionario histórico y moderno de la lengua española (Siglos XII al XX). 3 vols. Madrid: Aguilar, 1958.
Enciclopedia universal ilustrada. Barcelona: Espasa, 1912.

Enders, Victoria, and Pamela Radcliffe, eds. *Constructing Spanish Womanhood: Female Identity in Modern Spain*. Albany: State University of New York Press, 1999.
Esteban Mateo, León. *Hombre-Mujer en Vives: Itinerario para la reflexión*. Valencia: Ayuntamiento de Valencia, 1994.
Even, Yael. "Daphne (Without Apollo) Reconsidered: Some Disregarded Images of Sexual Pursuit in Italian Renaissance and Baroque Art." *Studies in Iconography* 18 (1977): 143-159.
Eiximenis, Francesc. *Texto y concordancia del* Libro de las donas. Ed. Gracia Lozano López. El Escorial. Madison, Wis.: Hispanic Seminary of Medieval Studies, 1992. Microfiche.
———. *Vita Christi*. 1496. Cambrigde, Mass.: General Microfilm, 1969.
Ezell, Margaret. *Writing Women's Literary History*. Baltimore: Johns Hopkins University Press, 1993.
Ezquerra Abadía, Ramón. *La conspiración del Duque de Híjar (1648)*. Madrid: n.p., 1934.
Feder, Lillian. *The Meridian Handbook of Classical Literature*. New York: Meridian, 1986.
Fisher, Sheila and Janet Halley. *Seeking the Woman in Late Medieval and Renaissance Texts*. Knoxville: University of Tennessee Press, 1989.
Formichi, Giovanna. "Saggio sulla bibliografia critica della novella spagnola seicentesca." In *Lavori della Sezione Fiorentina del Gruppo Ispanistico C.N.R.*, Vol. 3. Florence: n.p., 1973.
Foucault, Michel. *The History of Sexualty*. Trans. Robert Hurley. 3 vols. New York: Vintage, 1980.
Franciosini, Lorenzo. *Vocabulario español e italiano*. 2 vols. Rome, 1620.
Fraser, Nancy. *Revaluing French Feminism: Critical Essays on Difference*. Bloomington: Indiana University Press, 1992.
Frías, Damasio de. *Diálogos de diferentes materias ́inéditos hasta ahora*. 1529. Ed. Justo García Soriano. Madrid: G. Hernández y G. Sáez, 1929.
Frye, Northrop. *Anatomy of Criticism: Four Essays*. Princeton, N.J.: Princeton University Press, 1957.
Gacto, Enrique. "El grupo familiar de la edad moderna en los territorios del mediterráneo hispánico: una visión jurídica." In *La familia en la España mediterránea (Siglos XV-XIX)*, eds. James Casey et. al., 37-64. Barcelona: Crítica, 1987.
Galindo, Pedro. *Verdades morales en que se reprenden y condenan los trajes vanos, superfluos y profanos; con otros vicios y abusos que hoy se usan; mayormente los escotados deshonestos de las mujeres*. Madrid: Francisco Sáenz, 1639.

García Márquez, Gabriél. *El otoño del patriarca*. Madrid: Mondadori, 1992.
Genette, Gérard. *Narrative Discourse*. Ithaca, N.Y.: Cornell University Press, 1980.
Godzich, Wlad and Nicholas Spadaccini, eds. *Literature Among Discourses: The Spanish Golden Age*. Minneapolis: University of Minnesota Press, 1986.
Goffman, Erving. *Interaction Ritual: Essays on Face-To-Face Behavior*. Garden City, New York: Anchor/Doubleday, 1967.
Goldsmith, Elizabeth. *"Exclusive Conversations": The Art of Interaction in Seventeenth-Century France*. Philadelphia: University of Pennsylvania Press, 1988.
González de Amezúa y Mayo, Agustín. *Formación y elementos de la novela cortesana. Discurso leído ante la Real Academia Española*. Madrid: Real Academia Española, 1929.
González de Cellorigo, Martín, José Luis Pé rez de Ayala, and Conde de Cedillo. *Memorial de la política necesaria y útil restauración a la República de España y estados de ella y del desempeño universal de estos reinos*. 1600. Reprint, Madrid: Instituto de Cooperación Iberoamericana, 1991.
González Muñoz, María del Carmen. *La población de Talavera de la Reina (siglos XVI-XX)*. Toledo, Spain: Disputación Provincial, 1974.
Gossy, Mary. *The Untold Story: Women and Theory in Golden Age Texts*. Ann Arbor: University of Michigan Press, 1989.
Gracián, Baltasar. *El criticón. Obras completas*. Ed. Arturo de Hoyo. Madrid: Aguilar, 1960.
———. *El discreto*. 1641. In *El héroe, El discreto, El oráculo manual y arte de prudencia*, ed. Luys Santos Marina, 41-136. Barcelona: Planeta, 1990.
———. *Oráculo Manual y arte de prudencia / The oracle: A manual of the art of discretion*. 1647. Ed. and trans. L. B. Walton. New York: William Salloch, 1953.
Greenblatt, Stephen. *Renaissance Self-Fashioning: From More to Shakespeare*. Chicago: University of Chicago Press, 1980.
Greer, Margaret. *Desiring Readers: María de Zayas Tells Baroque Tales of Love and the Cruelty of Men*. University Park, Pa.: Pennsylvania State University Press, in press.
———. "The (Self)Representation of Control in *La dama duende*." In *The Golden Age* Comedia*: Text, Theory and Performance*, eds. Charles Ganelin and Howard Mancing, 86-106. West Lafayette, Ind.: Purdue University Press, 1994.

Grieve, Patricia. "Embroidering with Saintly Threads: María de Zayas Challenges Cervantes and the Church." *Renaissance Quarterly* 44.1 (1991): 86-106.
Griffin, Dustin. *Literary Patronage in England: 1650-1800*. Cambridge: Cambridge University Press, 1996.
Griswold, Susan. "Topoi and Rhetorical Distance: The 'Feminism' of María de Zayas." *Revista de estudios hispánicos* 14 (1980): 97-116.
Hernández Franco, Juan, ed. *Familia y poder. Sistemas de reproducción social en España (Siglos XVI-XVIII)*. Murcia, Spain: Universidad de Murcia, 1995.
Hernández-Sacristán, Carlos. "*The Art of Worldly Wisdom* as an Ethics of Conversation." In *Rhetoric and Politics: Baltasar Gracián and the New World Order*, eds. Nicholas Spadaccini and Genaro Talens, 287-304. Hispanic Issues, Vol. 14. Minneapolis: University of Minnesota Press, 1997.
Hernández Sánchez-Barba, Mario. *Monjas ilustres en la historia de España*. Madrid: Temas de hoy, 1996.
Herrera y Molina, Alonso de. *Espeio de la perfecta casada. En qve se contienen las condiciones que han de tener los benos casados para que se conseruen en paz: y como han de criar sus hijos, y gouernar su familia en amor y temor de Dios: a cuyo proposito se vá declarando toda aquella epistola de la sabiduria que canta la iglesia, y comiença: Mulierem fortem quis inueniet?* 1637. Granada, Spain: Andres de Santiago Palomino, 1638.
Huarte de San Juan, Juan. *Examen de ingenios*. Ed. Guillermo Seres. Madrid: Catedra, 1989.
Hufton, Olwen. "Women, Work and Family." In *Renaissance and Enlightenment Paradoxes*, eds. Natalie Zemon Davis and Arlette Farge, 15-45. In Vol. 3 of *A History of Women in the West*, eds. Georges Duby and Michelle Perrot. Cambridge: Harvard University Press, Belknap Press, 1993.
Huizinga, Johan. *Homo ludens: A Study of the Play Element in Culture*. Boston: Beacon Press, 1955.
Hume, Martin. *The Court of Philip IV of Spain in Decadance*. New York: Brentanos, 1927.
Ife, B. W. *Reading and Fiction in Golden-Age Spain*. Cambridge: Cambridge University Press, 1985.
Irigaray, Luce. *This Sex That Is Not One*. Trans. Catherine Porter. Ithaca, N.Y.: Cornell University Press, 1985.
Jardine, M. D. "New Historicism for Old: New Conservatism for Old? The Politics of Patronage in the Renaissance." In *Patronage, Politics and Literary Traditions in England, 1548-1658*, ed. Cedric C. Brown, 291-309. Detroit: Wayne State University Press, 1993.

Jesús, Fray Francisco de. *Narratives of the Spanish Marriage Treaty.* Ed. S. R. Gardiner. N. p.: Camden Society, Vol. 101, 1869.

Jesús, Teresa de. *Libro de la vida.* Ed. Otger Steggink. Madrid: Castalia, 1986.

Jonson, Ben. *The works of Ben Jonson: which were formerly printed in two volumes, are now reprinted in one: to which is added a comedy, called* The new inn: *with additions never before published.* 1692. London: Thomas Hodgkin, 1692. Ann Arbor, Mich.: University Microfilms, 1970.

Jordan, Constance. *Renaissance Feminism: Literary Texts and Political Models.* Ithaca, N.Y.: Cornell University Press, 1990.

Joset, Jacques. *Juan Ruiz, Arcipreste de Hita: Libro de Buen Amor.* Madrid: Taurus, 1990.

Juárez, Encarnación. "La autobiografía como búsqueda y afirmación de identidad." In *La Chispa '95: Selected Proceedings of the 16th Louisiana Conference on Hispanic Languages and Literatures*, ed. Claire Paolini, 185-195. New Orleans: Tulane University, 1995.

Kagan, Richard. *Students and Society in Early Modern Spain.* Baltimore: Johns Hopkins University Press, 1974.

Kamen, Henry. *Spain in the Later Seventeenth Century: 1665-1700.* London: Longmans, 1980.

Kaminsky, Amy, ed. *Water Lilies: An Anthology of Spanish Women Writers from the Fifteenth through the Nineteenth Century.* Minneapolis: University of Minnesota Press, 1996.

Keeble, N. H. *The Cultural Identity of Seventeenth-century Woman: A Reader.* New York: Routledge, 1994.

King, Williard. *Prosa novelística y académica en el siglo XVII.* Madrid: Anejos del BRAE, 1963.

León, Luis de. *Cantar de Canteres de Solomón.* 1561. Ed. José Manuel Blecua. Biblioteca Románica Hispánica, Vol. 22. Madrid: Gredos, 1994.

———. *La perfecta casada.* 1583. Barcelona: Grandes Autores, 1990.

Levin, Linda Gould, Ellen Engleson Marson and Gloria Reiman Waldman, eds. *Spanish Women Writers: A Bio-Bibliographical Source Book.* Westport, Conn.: Greenwood Press, 1993.

Livermore, H. V. *A New History of Portugal.* Cambridge: Cambridge University Press, 1966.

———. *Portugal and Brazil: An Introduction.* Oxford: Clarendon, 1953.

López de Úbeda, Francisco. *La pícara Justina.* 1605. Ed. Bruno Damiani. Ed. Facsim. Potomac, Md.: Porrua-Studia Humanistica, 1982.

López, Diego, ed. *Declaración magistral sobre las Emblemas de Andres Alciato con todas las historias, antiguedades, moralidad, y*

doctrina, tocante a las buenas costumbres. In Latin, with Spanish commentary. Valencia: Francisco Mestre, 1684.
López, Nelson. "Edición crítica para actores de *El valiente negro en Flandes* de Andrés de Claramonte." Ph.D. diss., University of Florida, 1998.
Lugo y Dávila. *Teatro Popular.* Ed. Emilio Cotarelo y Mori. Madrid: Viuda de Rico, 1906.
Luna, Lola. *Leyendo como una mujer: la imagen de la Mujer.* Barcelona: Anthropos; Seville: Instituto Andaluz de la Mujer, Junta de Andalusía, 1996.
Lynch, John. *The Hispanic World in Crisis and Change: 1598-1700.* Oxford: Blackwell, 1992.
Machiavelli, Niccoló. *El príncipe.* Trans. Guillermo Cabanellas de Torres. Buenos Aires: Heliasta, 1998.
Malón de Chiade, Pedro. *Conversión de la Magdalena.* Ed. Félix García. 3 vols. Clásicos Castellanos. Madrid: Espasa-Calpe, 1947.
Manuel, don Juan. *El Conde Lucanor.* Ed. Reinaldo Ayerbe-Chaux. Madrid: Alhambra 1983.
Maravall, José Antonio. *El mundo social de* La Celestina. Madrid: Gredos, 1976.
Marks, Elaine and Isabelle de Courtivron. *New French Feminisms.* Amherst: University of Massachusetts Press; Boston: Harvester, 1980.
Marques, A. H. de Oliveira. *History of Portugal: From Lusitania to Empire.* New York: Columbia University Press, 1972.
Marques, João Francisco. *A Parenética Portuguesa e a Restauração 1640-1668.* Oporto: Instituto Nacional de Investigação Científica, 1989.
Martín Gaite, Carmen. *Desde la ventana: Enfoque femenino de la literatura española.* Madrid: Espasa Calpe, 1993.
Martínez de Bujanda, Jesús. "Literatura e Inquisición en España en el Siglo XVI." In *Inquisición española y mentalidad inquisitorial*, ed. Ángel Alcalá, 579-592. Barcelona: Ariel, 1984.
Matthews Greico, Sara F. "The Body, Appearance, and Sexuality." In *Renaissance and Enlightenment Paradoxes*, eds. Natalie Zemon Davis and Arlette Farge, 46-84. . In Vol. 3 of *A History of Women in the West,* eds. Georges Duby and Michelle Perrot. Cambridge: Harvard University Press, Belknap Press, 1993.
Matulka, Barbara. *The Feminist Theme in the Drama of the* Siglo de Oro. New York: Columbia University Press, 1936.
McKendrick, Geraldine and Angus Mackay."Visionaries and Affective Spirituality During the First Half of the Sixteenth Century." In *Culture and Control in Counter-Reformation Spain*, eds. Anne

Cruz and Mary Elizabeth Perry, 93-104. Hispanic Issues, Vol 7. Minneapolis: University of Minnesota Press, 1992.

McKendrick, Melveena. *Women and Society in the Spanish Drama of the Golden Age: A Study of the* Mujer varonil. Cambridge: Cambridge University Press, 1974.

Melgarejo, Pedro. *Compendio de contratos públicos, autos de particiónes, executivos, y de residencias* (1652). Madrid: Joseph García Lanza, 1758.

Meneses, Leonor de [Laura Mauricia, pseud.]. *El desdeñado más firme.* 1655. Ed. and introduction by Judith Whitenack and Gwyn E. Campbell. Potomac, Md.: Scripta Humanistica, 1994.

———. *El desdeñado más firme.* N.p., n.d. Dedication signed "Paris, 1665." Biblioteca Nacional, R-25004.

Mercer, Ramona, Elizabeth Nichols and Glen Doyle, eds. *Transitions in a Woman's Life.* Focus on Women Series, Vol. 12. New York: Springer, 1989.

Mexía, Fray Vicente. *Saludable instrucción del estado de matrimonio.* Córdoba, Spain: Juan Baptista Escuerdo, 1566.

Molina, Tirso de. *El burlador de Sevilla. y convidado de piedra.* Ed. Rodríguez López-Vázquez. Madrid: Cátedra, 1990.

Moreto, Agustín. *El lindo don Diego.* Eds. Frank Casa and Berislav Primorac. Madrid: Cátedra, 1995.

Morreale, Margherita. *Castiglione y Boscán: El ideal cortesano en el renacimiento español.* Vol. 1. Madrid: Anejos del Boletín de la Real Academia, 1959.

Muñoz Fernandez, Angela. *Acciones e intenciones de mujeres en la vida religionsa de los siglos XVI y XVII.* Madrid: Mujeres en Madrid, 1995.

———. "Castiglione y 'El Héroe': Gracián y 'despejo.'" In *Homenaje a Gracián*, 137-143. Zaragoza, Spain: Institución Fernando el Ca-tólico, 1958.

Nalle, Sara. "A Saint for All Seasons: The Cult of San Julián." In *Culture and Control in Counter-Reformation Spain*, eds. Anne Cruz and Mary Elizabeth Perry, 25-50. Hispanic Issues, Vol. 7. Minneapolis: University of Minnesota Press, 1992.

———. "To Sin in Thought and in Deed: Ideas and Actions in Counter-Reformation Spain." Paper presented at the 2º Seminario de Historia Moderna de España, Soria, Spain, July 1992.

Nash, Mary. "Un/Contested Identities: Motherhood, Sex Reform and the Modernization of Gender Identity in Early Twentieth-Century Spain." In *Constructing Spanish Womanhood: Female Identity in Modern Spain*, eds. Victoria Enders and Pamela Radcliffe, 25-49. Albany: State University of New York Press, 1999.

Nicholson, Eric A. "The Theater." In *Renaissance and Enlightenment Paradoxes*, eds. Natalie Zemon Davis and Arlette Farge, 295-314. In Vol. 3 of *A History of Women in the West,* eds. Georges Duby and Michelle Perrot. Cambridge: Harvard University Press, Belknap Press, 1993.

Nieto Nuño, M., ed. *Diario del Conde de Pötting, Embajador del Sacro Imperio en Madrid (1664-1674)*. Madrid: Biblioteca diplomática española, 1990.

Olsen, Glending. *Literature as Recreation in the Later Middle Ages.* Ithaca, N.Y.: Cornell University Press, 1982.

Ong, Walter J. *Interfaces of the Word: Studies in the Evolution of Consciousness and Culture.* Ithaca, N.Y.: Cornell University Press, 1977.

Orso, Steven. *Art and Death at the Spanish Hapsburg Court: The Royal Exequies for Philip IV.* Columbia, Mo.: University of Missouri Press, 1989.

Os Restauradores de 1640 e a sua descendéncia. Lisbon: Publipor, 1990.

Oudin, César. *Tesoro de las dos lenguas, francesa y española.* Paris: M. Orry, 1807.

Pabst, Walter. *La novela corta en la teoría y en la creación literaria.* 1953. Trans. Rafael de la Vega. Madrid: Gredos, 1972.

Pacheco-Ransanz, A. "El concepto de la novela cortesana y otras cuestiones taxonómicas." In *What's Past Is Prologue,* eds. Salvador Bacarisse and J.L. Woodward, 114-123. Edinburgh: Scottish Academic Press, 1984.

Palomo, María del Pilar. *La novela cortesana: forma y estructura.* Barcelona: Planeta, 1976.

Parker, A. A. "The Meaning of 'Discreción' in *No hay más fortuna que Dios.*" In *Calderón de la Barca,* ed. Hans Flasche, 218-234. Darmstadt, W. Germany: Waassenschaftliche Buchgesellschaft, 1971.

Pellicer de Tovar, Joseph. *Idea del principado de Cataluña: recopilación de sus momentos antiguos: modernos y examen de svs privilegios.* Antwerp, Belgium: Geronimo Verdus, 1642.

Pérez-Erdelyi, Mireya. *La pícara y la dama. La imagen de las mujeres en las novelas picaresco-cortesanas de María de Zayas y Sotomayor y Alonso de Castillo Solórzano.* Miami: Ediciones Universal, 1979.

Perry, Mary Elizabeth. "Crisis and Disorder in the World of María de Zayas y Sotomayor." In *María de Zayas: The Dynamics of Discourse,* eds. Amy Williamsen and Judith Whitenack, 23-39. Cranbury, N.J.: Associated University Press, 1995.

———. *Gender and Disorder in Early Modern Seville*. Princeton, N.J.: Princeton University Press, 1990.
———. *Ni espada rota ni mujer que trota*. Trans. M. Fortuny Minguella. Barcelona: Crítica, 1993.
Perry, Mary Elizabeth and Cruz, Anne, eds. *Cultural Encounters: The Impact of the Inquisition in Spain and the New World*. Berkeley: University of California Press, 1991.
Pfandl, Ludwig. *Historia de la literatura nacional española en la Edad de Oro*. 1929. Trans. J. Rubió Balaguer. Barcelona: Sucesores de Juan Gili, 1933.
Pisan, Christine de. *Livre des Trois Virtús: edicion critique*. Ed. Charity Cannon Willard. Paris: H. Champion, 1989.
Place, Edwin. *Manual elemental de novelística española*. Madrid: Victoriano Suárez, 1926.
Postigo Castellanos, Elena. *Honor y privilegio en la corona de Castilla: El Consejo de las Ordenes y los Caballeros de Hábito en el s. XVII*. Almazán, Soria, Spain: Junta de Castilla y León, 1988.
Quevedo, Francisco de. *Poesía original completa*. Ed. José Manuel Blecua. Barcelona: Planeta, 1990.
———, ed. *El Parnaso español o, Las nueve musas castellanas*. 1668. Barcelona: L. de Ramón Pujal, 1869.
Raposo, Hipólito. *Dona Lvisa De Gvsmão, Dvquesa e Rainha (1613-1666)*. Lisbon: Empresa Nacional de Publicidade, 1947.
Rebhorn, Wayne, A. *Courtly Performances: Masking and Festivity in Castiglione*'s Book of the Courtier. Detroit: Wayne State University Press, 1978.
Reher, David. *Perspectives on the Family in Spain, Past and Present*. Oxford: Clarendon, 1997.
Rey Hazas, Antonio. "El erotismo de la novela cortesana." In *Edad de Oro*, ed. Departamento de literatura española de la Universidad Nacional Autónoma de Madrid, 271-288. Madrid, 1982.
Riley, Denise. "Does a Sex Have a History?" In *Feminism and History*, ed. Joan Wallach Scott, 17-33. Oxford: Oxford University Press, 1996.
Riley, Edward C. *Cervantes's Theory of the Novel*. Oxford: Clarendon, 1962.
Rimmon-Kenan, Shlomith. *Narrative Fiction: Contemporary Poetics*. London: Methuen, 1983.
Ringrose, David. *Madrid and the Spanish Economy (1560-1860)*. Berkeley: University of California Press, 1983.
Ripoll, Begoña. *La novela barroca: Catálogo bio-bibliográfico (1620-1700)*. Salamanca, Spain: University of Salamanca Press, 1991.

Rivers, Elias, ed. *Poesía Lírica del Siglo de Oro*. Madrid: Cátedra, 1979.
Rodríguez, Evangelina. *Novela corta marginada del siglo XVII español*. Valencia, Spain: Universidad de Valencia, 1979.
―――, ed. *Novelas amorosas de diversos ingenios del siglo XVII*. Madrid: Castalia, 1987.
Rodríguez Sanchez, Angel. *Cáceres: población y comportamientos demográficos en el siglo XVI*. Cáceres, Spain: Aula de Cultura de la Caja de Ahorros y Monte de Piedad, 1977.
Rojas, Fernando de. *La Celestina: Tragicomedia de Calixto y Melibea*. Ed. Dorothy S. Severin. Madrid: Alianza, 1979.
Ruiz, Juan. *Libro de buen amor*. Ed. Jacques Joset. Madrid: Taurus, 1990.
Ruiz de Alarcón, Juan. *La verdad sospechosa*. 1634. Ed. Alva Ebersole. Madrid: Cátedra, 1984.
Russ, Joanna. *How to Suppress Women's Writing*. Austin: University of Texas Press, 1983.
Russell, Peter E. *Temas de* La Celestina *y otros estudios*. Barcelona: Ariel, 1978.
Salas Barbadillo, Alonso Jerónimo de. *El curioso y sabio Alexandro: fiscal y juez de vidas agenas*. 1634. Madrid: Impr. de F.X. Garcia, 1753.
Salazar, Hernando de. *Tratado que se dio el Rey el año 1643 sobre materias de gobierno y hacienda*. Biblioteca Nacional de Madrid.
Sánchez, Elizabeth. "Magia en *La Celestina*." *Hispanic Review* 46.4 (autumn 1979): 481-94.
Sánchez, Magdalena. *The Empress, the Queen and the Nun: Women and Power at the Court of Philip III*. Johns Hopkins University Studies in History and Political Science. Series 2.116. Baltimore: Johns Hopkins University Press, 1998.
Sánchez Ortega, María Helena. "Sorcery and Eroticism in Love Magic." In *Cultural Encounters: The Impact of the Inquisition in Spain and the New World*, eds. Mary Elizabeth Perry and Anne Cruz, 58-92. Berkeley: University of California Press, 1991.
San José, María de. *Libro de recreaciones, ramillete de mirra, avisos, máximas y poesías*. [1585]. Reprint, with an introduction by P. Silverio de Sta. Teresa, Burgos, Spain: El Monte Caramelo, 1913.
Schulte van Kessel, Elisja. "Virgins and Mothers between Heaven and Earth." In *Renaissance and Enlightenment Paradoxes*, eds. Natalie Zemon Davis and Arlette Farge, 132-166. In Vol. 3 of *A History of Women in the West*, eds. Georges Duby and Michelle Perrot. Cambridge: Harvard University Press, Belknap Press, 1993.
Scott, Joan Wallach. "Gender: A Useful Category of Historical Analysis." *American Historical Review* 91.5 (1986): 1053-1075.

Scott, Lynn. "Carmen de Burgos: Piecing a Profession: Rewriting Women's Roles." Ph.D. diss., University of Florida, 1999.
Sears, Theresa Ann. *A Marriage of Convenience: Ideal and Ideology in the Novelas ejemplares.* New York: Peter Lang, 1990.
Sebastián, Santiago. *Emblemática e historia del arte.* Madrid: Cátedra, 1995.
Segal, Elizabeth. "'As the Twig is Bent. . .': Gender in Childhood Reading." In *Gender and Reading: Essays on Readers, Texts, and Contexts*, eds. Elizabeth Flynn and Patrocinio Schweickart, 165-186. Baltimore: Johns Hopkins University Press, 1986.
Serrano y Sanz, Manuel. *Apuntes para una biblioteca de escritoras españolas desde el año 1401 al 1833.* 2 vols. Madrid: Sucesores de Rivadeneyra, 1903-1905.
Showalter, Elaine. "Feminist Criticism in the Wilderness." *Critical Inquiry* 8.2 (winter 1981): 179-205.
―――. *A Literature of Their Own.* Princeton, N.J.: Princeton University Press, 1977.
Sieber, Harry. "Literary Continuity, Social Order and the Invention of the Picaresque." In *Cultural Authority in Golden Age Spain*, eds. Marina Brownlee and Hans Ulrich Gumbrecht, 143-164. Baltimore: Johns Hopkins University Press, 1995.
Simone de Beauvoir. *The Second Sex.* Trans. H. M. Parshley. New York: Knopf, 1952. Reprint, New York: Bantam, 1970.
Sinfield, Alan. "Power and Ideology: An Outline Theory and Sidney's Arcadia." *English Literary History* 52.2 (1985): 259-277.
Smith, Paul Julian. "The Rhetoric of Allegory in *El criticón*." In *Conflicts of Discourse: Spanish Literature in the Golden Age*, ed. Peter W. Evans, 92-109. Manchester, England: Manchester University Press, 1990.
Sobrino, Francisco. *Diccionario nuevo de las lenguas españoals y francesas.* Brussels, Belgium, 1705.
Soufas, Teresa Scott. *Melancholy and the Secular Mind in Spanish Golden Age Literature.* Columbia, Mo.: University of Missouri Press, 1990.
Spadaccini, Nicholas and Genaro Talens, eds. *Rhetoric and Politics: Baltasar Gracián and the New World Order.* Hispanic Issues, Vol. 14. Minneapolis: University of Minnesota Press, 1997.
Spieker, Joseph. "El femenismo como clave estructural en las *Novelle* de Doña María de Zayas." *Explicaciones de textos literarios* 6.2 (1978): 153-160.
Spielman, John. *Leopold I of Austria.* New Brunswick, N.J.: Rutgers University Press, 1977.
Stanton, Domna. *The Aristocrat as Art.* New York: Columbia University Press, 1980.

Steele, Meili. *Theorizing Textual Subjects.* Cambridge: Cambridge University Press, 1997.
Suárez de Mendoza y Figueroa, Enrique. *Eustorgio y Clorilene, historia moscovica.* 1629. Zaragoza, Spain: Iván de Ybar, 1665.
Surtz, Ronald. *Writing Women in Late Medieval and Early Modern Spain: The Mothers of Saint Teresa of Ávila.* Philadelphia: University of Pennsylvania Press, 1995.
Sylvania, Lena. "Doña María de Zayas y Sotomayor: A Contribution to the Study of Her Works." *Romanic Review* 13 (1922): 197-213.
Talavera, Hernando de. *Tractado prouechoso que demuestra commo en el uestir y calçar comunmente se cometen muchos pecados y aun tanbien en el comer y beuer.* Ed. Hannah Marie Nyholm. N.p., 1956.
Teresa de Ávila, Santa. *Libro de la vida.* Ed. Otger Steggink. Madrid: Castalia, 1986.
Thompson, I. A. A. *War and Government in Habsburg Spain 1560-1620.* London: The Athlone Press, 1976.
Thompson, Stith. *Motif-Index of Folk Literature.* 6 vols. Bloomington, Ind.: Indiana University Press, 1966.
Ticknor, George. *History of Spanish Literature.* New York: Harper, 1849.
Tirso de Molina. *Don Gil de las Calzas Verdes.* Ed. Xabier Veira. Madrid: Edicomunicación, 1997.
Torres Sánchez, Concha. *La clausura femenina en la Salamanca del Siglo XVII: Dominicas y carmelitas descalzas.* Acta salmanticensia. Estudios históricos y geográficos 73. Salamanca, Spain: University of Salamanca, 1991.
Traub, Valerie, M. Lindsay Kaplan, and Dympna Callaghan, eds. *Feminist Readings of Early Modern Culture: Emerging Subjects.* Cambridge: Cambridge University Press, 1996.
Trevor Davies, Reginald. *Spain in Decline.* London: Macmillan,1957.
Valbona, Rima de, ed. *Vida i sucesos de la Monja Alférez: Autobiografía atribuida a Doña Catalina de Erauso.* Tempe, Ariz.: Arizona State University Center for Latin American Studies, 1992.
Valis, Noël. "The Spanish Storyteller: Mariana de Caravajal." In *Women Writers of the Seventeenth Century*, eds. Katharina Wilson and Frank Warnke, 251-282. Athens, Ga.: University of Georgia Press, 1989.
Vasvari, Louise."Vegetal-Genital Onomastics in the *Libro de buen amor.*" *Romance Philology* 43.1 (1988): 1-29.
Vega, Lope de. "El arte nuevo de hacer comedias." Monograph Reprint 2. Liverpool, England: BHS, 1935.

———. "El laurel de Apolo." 1631. *Colección escogida de obras no dramáticas*. Biblioteca de autores españoles 38. 1856. Ed. Cayetano Rosell, 185-229. Madrid: Los sucesores de Hernando, 1918.
Vélez de Guevara, Luis. *El diablo cojuelo*. Ed. Enrique Rodríguez Cepeda. Madrid: Cátedra, 1984.
Vigil, Mariló. "La importancia de la moda en el barroco." In *Literatura y vida cotidiana*, Actas de las Cuartas Jornadas de Investigación Interdisciplinaria, eds. María Ángeles Durán and José Antonio Rey, 187-200. Madrid: Universidad Autónoma de Madrid; Zaragoza: Universidad de Zaragoza, 1987.
Villalón, Cristobál de. *El scholástico*. 1550?. Ed. Mare celino Menéndez Pelayo. Madrid: n.p., 1911.
Villa-Urrutia, W. R. de. *Relaciones entre España y Austria*. Madrid: n.p., 1905.
Vives, Juan Luis. *Instrucción de la mujer cristiana*. 1523. Trans. Juan Justiano. 1528. Ed. E. T. Howe. Salamanca, Spain: Univ. Pontificia de Sa-lamanca; Madrid: Fundación Universitaria Española, 1995.
Wall, Wendy. *The Imprint of Gender*. Ithaca, N.Y.: Cornell University Press, 1993.
Weinberg, Bernard. *A History of Literary Criticism in the Renaissance*. 2 vols. Chicago: University of Chicago Press, 1961.
Whigham, Frank. *Ambition and Privilege: The Social Tropes of Elizabethan Courtesy Theory*. Berkeley: University of California Press, 1984.
Whinnom, Keith. *Spanish Literary Historiography: Three Forms of Distortion*. Exeter, England: University of Exeter, 1967.
Wiesner, Merry. *Women and Gender in Early Modern Europe*. Cambridge: Cambridge University Press, 1993.
Williamson, Amy R. and Judith A. Whitenack, eds. *María de Zayas: The Dynamics of Discourse*. Cranbury, N.J.: Associated University Presses, 1995.
Yudin, Florence. "The *novela corta* as *Comedia*: Lope's *Las fortunas de Diana*." *Bulletin of Hispanic Studies* 45 (1968): 181-188.
Zavala, Iris. *La mujer en la literatura española*. Barcelona: Anthropos; Madrid: Comunidad de Madrid, 1995.
Zayas, María de. *Novelas amorosas y ejemplares*. 1647. Ed. Augustín González de Amezúa. Biblioteca Selecta de Clásicos Españoles 2. Vol. 8. Madrid: Real Academia Española, 1948.
———. *Parte segunda del Sarao y entretenimiento honesto [Desengaños amorosos]*. Ed. Alicia Yllera. Madrid: Cátedra, 1983.
Zook, Melinda. "Contextualizing Aphra Behn: Plays, Politics and Party, 1679-1689." In *Women Writers and the Early Modern British Political System*, ed. Hilda L. Smith, 75-93. Cambridge: Cambridge University Press, 1998.

Index

Ágreda, María de, 55
Alciati, Andrea, 119, 128-29
Alemán, Mateo, 58n2
Angela of Foligno, Saint, 22
Antonio, Nicolás, 116, 155
Astete, Gaspar de, 30-31

Barca de Bolea, Ana Francisca, 14n1
Behn, Aphra, 147
Bernal, Beatriz, 14n1
The Book of the Courtier. See Castiglione, Baldassare
Boscán, Juan, 3, 71-72, 110, 119, 128, 130-31, 141n6, 154

Calderón de la Barca, Pedro, 24, 63n38, 102, 108n25, 121, 122, 148
El Cantar del Mío Çid, 36
Caro, Ana, 116, 142n8, 193
Carvajal y Saavdra, Mariana de, xii, 4-5, 15n2, 43-44, 55, 123, 138-39; and patronage, 148, 154, 175-86. *See also* "Fábula de Dafne y Apolo"; "Fábula de Eurídice y Orfeo"; *Memorial*; *Navidades de Madrid y noches entretenidas*
Casa, Giovanni della, 111
Castiglione, Baldassare, 3, 16n10, 25, 69, 110-14, 116, 119, 121, 129-30, 140, 141nn5-6

Cellorigo, Martín González de, 51, 150
Cerda, Juan de la, 48
Cervantes, Miguel de, ix, xii, 9, 71, 187n1. *See also Don Quijote*; *Novelas ejemplares*
Cesti, Antonio, 186
Chambers, Ross, 154
Charnon-Deutsch, Lou, 54, 58
Chiade, Malón de, 30
Claramonte, Andrés de, 117
Coloma, Carlos de, 4
comedia. See marriage; theater
La conversión de la Magdalena. See Chiade, Malón de
Córdoba, Martín Alonso de, 28
El cortesano. See Milán, Luis
court society: attire, 25, 30-31; legitimacy of children, 50, 51, 63n40; social expectations, 50-51, 113-15, 115-18; theater, 25
courtesy manuals, 5, 27-30, 109-13, 141n4
Courtivron, Isabelle de, 105n2
courtship novel: and the church, 85-87; "courtly" v. "courtship," 3-5, 6, 13; courtship as a game, 67, 105n2; criteria of courtly novel, 2; and eroticism, 9-11, 17nn16-17; the law in, xi-xii, 82-85; and male perspective, 11-13; and mimesis, 70-72; and modern psychology, 7-8
Coutinho, Leonor, 14n1

Covarrubias Horozco, Sebastián de, 128
El criticón, 112, 147
Cruz, Juana de la, xi

damas cortesanas, 3-4, 6
Dantisco, Lucas Gracián, 109, 111, 118, 193
Davis, Natalie Zemon, 13, 19
Daza Pinciano, Bernardino de, 119, 121, 128-29
dedications, literary. *See* literary dedications and patronage
Delicado, Francisco, 3
El desdeñado más firme, 1, 78, 81, 88-93, 95, 98-99, 107n21, 127-28, 134, 139-40, 189n26, 193-94; and patronage, 145, 152, 202-4
"El desengañado amado y premio de la virtud," 156-57
Desengaños amorosos, 1, 55, 87, 99, 101, 104, 127, 133, 140, 193-94; "Amar sólo por vencer," 24, 86, 99, 101-2, 107n23, 108n25, 123-24, 127, 135-36, 199; Cornice, xvin2, 10, 69, 72, 79-81, 86, 87-88, 106n14, 134-35, 154, 162, 195-96; "La esclava de su amante," 74-75, 86, 98, 133, 162-63, 196; "Estragos que causa el vicio," 3, 61n20, 81, 97, 107n24, 108n25, 126-27, 201-2; "La inocencia castigada," 10, 18n21, 82-83, 85, 86, 94, 97-98, 101-4, 162, 198-99; "La más infame venganza," 77, 79-81, 86-87, 97, 98, 106n13, 197; and patronage, 145, 148-49, 152, 158, 160, 163-64, 180; "La perseguida triunfante," 75, 86, 99, 100, 102, 104, 161-62, 201; "Mal presagio casar lejos," 12, 74, 99-100, 107n17, 123, 161-62, 199-200; "Tarde llega el desengaño," 162, 160-61, 198; "El traidor contra su sangre," 84-85, 96-97, 200; "El verdugo de su esposa," 81, 94, 102-4, 162, 197
El diablo cojuelo. *See* Vélez de Guevara, Luis
discretion: definitions of, 118-22; observable facets, 122-28; subtle manifestations, 128-40
El discreto, 112, 156
Don Quijote, 81, 102, 103, 108n27, 111, 120

education, women's, 22, 27-30
El Saffar, Ruth, 49-50, 105n4
emblem books, 119
Los emblemas de Alciati en rhimas españolas. *See* Daza Pinciano, Bernardino de
Erasmus, 60n16
Erauso, Calalina de, 14n1
Espejo de la perfecta casada *See* Herrera, Alonso de
Exemplary Novels. *See* Novelas ejemplares

"Fábula de Dafne y Apolo," 191n36
"Fábula de Eurídice y Orfeo," 191n36
female agency, 116; beauty, 101-2; chaos, 88-93; cooperation of others, 77-81; familial opposition, 95-98, 107n22; favorable circumstances, 73; impediments, 94; kindness of strangers, 81-88; in marriage, 5-6, 32-36, 40-41; parental protection, loss of, 99-100; "power" v. "authority," 106n5; socioeconomic, 73-77; and the supernatural, 102-4; unscrupulous suitors, 98-99
Fernández Alarcón, Cristobalina, 116
Flos Sanctorum, 21
Formación y elementos de la novela cortesana. See Amezúa, González de
Fraser, Nancy, 69
Frías, Damasio de, 118-19, 120, 121
Frye, Northrop, 15n4, 69
"Fugitivo pajarillo," 158

Gaite, Carmen Martín, 18n25
Galateo. See Casa, Giovanni della
Galateo español. See Dantisco, Lucas Gracián
Galindo, Pedro, 31
García Márquez, Gabriel, 148
gender: attire, 25; and cultural symbols, 20-26; and identity, 46-58; and social norms, 26-31; and socioeconomic relationships, 31-46
gender density, x
gender roles, 19-20, 24, 47-50
Genette, Gérard, 18n23
Gibaldi, Joseph, 106n9
Goffman, Erving, 113
Goldsmith, Elizabeth, 115
González de Amezúa y Mayo, Agustín, 1-2, 6-13, 15n2, 193
Gossy, Mary, 62n32
Gracián, Baltásar, 112, 115, 121, 141n1. *See also El criticón*; *El discreto*; *El héroe*; *Oráculo manual y arte de prudencia*
Greenblatt, Stephen, 109
Greer, Margaret, 107n16, 107n24, 108n25
Grieve, Patricia, 107nn19-20
Griffin, Dustin, 149, 150
Guevara, Luis Vélez de, 187n7

Hapsburg court crisis, 150-55
El héroe, 112, 131
Herrera, Alonso de, 30
Huizinga, Johan, 114

Instruction of the Christian Woman. See Vives, Juan Luis
intercalated narrative, 142n10

Jardín de las nobles doncellas. See Alonso de Córdoba, Martin
Jardine, M. D., 147
Joceline, Elizabeth, x-xii

Kagan, Richard, 48-49, 106n8

Lazarillo de Tormes, 9, 18n19
León, Luis de, 17n16, 20, 24, 28-29, 56
Leyes de la Esposa. See Ágreda, María de
Libro de recreaciones. See San José, María de
literary dedications and patronage, 145-50, 187n2
López, Diego, 129
Lugo y Dávila, Francisco de, 111

marriage: and *comedia*, 26; exogamy, 99-100; finances of dowry, 33-35; and social elevation, x, 16nn12-13, 35-41, 62n27, 62n29; and widowhood, 54-55. See also female agency
Mauricia, Laura. See Meneses, Leonor de
McKendrick, Geraldine, xi
Memorial, 43-44, 62n33
Mendoza, Mencía de, 22
Meneses, Leonor de (pseud. Mauricia, Laura), 55, 62n27, 116, 139, 142n8, 152, 154, 164-75. See also *El desdeñado más firme*
Mexía, Vicente, 30
Milán, Luis, 111
Montalvo, Gálvez de, 104-5, 109-10, 118, 138
Moreto, Agustín, 89
The Mother's Legacie to her Unborn Childe. See Joceline, Elizabeth
Murillo, Bartolomé, 21

mythology and women, 23

Nalle, Sara, 21
Navidades de Madrid y noches entretenidas, 1, 44, 67-69, 71, 106n8, 127, 138, 140, 143n15, 190n33, 191nn34-35, 193-94; "El amante venturoso," 11-12, 82, 101, 182-83, 206; "Amar sin saber a quién," 18n26, 78-79, 88, 89, 138, 180-81, 191n38, 208; "Celos vengan desprecios," 98, 127, 135, 138, 183, 207; Cornice, 77-78, 106n12, 126, 204; "La dicha de Doristea," 32-33, 74, 81-82, 86, 95, 98, 107n22, 124-26, 135-36, 138, 180, 183-84, 185, 205; "El esclavo de su esclavo," 75-76, 81, 95, 107n22, 133-34, 184-85, 191n37, 206; "La industria vence desdenes," 62n31, 75, 76, 85-86, 101, 107n22, 131-33, 136-37, 138, 142n13, 180, 185-86, 191n38, 208; and patronage, 114, 145, 153, 190n28; "Quien bien obra siempre acierta," 4-5, 78, 81, 83-84, 86, 95-96, 138, 181-82, 207; "La Venus de Ferrara," 73-74, 76-77, 95, 106nn10-11, 107n22, 137-38, 185-86, 205
novela cortesana. See courtship novel
Novelas amorosas, 1, 159

novelas de cortejo. See courtship novel
Novelas ejemplaras, 1, 6, 10-11, 157-58; "El coloquio de los perros," 9, 15n3, 18n18, 122; "El casamiento engañoso," 15n3; "La fuerza de la sangre," 10, 11; "La ilustre fregona," 15n3; "Rinconete y Cortadillo," 15n3

The Odyssey, 142n14
Oráculo manual y arte de prudencia, ix, xiii, 119, 120-21, 128, 129-30, 140, 187n3

Pacheco-Ransanz, A., 2-3
Palmerín de Oliva, 14n1
Parte segunda del Sarao y entretenimiento honesto. See *Desengaños amorosos*
patronage. *See* literary dedications and patronage
Pellicer de Tovar, Joseph, 155
Pérez de Montalbán, Juan, 15n6
La perfecta casada. See León, Luis de
picaresque novel, 3, 50
politics and women, 5, 16nn11-12
Primaleón, 14n1

religion, 21-22, 27-28, 29, 30-31, 102-3; and gender, 60nn11-12; and status, 62n30 religious vocation, women and, 41-43, 45, 55-57, 64n47, 64n49, 86-87
Riley, Denise, x, 47

Rojas, Fernando de, 22-23, 64n41, 108n27
Ruiz de Alarcón, Juan, 63n38

Salazar, Hernando de, 49
San Félix, Marcela de, 57
San José, María de, 56
San Juan, Huarte de, 27, 60n12
Santo Domingo, Sor María de, xi
Sbarra, Francesco, 186
El scholástico. See Villalón, Cristóbal de
Scott, Joan Wallach, 13, 19, 26, 160
Scudéry, Madame de, 153
Serrano y Sanz, Manuel, 62n28
Shakespeare, William, 105n4
Sieber, Harry, 10
Silva, Rodrigo de, 62n29, 156-58, 162
Solórzano, Castillo, 3
Steele, Meili, 68-69
Suárez de Mendoza y Figueroa, Enrique, 158

Talavera, Hernando de, 28
The Taming of the Shrew, 105n4
Teresa of Ávila, Saint, 48, 56, 63n36, 64n47
Teatro popular. See Lugo y Dávila, Francisco de
Texeda, Isabel de, xi
theater, 22-25; *comedia*, 23, 105n4. *See also* marriage
Thomas Aquinas, Saint, 42
Thompson, Stith, 70, 106n6, 142n12

Tragicomedia de Calixto y Melibea. See Rojas, Fernando de

Úbeda, López de, 3

El valiente negro en Flandes. See Claramonte, Andrés de
Vega, Lope, 59n6
Vélez de Guevara, Luis, 155-56
Verdades morales. See Galindo, Pedro
Villalón, Cristóbal de, 111
Virgil, 52
Vives, 28-29, 52-53, 60n16, 95

Whinnom, Keith, 17n14
Wiesner, Merry, 5, 53

Zayas, María de, xii, 15n2, 54, 84-85, 104, 107n16, 107nn19-20, 139; and patronage, 152, 154, 155-64, 175, 188n12. *See also* "El desengañado amado y premio de la virtud"; *Desengaños amorosos*; "Fugitivo pajarillo"; *Novelas amorosas*

About the Author

Shifra Armon is associate professor of Spanish at the University of Florida. She has published articles on topics of early modern literary and culture studies in Spain in *Cervantes: Bulletin of the Cervantes Society of America*, *Caliope: Journal of Renaissance and Baroque Poetry* and *Revista canadiense de estudios hispánicos*. Her book reviews have appeared in *MLN* and *South Atlantic Review*.